TRADITION AND DESIGN
IN LUKE'S GOSPEL

TRADITION AND DESIGN IN LUKE'S GOSPEL

A Study in Early Christian Historiography

JOHN DRURY

JOHN KNOX PRESS
ATLANTA

First published in Great Britain in 1976
by Darton, Longman and Todd Ltd
Published in U.S.A. in 1977
by John Knox Press

Library of Congress Cataloging in Publication Data
Drury, John.
    Tradition and design in Luke's Gospel.

    Bibliography: p.
    Includes index.
    1.   Bible.   N.T.   Luke—Criticism, interpretation,
etc.   I. Title.
BS2595.2.D78   1977   226'.4'06   77-79586
ISBN 0-8042-0451-9

Printed in the United States of America
John Knox Press
Atlanta, Georgia

TO
THE RECTOR AND FELLOWS
OF EXETER COLLEGE, OXFORD
AND
THE DEAN AND CHAPTER
OF NORWICH CATHEDRAL

Among the inquiries to which this ardour of criticism has naturally given occasion, none is more obscure in itself, or more worthy of rational curiosity, than a retrospection of the progress of this mighty genius in the construction of his work; a view of the fabric gradually rising, perhaps from small beginnings, till its foundation rests in the centre and its turrets sparkle in the skies; to trace back the structure, through all its varieties, to the simplicity of its first plan; to find what was first projected, whence the scheme was taken, how it was improved, by what assistance it was executed, and from what stores the materials were collected, whether its founder dug them from the quarries of nature, or demolished other buildings to embellish his own.

Samuel Johnson

Preface to William Lauder's.
Essay on Milton's Use and
Imitation of the Moderns in
His Paradise Lost, 1750.

The Revised Version has usually been
used for the New Testament, the
Revised Standard Version for the
Old Testament.
Instead of the Septuagintal title of the
Books of Samuel and numbers of
the Psalms, the more common ones
have been used.

Contents

Preface   xi

1   Introduction—The Well of the Past   1

2   A Place on the Map   15
     1. The Theological Climate   15
     2. Gospels and Neighbours   25

3   Critical Method   39
     1. Source Criticism   40
     2. Form Criticism   41
     3. Redaction Criticism   42
     4. The Next Step   43

4   Using Scripture   46
     1. The Infancy Stories and Beyond   46
     2. Some Turning Points   66
     3. 'Today'   70
     4. Some Stories Only in Luke   71
     5. Parables Peculiar to Luke   75

5   Using Mark   82
     1. Luke's Edition of the Beginning of Jesus's
        Ministry in Mark   85
     2. Luke's Edition of theMinistry in Mark   91
     3. The Great Omission and the Gospel's Axis   96

      4. Luke's Edition of Mark's Passion:
            Part i—Prelude   103
            Part ii—The Process   109

6   Using Matthew   120
      1. Infancy and Resurrection Stories   122
      2. In Order   128
      3. The Sermon   131
      4. A Christian Deuteronomy   138
      5. Historical Development in Matthew   164

7   Historical Relativity and Christian Faith   174

Appendices
      A Some Septuagintal Phrases in Luke 1 and 2   185
      B Psalmody in Luke 1 and 2   187
      C The Census   189
      D Some Notes of Time in Matthew which are not
            in Mark   191

Select Bibliography   193

Indexes
      Biblical   197
      General   205

Preface

In all fairness a book about how another book came into existence ought to contain some explanation of its own provenance. When I was invited to write a short commentary on Luke, I shared the dislike of his work which is common in a generation and tradition devoted to the more drastic teachings of Paul, Mark and John. Writing the commentary turned hostility into admiration: largely because I was also engaged in another book, *Angels and Dirt* (Darton, Longman and Todd, 1972) which sought to explore points of intersection between Christianity and ordinary unecclesiastical experience—and Luke was the first Christian writer to do that in a thorough-going fashion. Modern apologetic found kinship with his secular gospel. Two more things emerged from work on that commentary. First, I discovered that I could do it without resort to the hypothesis of Q, though it is commonly thought to be an indispensable exegetical tool. Second, I found that the Old Testament had so much more influence on Luke than traditional criticism supposes that it could well be as important a source for Luke's work as his Christian documents. There was not space in the commentary for full treatment of these theses and a dead-line had to be met. While I was working them out at Exeter College, Oxford, I had a stroke of luck. M. D. Goulder was giving his Speaker's Lectures on the midrashic interpretation of the synoptic gospels (part since published as *Midrash and Lection in Matthew*, S.P.C.K., 1974) just across the street in Trinity. They brought into focus two vague but pressing concerns of mine. The first was with the gospels as literature and the sense that the evangelists ought to be appreciated by the same disciplines as are used in non-theological literary studies. I am fond of poetry and fiction, which are not universally popular amongst New Testament critics. The second was with history. I had read the first part of the History Tripos at Cambridge and this led, as I see now, to a certain bafflement and unease when I changed to theology. History was much pondered and invoked in New Testament studies but practised in a less pervasive and delicate way. The gospels were studied with painstaking scholarship but in relative isolation and with little more than the occasional glance at similar and contemporary literature. Goulder brought these two lines together and into the light by expounding *midrash* as the imaginative literary discipline by which the writers of the New Testament's time and *milieu* did their work.

Other strokes of luck followed. I lectured in Oxford in harness with Dr Morna Hooker and with my father-in-law, Dennis Nineham. This meant that my ideas were aired under the scrutiny of two exceptionally exacting and friendly scholars and formed in the market-place of teaching. Robin Baird-Smith of Darton, Longman and Todd trustingly agreed to take them on as a book. Moving to Norwich at this point put me among colleagues, the Dean and Chapter, who have been more than tolerant of my many hours in the study, and amongst parochial clergy and laity with whom I could test the implications of my notions for faith and its practice. An invitation from the diocese of Durham finally allowed me to put much of the final version before a sympathetic and vivaciously critical gathering of parish priests. A version of Chapter III appeared as an article in *Theology*, June 1974, entitled 'Midrash and Gospel'.

I would like to thank others who have given me particular help. Professor G. W. H. Lampe and Professor C. F. D. Moule of Cambridge have been generous in encouragement and the answering of queries. Professor C. F. Evans's essay on 'The Central Section of St Luke's Gospel' in *Studies in the Gospels*, edited by D. E. Nineham, with its synoptic table, will prove as necessary to the reader of this book as it has been to its writer. To the great works of Creed, Cadbury, Conzelmann and Haenchen I owe more than I can acknowledge. Miss Jean Cooper, Secretary to the Dean and Chapter of Norwich, has spent much time and patience on the typescript. The Revd J. L. Houlden read it and made valuable suggestions. The Revd T. Colman undertook the exacting task of compiling the indexes. My greatest stroke of luck has been my wife who has given me constant help and understanding. Together with our daughter, who is not in a position to give the same skilled support, she has fostered that *joie de vivre* which writers need so much and which delights the reader of Luke's Gospel.

JOHN DRURY
Norwich 1975

I

Introduction—The Well of the Past

CHRISTIANITY, LIKE ITS Jewish parent, is an historical religion with events in time bound inextricably into the centre of its theology and devotion. Its creeds have an epic sweep from creation through redemption to doomsday. The sacred scriptures of the New Testament show its character by their proportions: seventeen parts narrative (the gospels and the Acts of the Apostles) to ten parts instruction (the epistles), with the historical prophecies of Revelation adding a further, undistributed two parts. The pattern is also reflected in current Christian preferences. The ordinary believer owes more to the narratives, and likes them better, than the epistles —where he probably understands little and does not much like the little he understands. In academic circles the study of Paul and the other letter-writers goes ahead fruitfully but in some seclusion. Work on the gospels, by digging up ground with which the Church at large is more affectionately familiar, is done in more public and explosive conditions. The critic hears an ecclesiastical voice beseeching him to tread softly, for he treads on its dreams.

History, and particularly religious history, is an affair of the heart as well as the head, of dreams as well as dates. Stories (to use a term which deliberately begs the question of fact or fiction) communicate doctrines to the ordinary man more vividly than abstract schemes or moral advice because they are more concrete and more fun. By hearing them, telling them, modifying and retelling them, people find their way about and explore human possibilities. They are attached to them, in both senses, because they nourish and authenticate their existence by giving it roots in the venerated past. When new men or new movements arrive on the scene they commonly display a voracious historical appetite. The millionaire wants a pedigree and family portraits, and is not unduly worried by nice questions of authenticity. The Tudor chroniclers boosted the authority of the new dynasty, descended from a line of Welsh squires, by genealogies which connected them to King Alfred, the mythical Lud of London's Ludgate, and went back through David and Jesse to Adam himself. Eminent subjects of the crown claimed Trojans and Roman consuls as their ancestors. Heraldry ran riot. Reviewing this phenomenon, J. H. Plumb[1] insists that 'this was no joke, no game, no fantasy; both arms and pedigrees were of vital use. The great painted genealogies had a purpose, every whit as definitive as the great *stele* of Sethy the First at Abydos where he is depicted venerating the names of his seventy-six ancestors. . . . So he has the power descended, so is the power confirmed.'

Thomas Mann's four-volume saga *Joseph and His Brothers*[2] explores the nexus of history and personal identity by retelling biblical narrative. It begins with the sentence 'very deep is the well of the past, unfathomable' and goes on to describe a Jacob whose identity merges back, with his story, into that of his father, Isaac, and grandfather, Abraham. 'History', says Mann, 'is that which has happened and that which goes on happening in time. But also it is the stratified record upon which we set our feet, the ground beneath us; and the deeper the roots of our being go down into the layers that lie below and beyond the fleshy confines of our ego, yet at the same time feed and condition it—so that in our moments of less precision we may speak of them in the first person and as though they were part of our flesh-and-blood experience—the heavier is our life with thought, the weightier is the soul of our flesh.'[3]

Mann acknowledges 'the difficulty of writing about people who do not exactly know who they are. But I also make no question of the necessity of reckoning with those vacillating states of consciousness.'[4] A similar state of affairs confronts the student of the New Testament and he too has to reckon with it. The search for a Jesus who is Son of God and Son of Man necessarily slips back into the Old Testament where these titles first appear and into the antecedent culture where they were used before they were written down. Curiosity about Jesus's self-understanding has not got much satisfaction out of this quest, but it is at least certain that Jesus thought of himself in terms derived from the Old Testament scriptures which were his education—and so had something important in common with

Mann's patriarchs. Paul identified him by likeness and contrast with Adam. The old stories and prophecies bear continually on the gospel narratives of his life and, in different ways, shape them. So the critic who lets down his bucket into the well of Christian history never finds bedrock, but rather has the unnerving experience of paying out more and more line. The people he is dealing with not only have identities open to history and happily confused with the past. The writers are also making a determined bid for historical authority and historical roots because, like Plumb's Tudor monarchs and their servants, they are new men. So has the power descended, and so is power confirmed.

Rooted in the Jewish past, it was inevitable that the early Christians' thinking about history should be determined by Jewish historiography. To the modern mind the most striking feature of this tradition is that it gave to creative belief the governing position which is now occupied by analytic understanding. There is therefore a rift between the biblical critic and the old writers he is studying. While he knows that twentieth-century historians have formative beliefs and axes to grind, he also acknowledges that they have a different idea of success in history writing from the ancients, who felt certain at points where he is uneasy and checked differently. If he is a believer he becomes sharply aware of belonging to an ancient historical faith which has survived into an ice-age of scientific historical analysis. The stories which are integral to his faith, nourish and authenticate his religious identity, have come within reach of the knives of criticism. As with the patient on the psychoanalyst's couch, the ominous tension of the situation is compensated by the pleasure of seeing the past more in its own terms and colours than before—he will not dress Solomon as a renaissance prince or foist upon Jesus the mentality of a Victorian liberal. The times have changed. The days of man's historiographical innocency have gone. Critical technology now shares the stage with integrating belief and he has the task of getting them to terms with one another. In approaching the Jewish historical tradition which fostered the Christian he aims at objective appreciation rather than direct identification. How did the writers of the Old Testament histories do their work?

From the collections of tales which every group treasures as a kind of moral scrap book, they drew what Momigliano calls 'the idea of an historical continuum from the creation'.[5] 'The uniqueness of this development', comments Plumb in turn, 'lay in the idea of development. The past was not static, a mere story of information, example and event, but dynamic, an unfolding story.'[6] The techniques by which this very thorough-going historicism was done owed more to historical intuition and imagination than to the detailed historical research of which the twentieth century approves. There were plenty of tales floating loose and higgledy-piggledy in the great pool of oral tradition. The need was for links by which one tale might be connected to another in a coherent order (Lk 1:3—'to write to you consecutively'), which expressed their faith in the one God who was the supreme disposer and Lord of the whole historical process. The all-important links had to be made out of the existing tales themselves, worked upon until link shapes had been fashioned where necessary. There was no other material. To use Paul's metaphor,[7] it was like the grafting process by which the fruit grower makes a new apple tree. Incisions are made in a tree of one kind into which he sticks shoots from another stock. To put it in another horticultural image, the seeds of one event are in the established plant of another. According to Moshe Weinfeld[8] this was the technique of the Deuteronomic historian. 'Every national achievement or failure in this scheme is the result of the prophetic word which fore-ordained it. . . . The divine word acted in all stages of Israelite history and the national catastrophes were the consequences of the sins of Israel and Judea and their kings.'[9] A dialectic of prophecy and fulfilment was thus history's sustaining rhythm. The redactional method was to work on early prophecies and tales in such a way as to join them to others until the whole thing is set in a frame of historico-national significance. Set speeches or orations do the job particularly well, drawing on the narrative and serving as plateaux from which time past could be seen reaching a fulfilment in the present, time present being set on its course of destiny into the future.[10]

The process did not stop with this monumental achievement, crowned by the Deuteronomist's work, of linking material in connected historical epic. Life goes on after such books have been written and issues are raised with which they do not cope directly. There must be further interpretation, or *midrash*, to use the Hebrew word. New contingencies must be grafted to the old and hallowed stock. It is seen happening within the Old Testament canon in Nehemiah 8: a great tableau of the entire nation returned from exile gathered in the square before the Water Gate to hear Ezra the scribe read 'the Book of the Law of Moses which the Lord had given

4

to Israel'. But it is an old book, written before the catastrophe, so it is necessary that a corps of exegetes help the people understand the law. 'They read from the book clearly (or, with interpretation) and they gave the sense so that the people understood the reading.' Genesis 41:45 triggered narratives which are not in the Bible. 'Pharaoh gave Joseph in marriage Asenath the daughter of Potipherah priest of On.' A Rabbi in the strict pharisaical tradition knows that scripture cannot, at this point, possibly mean what it says. A law-abiding patriarch would never have married the daughter of a pagan clergyman. Asenath was not what she seemed, but the daughter of Dinah by the son of the King of Shechem, exposed by the righteous Jacob and transported by the archangel Michael to the temple at On where she is reared by Potipherah's childless wife until Joseph comes to marry her.[11] The embarrassment of this Rabbinic special-pleading contrasts with the gratification of a Jew living co-operatively amongst gentiles in Alexandria who must have known, such is life and love, of serious Jewish boys falling for acceptable gentile girls. Scripture to him means just what it says. It has only forgotten to mention that Asenath repented of her heathen ways and embraced the true faith before marriage. The romance of *Joseph and Asenath* (*circa* 100 B.C.–A.D. 100) results. The Dead Sea sect is another example of a new way of living, not dreamt of in scripture, insisting that it is precisely what scripture foresaw and commandeering by *midrash* the Holy Books to be its own root. So is Josephus at the end of the first century, contemporary with the Christian gospel-writers, editing Jewish scriptures into a form which would impress and attract the Graeco-Roman public.

Into this world early Christianity was born: the perennial human appetite for historical roots sharpened both by being a new arrival and by being sprung of a stock in which history *was* theology to such an extent that fragments of individual story were joined into an extended epic development. 'About the time when Christianity arose . . . historiographical productivity on really pure Jewish soil was very thin, and it was where Jewish life was in contact with the Greek historiographical tradition that it was productive in historical writing.'[12] So it was natural that historical writing flourished among the Christians as they established themselves in the same realm of contact as Hellenistic Judaism. As with Josephus and others, it was commerce with Hellenism which excited Luke to his renaissance of Old Testament historiography. Judaism also provided the set of tools, *midrash*, by which new shoots could be grafted into the tree of that great old history, still alive and developing. The Christians took it up and used it. Paul saw the story of the childhood of Ishmael and Isaac as a prophetic allegory of the relations of the Church and Judaism. He even has the young Ishmael persecute the young Isaac (Ga 4:29), although Genesis 21:9 depicts them playing together, to fit his contemporary situation. Harrying the Corinthians for some material reward for his labours among them he quotes Deuteronomy 25:4, 'You shall not muzzle the ox when it is treading out the grain', insisting that God is not here concerned about oxen but about himself (1 Co 9:9-10). Christian writing continued as midrashically as it began.

Luke is the best vantage point from which to see early Christianity in search of its past, because he is generally and rightly acknowledged to be the master historian amongst the New Testament writers, even if this acknowledgement is frequently followed by industrious wishful thinking about his methods. To open his gospel is to start at a point further back in time than with his predecessors which in itself signals the historian. For Paul the gospel begins with the death of Christ. According to him this is traditional (1 Co 15:3 ff.) and it shows how far he and his predecessors were from any of the biographical interest which is essential to history. His gospel is a story in the long history of God's dealing with his people, but told as a story it is unsatisfactory. It is a fish out of water when it is lifted away from the ocean of doctrine which sustains it: an element more friendly to the development of existential myth than of story-telling. Dazzled by the glory of the cross, Paul sees all before it, save Abraham's faith, as darkness. Centuries elapsed before God gave the Law as a remedy for Adam's sin. When it failed to work, more centuries passed until his definitive act of salvation in Jesus—which had yet to reach complete fulfilment at the day of judgement. Paul's sense of history was strong but crude. Mark took the momentous step of presenting the (Pauline) gospel of the cross entirely as history, beginning with the baptism of Jesus preceded by the Old Testament's prophecy and the expectant mission of John. As Ezra Pound says in his *ABC of Reading*, after the inventors who do a thing powerfully and roughly for the first time, come the masters who work it into something more elegant and digestible at the cost of a diminution of the primal power. Matthew picks up Mark not only to moralise him with a wealth of didactic material, but to historicise him further by frequent and conscious reference to the seeds of past prophecy which now flower into fulfilment. He also takes things further back in time, beginning with the genealogy from Abraham and Joseph's discovery of Mary's pregnancy. Luke (dispensing with Q[13]) then re-moralises, giving Matthew's decidedly ecclesiastical ethics a wider secular reference, and re-historicises Mark (who is his leading source for narrative) more thoroughly still. Where Matthew makes prophecy and fulfilment so blatant with his formulae of introduction ('To fulfil what was spoken by the prophet' etc.) that they are 'asides' from the drama, Luke feeds them into the tale so skilfully that there is no interruption and they need, from the modern reader who does not know his Old Testament as well as the first Christians, some digging out. Nowhere is this more striking than at the beginning of his book. This is at a point still further into 'the dark backward and abysm of time'[14] than before, with the appearance of the father-to-be of John the Forerunner and the promise, in the thoroughly traditional setting of temple worship, of John's birth. Only after eighty-six verses is Jesus born. This deep historical sounding is out-bid only by the Protevangelium of James[15] which is in the synoptic tradition and begins with Jesus's grandparents still childless, and John's ace of trumps in origins 'In the beginning the Word was'. Matthew's genealogy goes back to Abraham, Luke's to Adam.

But more than that, examination of Luke's first two chapters shows that they are in the septuagintal tradition from top to toe. Harnack noticed that in Luke 1 and 2 'The whole style is artificial and is intended to produce an impression of antiquity—a purpose which has been really fulfilled.'[16] H. F. D. Sparks more precisely says that the style is that of the Septuagint. 'A high percentage of Luke's most striking phrases have either exact, or very close parallels in the Septuagint.'[17] But it is more than a matter of style. The content of the drama is septuagintal too: the childless couples promised children by angelic visitation revive the tales of Abraham and Sarah, Manoah and his wife, Elkanah and Hannah. The Psalms which celebrate the action are an Old Testament stock-in-trade as a form, and in content a collage of Old Testament texts. The seam opened by Professor Sparks seems to be inexhaustible. Old Testament references in both style and content can be got out of Luke 1 and 2, and indeed out of his gospel at large, in such quantity that there can be no doubt that the Septuagint, handled with skill and conservative reverence, is a source: and for the first two chapters *the* source. To turn from Luke to Old Testament narrative, the story of Samuel's birth, for example, or the books of Tobit and Judith, is to cross no

7

boundaries but to remain in the same country, to hear the same language in the same forms describing similar events. Why? The answer is simple and takes us deeper still: because the same God, who as Lord of history works his purpose out by prophecy and fulfilment as year succeeds to year, is working all in all. There is no interruption because Luke is joined to Judaism at the deepest and most unbreakable point: historical monotheism. What Haenchen has said of Acts is true of the gospel. 'In reality it is God himself—the supreme authority—who governs and prescribes, in accordance with his plan, the course to be followed by the "Word of God".'[18]

Monotheism was the distinguishing mark of Judaism in the ancient world: the key-stone of the apologetic by which it courted the favour of the gentiles, as of the polemic by which is resisted them. Its transcendence sets the problem of how this Most High God (a phrase from the later Old Testament books, common in *Joseph and Asenath* which Luke found once in Mark but used eight times himself in Luke–Acts), can have to do with men. The answer of Old Testament history is plain: by sending down heavenly messengers to announce his inexorable will and by raising up men of his choice, patriarchs, prophets, kings, wise men, to do the same. Thus monotheism becomes historical and enables history. The Most High allows the secular, setting it at a distance from himself which gives independence, and on its own course of development in the seed-time-and-harvest rhythm of prophecy and fulfilment. Luke is thus consciously at one with Judaism in being monotheistic (see the canticles of Luke 1 and 2 and Paul's speeches at Lystra and Athens—Acts 14:15–17 and 17:22–31), and in expressing it by writing history. The graft is so deeply and sensitively made that it is possible not to notice it. Whereas Luke is patently an historian in the Jewish tradition, C. K. Barrett[19] and other excellent scholars, while allowing for much Old Testament influence, have tried to plant him with the Greeks, working on scanty resemblances rather than the wealth which is opened up by the acknowledgement of Luke's Jewishness. Matthew is usually thought the Jewish evangelist, Luke the gentile. Certainly Matthew is Jewish, a close neighbour of the Tannaitic rabbis who did their casuistic moralising out of scripture and sayings of the wise. He lives as it were next door to them and quarrels with them stridently. Luke is Jewish in the story-telling tradition of the books of Genesis, Judges, Samuel and Kings and the tales in the Apocrypha, a tradition still alive in Josephus's grand historical *midrash*, *The Jewish Antiquities*, and in *Joseph and Asenath*.

8

The young community's search for its past is resolved by being thoroughly at home in it—a home which, according to Luke, it has never left. The elder brother was the apostate.

Luke's Jewish historical faith determines his theology of Christ, notoriously lower than some. It is in fact as high as a traditional historical monotheism will allow and no higher. John gets higher by cutting loose from history in order to philosophise about it rather than stick exclusively to telling it. And when he does tell it, it is archetypally eternal. Nicodemus and Thomas are always with us. The Johannine Passion narrative is a profound diagnosis of the sickness of the religious and political establishments in God's presence. Luke's Jesus is the epitome and compendium of the men whom God raised up: he is Son of God like the kings, wise men and Joseph in *Joseph and Asenath*, he is Son of David born in David's city, teacher, and, most striking of all, a prophet in the mould of Elijah, which role Luke deliberately takes from John (leaving him, like Elisha, 'the spirit and power of Elijah') and gives to Jesus. Last, but not least, he is the founder of Christianity, and *the* Christ (Luke's preference for that definite article) prophesied in scripture. So in Christology there is a levelling down of Paul's doctrine of the unique interruption, a muffling of the crash of the descent of the Redeemer causing a radical discontinuity in the conditions of life. Instead we have a Jesus who is a link in time's chain, himself the ligature of old and new, the middle of time. History is no longer, as in Paul, the anvil on which God hammers out salvation at white heat, but the medium in which he is known in its rhythm of prophecy and fulfilment. Eschatology is subtly affected. It remains but is very deliberately 'not yet'. Jesus is not the end but its prophet (John takes the opposite line on both counts: the end is now and it is Jesus). It follows from this that Luke has nothing of Paul's doctrine of a mystical indwelling of Christ in the Church and the believer. The phases of history are connected but distinct, and from the point of view of the Church's 'today', Jesus is of the yesterday of his earthly life and the tomorrow of his return. Meanwhile he is in heaven 'until the times of the restoration of all things' (Ac 3:21). 'We are left with the impression', says C. P. M. Jones, 'that Christ is one thing and the Church another, and that the Church (and the Holy Spirit) carry on the work of an absentee Christ.'[20] Only monotheism could allow this or make it a secure Christian position.

Out of the Christology we can draw two major strands for brief introductory notice. As prophet, Jesus, like his predecessors,

9

addresses the nation. The famous 9:51, packed with septuagintal reference, says that the time drew near for his assumption (like Elijah and, in later Jewish tradition, Moses) and he set his face to go to Jerusalem (as in the prophecy of Jeremiah 21:10, 'For I have set my face against this city for evil and not for good, saith the Lord; it shall be given into the hand of the King of Babylon and he shall burn it with fire.') The nation's dark destiny is the real shadow in Luke's passion, the destruction of Jerusalem emerging in the eschatological prophecy which precedes it in graphic detail out of Mark's obscure 'desolation of abomination'. On the way to the cross Jesus pauses for his last oracle. It is to the daughters of Jerusalem (septuagintal phrase) and is of doom, cast in septuagintal terms. Christ's *via dolorosa* is an irrevocable bend in the longer path of the nation's road to ruin. 'If they do these things in the green tree, what shall be done in the dry?' (Lk 23:31). At the same time the Passion story opens another road. At the Last Supper Luke has Jesus give the Church its charter, its discipline and its destiny. Peter's denial will be reversed and he will return to strengthen the brethren, to be the wise apostle of Acts. Throughout, the Church's ministry has been carefully woven into its founder's. The miraculous catch at 5:1ff. anticipates Acts, as does the added mission of the seventy. Mark's treatment of the disciples as invincibly stupid men is edited so that, for all their weak humanity and need for repentance, they can be credible links, men who really could have been the Church's founding fathers under the Christ. Again we notice the difference from Matthew who, ethically concerned for the Church, amplifies Mark's narrative with Church teaching. Luke's concern for the Church is historical. He prunes and adorns Mark's narrative until its founding emerges as a clear theme.

Compared with the brimstone of Mark, Paul and even Matthew, Luke's book is notoriously bland. This is an effect of his unequalled success in providing the Church with a past. Even theologians cannot have everything. He has given the community roots as strong and nourishing as it could ask. He is also a bourgeois (how else could he devote a large part of a chapter to table manners and add to the horror of a demoniac's plight that he did not live in a house?). His thoroughgoing historicism makes him a catholic too, his Jesus the Christ set in the company of the men of God's past and the men of God's future. Graphically, the carved reredos or the east window familiar in our churches is a Lukan thing—Christ in the middle in his mother's arms, prophets and kings underneath, apostles to either side, above them the Church's doctors and the angels in the tracery, and God, undepicted, over all. So is the Church's year by which Christianity moves with the seasons to the music of time.

Luke's smooth continuity should not, however, be exaggerated. If there were not some discontinuity there would be no story, and this Luke found in the tragic catastrophe of the Jewish nation. Yet again, before that tragedy falls, the elements which will carry through it historically are established. The admission of the gentiles into the people of God is prophesied in the gospel, from Simeon's song and Jesus's manifesto at Nazareth in Chapter 4 onwards. In Acts it is accomplished. The Church, too, we have seen, is established before God's break with Judaism. Or again, it is noticeable that Luke's attitude to the Jews turns harder in Acts. The seeds of this too are in the gospel (see Chapter 4 again), and explained by Luke's emphasis on repentance and his antagonism to those who refuse it. The prodigal son, the unjust judge, the unjust steward, Zacchaeus and the penitent thief are only in Luke—all men who changed their minds and their ways in exemplary fashion. The Jewish nation refused this, acting (in Luke's view) true to form and in the tradition of its shameful treatment of those former envoys of God who had made the same call. 'Which of the prophets did you not persecute?' (Ac 7:52). Discontinuity within historical continuity finds focus and a concrete instance in any act of repentance. Changes of heart carried into changes of religious allegiance were a phenomenon of the pluralistic, hybrid world which Luke shared with the writer of *Joseph and Asenath*.[21] Judaism of the dispersion, scattered abroad from the confined security of the homeland, discovered in the proselyte a new kind of member of God's people. As a new religion, Christianity depended on conversions for its existence. The story of its growth, as told by Luke, turns upon them. They are the subject of many of the famous parables peculiar to him. Where Matthew's parables see the crisis of judgement as the end, in Luke's it forms the middle of the tale and sets it off on a new tack—usually in this world (the unjust steward), sometimes in the next (the rich man and Lazarus). Acts of repentance by Peter, implying discontinuity as well as continuity, mark each turning point in Luke's tale: at the miraculous catch with which the joint ministry of Jesus and the Apostles begins, at the Passion ('When you have turned again strengthen your brethren' Lk 22:32), and at the admission of gentiles (Ac 10 and 11).

Luke has drawn upon himself the hatred of some modern theologians who have good and tragic reason to suspect such a marriage of God's will with history. His work must appear to be something of a glamorising falsification to the reader who compares the statesmanlike council of Acts 15 with the bitter tangle reflected in Paul's letter to the Galatians, or his editing of Mark with the original. Luke's superior historical realism and plausibility makes the reader feel all the more let down when he makes such contrasts and draws his conclusion. A further annoyance to one school of recent theology is that Luke believed in the fatherhood of God and the brotherhood of man (Ac 17:24–9), which Harnack made a corner-stone of the liberalism against which Barth and his successors reacted so explosively. The *Frühkatholizismus* attributed to him since Harnack is not ordinarily a term of praise. But he certainly has a contribution to make to the christological debate which is raging at present. John Robinson's insistent reminders that Jesus was a man[22] (and how much portraits of the human Jesus draw on Luke, whether by Loisy, Dodd or Jeremias!) imply that he too was fixed in time and had colleagues, predecessors and successors in his ministry. Of the men raised up by God he is *primus inter pares*, as such having the uniqueness which is a gift of the spirit bestowed on man: and most clearly on the men of the spirit who seek it and work it out. It does not seem necessary in the Lukan frame to posit that uniqueness of kind which has been the rampart of Christian separatism and one of the reasons why Simone Weil was at odds with the Church. Monotheism reserves that transcendent uniqueness for God and fosters catholicism, the *communio sanctorum* which best describes how a Christian lives: with God as centre and with Christ the centre of God's will in history—but not in an isolated sense, for a debt of inspiration is owed to the many others who witness to him and with him. Luke, the first Church historian who wrote that history deliberately to project the line of Old Testament history, is honest to that. Little will be said here of the factual value of Luke's work. If it were put high, a law of swings and roundabouts, not usually noticed by conservative critics, would demote his canonical colleagues. Nevertheless, it cannot be put very high if Luke's Gospel is sufficiently explained, as it seems to be, by his use of Mark, Matthew or Q and (much more than is generally supposed) the Old Testament—all deployed with the exact and leisurely skill of one of the greatest narrative Midrashists. And yet the reader of Luke feels that this is how it must have been. Jeremias[23] takes the Lukan parable as his yard-stick and

Caird[24] the Lukan prophetic Jesus as the historical one. This can be attributed to Luke's historical sense, rather than to any hot line to a source of historical fact denied to his predecessors. He simply knows that Jesus's ministry was at a particular time; not his own time or the time of the Old Testament, but the link between them. It was yesterday—not today, or the day before yesterday. He is, for example at pains to keep gentiles off stage in his gospel. Mark's Syrophoenician woman disappears and Matthew's centurion is kept off the scene by hectic stage management. For Luke knew that the mission of the gentiles was later and avoids the anachronism. This finer sense of time distinguishes Luke. He has the historian's nose.

Above all he shows the need of a community for strong, historical roots, how a talented writer went about providing them, and the problems which such an achievement solves and raises.

[1] *The Death of the Past,* Pelican Books, 1973, pp. 26–29

[2] Sphere Books, London 1968

[3] Ibid., p. 158

[4] Ibid., p. 112

[5] 'Time in Ancient Historiography' *History and Theory,* Middletown 1966, 6, 18–19

[6] Plumb, p. 57

[7] Romans 11:17–24

[8] *Deuteronomy and the Deuteronomic School,* Oxford 1972

[9] Ibid., pp. 15 and 16. An example, given by Weinfeld on pp. 18–20, is the Deuteronomist's editing of the tale of Ahab's punishment for killing Naboth to get his land in Jezreel. Elijah promises him that 'in the place where dogs licked up the blood of Naboth shall dogs lick your own blood' (I K 21:19), but when Ahab repents Elijah says that the curse will be delayed and transferred to his son (vv. 27–9): which is fulfilled in II Kings 9 when Jehu orders that the body of Ahab's son Joram be thrown onto the plot of ground belonging to Naboth the Jezreelite. The Deuteronomist was not satisfied with this diversion of the prophetic curse, the weakness of its historical link, and reshapes the death of Ahab accordingly. The dead king's chariot is washed out 'by the pool of Samaria and the dogs licked up his blood and the harlots washed themselves in it, according to the word of the Lord which he had spoken' (I K 22:38). The Deuteronomist, who is generally believed to have interpolated this verse, insists that God's word should have its course in spite of the earlier tradition—even if it has to be fulfilled at the wrong place: Samaria instead of Jezreel.

[10] See Weinfeld's chapter on 'The Prophetic Oration'

[11] Pirké of Rabbi Eliezer, 38, given in *Joseph et Aséneth* ed. M. Philonenko, Leiden 1968, p. 33

[12] James Barr, 'Trends and Prospects in Biblical Theology' *Journal of Theological Studies,* October 1974, p. 280

[13] See Chapter VI

[14] Shakespeare *The Tempest* I.ii

[15] In E. Hennecke *New Testament Apocrypha* ed. R. McL. Wilson, Lutterworth 1963, pp. 370–388

[16] *Luke the Physician*, London 1907, p. 217

[17] 'The Semitism of St Luke's Gospel' in *Journal of Theological Studies* 44 (1943), pp. 129–138

[18] *The Acts of the Apostles*, Blackwell, Oxford 1971, p. 98

[19] *Luke the Historian in Recent Study*, London 1961, particularly p. 9: 'His fellows are Polybius and Plutarch, Josephus and Tacitus.'

[20] 'The Epistles to the Hebrews and the Lucan Writings' in *Studies in the Gospels* ed. D. E. Nineham, Blackwell, Oxford 1955, p. 127

[21] See A. D. Nock *Conversion*, Oxford 1933, a classic study which depends much upon Luke–Acts when dealing with Christian beginnings.

[22] See his *The Human Face of God*, S.C.M., London 1973

[23] *The Parables of Jesus*, S.C.M., 1954

[24] *Jesus and the Jewish Nation*, Athlone Press, London 1965

2

A Place on the Map

1. *The Theological Climate*

THE LONGING FOR historical roots, which impinges on new institutions with particular force, always has to wait until such an institution has got a foothold in the world and a little leisure before it can be as thoroughly exploited as in the massive Church history of Luke–Acts—far the biggest literary unit in the New Testament. It is in the affluent evening of his life that the *nouveau riche* gets interested in his genealogy. Previously he had neither the position nor the time. The contrast between Paul's use of history and Luke's shows the same development in the early Church, and leads us to expect to find more in common between Luke and the Deutero-Pauline letters than between him and Paul's authentic writings. It is clear from Acts that Luke belongs to a generation of Christians for whom Paul had become a hero, made more glamorous by miracles, more acceptable to Christian leaders and congregations and more eirenically statesman-like in his approach to the Jews and their law, than he is in his own letters. Martyrdom had shed a calming glow on this restless and contentious figure. The prophet who had never been on the easiest terms with his fellow Christians during his lifetime is hallowed after his death by the erection of literary monuments—Acts and the letters written in his name. Hans von Campenhausen[1] believes that the Pastoral Epistles were written as a lever for the reinstatement of the radical Paul, who quarrelled with the apostles, into a hierarchically and historically minded Church. 'The Pauline epistles could not be abandoned—but if they were to be preserved they had to be balanced with needs and ideas of a wholly different kind. It is, in my view, indisputable that it was at this time and with this intention that the Pastoral Epistles must have been composed.' In order of the confidence with which ancient and modern scholars have linked them to Paul, these Deutero-Pauline letters are: Ephesians, the Pastoral Letters (1 and 2 Tm and Tt) and Hebrews.

The letter to the Ephesians is built on a sense of solid historical continuity and growth. 'The Church, like a building, will take time to construct and to attain to "the measure of the stature of the fullness of Christ". History continues; the Church is involved in tomorrow and tomorrow and tomorrow.'[2] It can look forward to tomorrow more calmly than before because it is in secure possession of its past. It had been in the mind of the creator from all eternity. 'To me', says the writer who has taken upon himself the cloak and person of Paul, 'this grace was given to preach to the gentiles the unsearchable riches of Christ, and to make all men see what is the plan of the mystery hidden for ages in God who created all things, that through the Church the manifold wisdom of God might be made known to the principalities and powers in the heavenly places. This was according to the eternal purpose which he has realised in Christ Jesus our Lord.' (Ep 3:8–11). The Church is the historical fruition of a 'plan for the fullness of time' (Ep 1:10). Luke's entire work rests upon the same conviction. Christianity is for him the historical fulfilment of God's design, a purpose which the Jews 'rejected for themselves' (Lk 7:30 and see Ac 28:25–28), so that the religious initiative passed to a Church which included gentiles. Gentile membership in Ephesians is a matter for historical celebration, rather than present argument as in Galatians, because the bitter struggle over the Law which was central to the discussion then is now seen to be past and settled. 'But now in Christ Jesus you who once were far off have been brought near in the blood of Christ, for he is our peace who has made us both one and has broken down the dividing wall of hostility by abolishing in his flesh the law of commandment and ordinances that he might create in himself one new man in place of the two, so making peace, and might reconcile us both to God in one body through the cross, thereby bringing the hostility to an end' (Ep 2:13–16). Christ's death is the reconciliation of inter-human hostility, and particularly of the division between Jew and gentile. The passage brings to mind that curious addition which Luke made to Mark's passion narrative, the trial before Herod at Luke 23:8–12. Source-wise it consists of jumbled reminiscences of Mark's trials before the Sanhedrin and before Pilate, and of the mockery by Pilate's soldiers (Lk 23:9–11), sandwiched between Luke's observations that Herod had long wished to see Jesus and that having seen him 'Herod and Pilate became friends with each other that very day: for before they were at enmity between themselves'. Judicially the incident is inconclusive and from the point of view of narrative it is a detour. Its thrust and point is in the last sentence. The Jewish ruler is reconciled to the gentile on the very day of the shedding of Christ's blood. The symbolic history of Ephesians appears in Luke as actual history. It is as impossible to say which writer depends upon the other, or whether they are both drawing on a common stock, as it is clear that they are very close in their theological history. As with the miraculous catch of 5:1–11, Luke is here planting in the Lord's ministry an acted prophecy of the Church's achievement.

Along with its sense of temporal order, the Church of Ephesians has an hierarchical order. It is 'built upon the apostles and prophets, Christ Jesus himself being the Chief cornerstone in whom the whole structure is joined together and grows into a holy temple in the Lord' (Ep 2:20f.). The chief gift of the ascended Christ (more in evidence than Paul's crucified Christ) is Church order: 'that some should be apostles, some prophets, some evangelists, some pastors and teachers' (Ep 4:11). Luke's share of the same concern is evident in the pains he goes to in order to have Jesus found the Church during his ministry with more detail and definition than the previous evangelists. Comfortably set in history and graded authority, the Church of Ephesians is given an ethic which accepts the conditions of ordinary life and finds theology within them. 'The exalted conception of human marriage is spectacularly different from the low and grudging doctrine of 1 Corinthians 7, that it is allowable as a remedy against incontinence—as if marriage under the new covenant has a status comparable to that of divorce under the old.'[3] Marriage is treated as an image of life's central mystery, and from it flows a theology of the family—husbands, wives, children, slaves and masters living in mutual service and peace. A well-to-do household is envisaged here as in Luke's tales of the unjust steward and the prodigal son and in the dinner parties of which he is (theologically) fond. The tendency to find salvation in the secular and ordinary binds the two authors together and distinguishes them from earlier Christian writers. Their Christ preached peace (Ep 2:17, Lk 1:79, 19:42, etc.), and set his disciples an example of kindness, tender-heartedness and forgiveness (Ep 4:32).

A bond of some kind between Luke and the Pastoral Epistles has long been recognised. They are so close, in the generalities of doctrine and the particularities of vocabulary and grammar, as to support theories of common authorship.[4] They certainly share concerns, attitudes and a modest standing in the world, together with the ideas and key words for dealing with them. Many of these are obviously rooted in Paul's own teaching, as with Ephesians, but again they stand out with a clearer definition because the arguments which exercised Paul have been settled and receded into the background, leaving concerns which were secondary to him in greater prominence.

Paul viewed the surrounding world in which rulers govern, money changes hands and people marry with a certain cavalier tolerance, sometimes coloured by indifference or irritation, before diving into matters of more profound moment. In the Pastoral Epistles and particularly the more spacious 1 Timothy, they get a positive assent which is not over-shadowed by the presence of deep symbolic theologising. In Romans 13:1–7 obedience to secular governance is laid on the Christians as an obvious obligation. But 1 Timothy 2:1–4 is more positive. 'Kings and all who are in high positions' are to be the subject of 'supplications, prayers, intercessions and thanksgivings', which include all humanity because the peaceful order which kings make is an integral condition of the realisation of God's desire that all men should be saved. Likewise in Luke–Acts judicial decisions made by rulers enable the spread of Christianity. With this goes an affirmative attitude to humbler secular institutions. Ascetics who 'forbid marriage and enjoin abstinence from food' are castigated by the pastor as demonically inspired liars for, as Peter learned by his vision in Acts 10, 'everything created by God is good' (1 Tm 4:1–5). Like a worldly-wise family doctor, the pseudo-apostle counsels Timothy to abandon drinking only water and prescribes 'a little wine for the sake of your stomach and your frequent ailments': has the hypochondria which attends upon leisurely and conscientious living made its first appearance in the Church? As in Ephesians family life is supported by godly admonitions. A widow's first duty is to her family if she has one, because failure to look after one's kin amounts to apostasy from the faith (1 Tm 5:3–8). Good household management and discipline is a duty of the bishop, no less important than his teaching. 'He must be well thought of by outsiders.' Deacons also should be respectable family men (3:1–13). Luke's familiarity with Mark and Matthew, together, no doubt, with his own experience, taught him the contrary truth that discipleship can mean an abandoning of family ties (Lk 9:57–62, 14:26),[5] but he can also make their restoration the climax of his miracle at Nain and his tale of the prodigal son.

Money is a problem for both Luke and the pastor. They see it as indispensable, useful to the cause—but transient and fraught with danger. The elder who teaches is a labourer who deserves his pay. (1 Timothy 5:18 is very much the same as Luke 10:7, sharing 'wages' against the 'food' of Matthew 10:10.) The philanthropic rich man lays up a good foundation for the future (1 Tm 6:19)—a form of life assurance which Luke found in Mark 10:21 and Matthew 6:19 and emphasised in his parable of the rich fool (12:21). The pursuit of money is the road to ruin and the cause of apostasies from the faith. 'The love of money is the root of all evil' (1 Tm 6:10). As Moule says, 'The themes of the distinctively Lukan parables of the rich fool and the dishonest bailiff are distinctly audible here', and particularly in the proverbial wisdom about the uncertainty of riches (1 Tm 6:17), and their transience (6:7) and the excellence of contentment. It is as evident here as in Luke that Christianity has made itself at home among the bourgeoisie, endorsing its values of family discipline, hospitality and hard work. Its practical piety is defended against the more exotic and highfalutin claims of asceticism and 'godless and silly myths'. No 'gazing into heaven' for them. Their concerns are at eye-level, just as in Luke the whole gospel is in history and the every-day world. The voice of middle-class religion speaks out as clearly at 1 Timothy 4:8 as in the works of Samuel Smiles, the Victorian prophet of pious prosperity: 'godliness is of value in every way, as it holds promise for the present life and also for the life to come'.

The theology of the Pastoral Epistles is notoriously sparse and second-hand. But such as there is chimes in with Luke's. 'There is one God and there is one mediator between God and men, the man Christ Jesus who gave himself as a ransom for all, the testimony to which was born at the proper time' (I Tm 2:5). Ransom is the only notion there which is foreign to Luke, who omitted Mark 10:45 ('a ransom for many'). God is 'the saviour of all men' (I Tm 4:10). The pastor's four-square monotheism requires a subordination of Jesus and an emphasis on his humanity—'the *man* Christ Jesus'. The same is true of Luke. When the pastor sets forth 'the mystery of our religion' by quoting a hymn about Christ (I Tm 3:16), Pauline theology of the cross is conspicuously absent. Instead the pattern is a path to glory, the purpose of its earthly section being seen at 1:15 as the salvation of sinners, a major Lukan theme.

The Church structured by its bishops, elders and deacons, needs no defence. It is God's household, 'the pillar and bulwark of the truth'. Instead of passionate dialectic, the stock-in-trade of its doctrine has become, if the pastor is as typical and ordinary as he looks, formulae and the proverbs favoured by Luke. It is not disturbed as in former days by dissension about the Law. Of Paul's diagnosis of the dark collusion of law and sin there remains only the unexceptionably banal view that law has its place as a corrective of bad conduct. Luke also knew nothing of these battles of yesterday, or if he did, concealed it. His Jesus and his apostles are law-abiding and in Acts the resurrection has taken the Law's place as the centre of dispute with Judaism. Indeed the only possible reference to that gigantic problem in the Pastorals is the pseudo-apostle's plea that in his Jewish days he 'acted ignorantly in unbelief'. This is Luke's solution too, put into the mouth of Peter at Acts 3:17 and of Paul at Acts 17:30 and parabolically presented at Luke 12:47, where the disobedient servant who did not know his master's will gets a lighter beating than the one who did. Luke acts on this conviction in the whole of his literary enterprise which, according to both its prefaces to Theophilus, is motivated by the belief that the great need is for people to be better informed. Last but not least, the sacred writings of the Old Testament have a sure and authoritative place in the Church. They are 'able to instruct you for salvation through faith in Christ Jesus', which is to say that for the pastor they are Christian books and a mine of material for such practical duties as teaching, reproof, correction and 'training in righteousness'. Apart from the solitary quotation of the Deuteronomic ox at 5:18 however, he pays the Old Testament as good as no attention at all. The mediocre mind reveres without exploiting. It cannot be Luke's who wove scriptural convictions and language into his work with such skill, but like his it is set within a Church in order and at peace.

Many of the characteristics which Luke and the pastor have in common are also shared by the writer of Hebrews, with the difference that here we have an intelligence not inferior to Luke's, though working in symbolic concepts rather than in narrative.[6] Ethics takes the lower place in Hebrews which theology takes in the Pastorals, but has the same orientation. Marriage is revered and protected, the love of money warned against, obedience to leaders (though ecclesiastical rather than secular) made into a leading virtue, together with steadfast sticking to the faith. Hospitality and sharing are to permeate Christian living (Heb 13:1–17). Monotheism again demands that Jesus should, as an indispensable part of his mediating work, occupy a position of subordinate and thoroughly human pre-eminence in the earthly life which was the path between his pre-existence and the present heavenly glory which now separates him from the life of the Church on earth. If the separation is less sharp in Hebrews it is because, unlike Luke, the writer is gazing into heaven and making a monumental symbolic scheme based upon history, rather than a narrative with symbolic references. He is therefore less bound by time's irrevocable differences. The Church reposes on solid foundations and draws upon a fund of doctrine and practice which has features also found in Luke–Acts, but not elsewhere.[7] Here too the status of the Law is not a matter for passionate argument. It has found its proper place, particularly in its cultic aspect, in pointing to its own fulfilment in Christ. The scriptures cohere in him. Like Luke and unlike the pastor, the writer of Hebrews uses them throughout as material for his Christian edifice with the same leisurely and learned thoroughness.

His construction rests upon an underlying and clearly articulated view of history. A temporal gap separates the writer from the origin of Christianity and he is conscious of it. 'It was declared at first by the Lord and it was attested to us by those who heard him, while God also bore witness by signs and wonders and various miracles and by gifts of the Holy Spirit' (Heb 2:3f.). The life of the Church is linked to its Lord's by the apostolic eye-witnesses and the providence of the Holy Spirit with God over all: Luke and Hebrews are fundamentally at one. Prophecy and fulfilment make sense of the relation between the Christian 'now' and the Jewish 'then' in both their schemes. In Hebrews the old cultic regulations are fulfilled in Christ's eternal and heavenly priesthood, the earnest looking forward of the old historical characters in the perfection of Christian existence. The earthly life of Jesus is the middle of time, the 'little while' which links these separate epochs by his coming as both fulfilment and forerunning pioneer. The faithful Christian is set between this centre and the end. In Hebrews as in Luke the fires of earlier eschatological expectation have cooled—not only because their fulfilment had been postponed, but also because the Church has found plenty to get on with in the present, not least the ordering and celebration of a generation and more of achievement. The future end still glimmers on the horizon and is by no means the object of scepticism, but there is now a past to balance it.

Luke belongs with these later writers of the New Testament by sharing their fundamental attitudes. The passage of time has brought about a recession of eschatology, a comfortable integration and dialogue with the secular world, and stress on the historical foundations of Christianity. Precise dating of the Deutero-Pauline letters is impossible, so they contribute little to the dating of Luke beyond a strong indication that he is, in New Testament terms, late. They direct the search for a date forwards rather than backwards, which contradicts the opposite tendency of many critics to make a gospel as early as possible, and gives general support to O'Neill's view that 'the *terminus a quo* for Luke–Acts is about A.D. 115, and the *terminus ad quem* is about A.D. 130, but the naming of these dates gives an air of precision to the case which is scarcely warranted. More important than the dates are the arguments, that Luke and Justin Martyr held common theological positions without being dependent on each other and that Luke–Acts was completed in time for Luke to be used by Marcion.'[8] O'Neill explains the verbal coincidences between Luke and Justin by independent use of a common source. He reaches this position by arguments which are detailed and persuasive, but not conclusive: for when writers say the same thing in the same or similar words, it is impossible, in the absence of other evidence, to close any of the three viable explanations—that A depends on B, B on A, or both B and A on a certain C which has not survived. (For this reason, incidentally, arguments against Q in this book fall short of killing it.) The importance of O'Neill's work, as he himself acknowledges, is to show Luke and Justin inhabiting the same intellectual realm. The atmosphere which sustains and informs the Deutero-Pauline letters is still present in Justin, Luke is linked to both and so can be dated within their parameter.

Justin was a gentile convert to Christianity who addressed his doctrine to Jews and Greeks outside the Church and built it upon the twin pillars of monotheism and scripture. There is, therefore, a distinctly Jewish tone to him—surprising at first, but understandable when he is seen like the later New Testament writers within a Church which has left Paul's struggles behind and is now engaged in establishing itself by continuity with the God of Israel and the sacred writings which testify to him. Authority belongs to the man

22

whose arguments are based on scripture and who believes in only one God (Dialogue with Trypho 56:16): 'the father and maker of all' is his favourite description. It derives from Plato (Republic 506 E), but could hardly be more appropriate to the heart of Judaism with which Justin shares a high and pure doctrine of transcendence. As with Luke this affects all the rest of his thinking. Christ is God's first offspring, the Word begotten before all creation and present throughout all history. He evidently wants to pitch his Christology as high as he can, and he gets it far higher than Luke who does not share his idea of pre-existence: 'Since he is the first-born of God, he is God.' But monotheism stands in the path to check this and prevent a resolution. Eusebius[9] says that he wrote a book on the *monarchia* or sole rule and unity of God. The Word 'cannot be the supreme Father since he is too far removed to have direct contact with this inferior realm, and cannot have abandoned his universal care for the cosmos as a whole, to be circumscribed by incarnation in one small corner of it'.[10] Christ, it seems, is God in the second rank, God subordinate.

This scheme, hovering between Luke's and John's, has happy results for Justin's attitude to the world and time. Monotheism is favourable to history and historical reflection. Justin believes that Christ was prevalent in the Old Testament as the glory of God, Son, Widsom, Angel, Lord, Word. Further, a pagan like Socrates or Heraclitus who lived 'with Logos', is a Christian along with Abraham and Elijah. Plato had preached the true God, having read the Pentateuch while in Egypt. History is theology—not a series of separate incidents of salvation, but a continuous development which declares God's activity through his mediators amongst whom the Word himself, and the prophets with Moses at their head, are pre-eminent. 'When you hear the words of the prophets spoken as by some person, do not think that they were spoken by the inspired person, but think rather that they were spoken by the divine word who moved them' (1 Apology 36:1). The Word who spoke by the mouth of the holy prophets (Lk 1:70), is, for Justin as for Luke, a prophet himself. 'That all these things should take place was foretold by our teacher who is Jesus Christ, the Son and Apostle of God, the Father and Lord of all. . . . Those things are indeed happening which he foretold in anticipation. This is the deed of God—to tell a thing before it happens, and then to show it happening as foretold' (1 Apology 12:10). His conviction that prophecy and fulfilment are history's driving rhythm keeps Justin—as Luke—in the Jewish tradition. They both see an overall three-fold pattern in prophetic history. Justin finds a dispersion of prophecy after Moses amongst his successors, then a concentration in Jesus followed by a further dispersion amongst his successors. He has exact dates for creation, the birth of Jesus and the second coming, and he fills the space between the ascension and the final consummation with the Church's spectacularly successful mission to every known race—which is itself used as an argument for Christianity. He views the world with triumphant affirmation and has, like Luke, 'a full-blooded and extremely literalistic doctrine of the resurrection of the flesh'.[11] For him, too, the problem of the law is historically settled. Prophecy is forever, but the old Law has had its day and is now replaced by a new and universal one. Here Luke takes another road, believing in the continuity of the old Law into the life of the Church—a difference largely explained by the exigencies of being a practitioner rather than a philosopher of history. But he shares Justin's belief that the destinies of the Church and the empire are bound up in the providence of God. 'It was, he believes, part of the providential plan that Rome should govern Judea at the time of the incarnation, and that in A.D. 70 Jerusalem should be sacked by the legions as the instruments of divine wrath.'[12] They are both as concerned as the pastor to show that Christians are respectable law-abiding folk who assent to *Pax Romana*.

Three other Christian writers of the same epoch fill out the picture. Clement of Rome, his mind 'saturated . . . with the language and ideas of the Old Testament, the only scriptures, properly so called, for Christians at this early time',[13] appealed to the scriptures, and particularly 'the blessed Moses' and his government of Israel, for the foundation of his doctrine of the Christian ministry of bishops and deacons. There he finds both an exemplar for the present and a prophecy of it.[14] The Epistle of Barnabas is 'the most thoroughgoing attempt to wrest the Bible absolutely from the Jews, and to stamp it from the very first word as an exclusively Christian book.'[15] This springs from the conviction that through the prophets the Master has laid open to us both past and present history, and has given us an anticipatory taste of the future as well. . . . We see events coming to pass step by step precisely as he told us.'[16] The writer proceeds by a process of relentless allegorisation which shows that the Christians, not the Jews who wrote the books, are their rightful owners and interpreters. But, having commandeered the scriptures, the Christians were to find them something of a mixed blessing.

Ignatius discovered to his vexation that heretics could quote these primary sources (*archeia*) as aptly as an orthodox bishop. He countered that 'for me Jesus Christ is the *archeia*; the inviolable *archeia* are his cross, his resurrection and the faith which he creates' (Philad 8:2). The old scriptures could not in the end be the Church's only or final court of appeal.

All these Christian writers belonged with Luke in a Christianity which had found a place in the sun and the leisure to make the celebration of its own existence a basic ingredient of its theology. At worst this is bourgeois in a complacent sense. At best it finds the intersection of God and man in the world around, in Church and family life and the whole process of human history. Luke, Justin and the writer of Hebrews took time to order history in Christian terms and in some detail, embarking on a thorough reinterpretation of the Jewish scriptures in the process. On this civilised ground they are ready to hold their own with polite firmness in debate with Greeks and Jews. They find themselves in that confluence of the Hellenistic and Judaic traditions where the more open-minded Jews of the dispersion were already at home. But there is one basic and obvious difference between them and Luke. They reflected upon history but he wrote it—a difference in the form for expressing the ideas which made a difference to the ideas themselves. Luke stands in succession to the Christian narrators Mark and Matthew whose work he revises to suit the new and kinder climate. His gospel is more of a secular history than theirs, a work of literature for a literary public. It so demonstrably belongs with them as well as with his letter-writing contemporaries, that a second bearing must be taken on the category of 'gospel'.

2. *Gospels and Neighbours*

There was nothing quite like the gospels in the literature of their time, and there has been nothing quite like them since. C. F. Evans in *The New Testament Gospels* (BBC 1975) asks us to suppose the Librarian at Alexandria received one of them—how would he have classified it? It was too doctrinal to put among the biographies, too much of a narrative to be at home amongst the theological treatises. 'The literary form of the gospels', says W. Schneemelcher, 'is a singular phenomenon in the literature of late antiquity, confined to the Christian world and having its origin in the special necessities of preaching and worship.'[17] It is an opinion which has come to be treated as axiomatic in New Testament studies—with some reason, since prolonged investigations have failed to extract from the mass of ancient literature a book which tallies exactly with the gospels in every important feature. But every axiom left to itself and unexamined has a way of fostering exaggeration. This is a particularly lively danger with the gospels, because they are pre-eminent amongst the holy books of Christianity. A religion which likes to think of itself as uniquely true amongst religions, and deduces that conviction from the unique status of its founder amongst the world's holy men, or projects such a status upon him, will naturally be enthusiastic about the discovery that the primary sources for knowing him are singular phenomena. Just as naturally it will tend to exaggerate the singularity into an isolation which puts the gospels clean off the map of the history of literature. Fortunately Christianity has in itself a corrective for this projection. Being an emphatically historical religion, it has not only been bound to attend to the disciplines of scientific, analytical history, it has fostered and promoted them. As a result its tendency to give an uncritical welcome to the notion of the historical singularity of the gospels is countered by a lively curiosity about how they came into existence—an enquiry which breaks the isolation in a practical fashion by taking its followers into the literary world of the first century. Modern biological studies have corrected the old way of lifting a specimen out of its environment into the laboratory by examining it within its native surroundings and as the nexus of all the factors which make it what it is. It will still be singular ('a rose is a rose is a rose'), but its individuality will have been made more intelligible and so more distinct by being seen amongst its neighbours. The old isolating way was not superseded because scientists have a rancorous, levelling mind which longs to conclude 'it is nothing but . . .' It was found that it imposed too much. The methods overpowered the subject and blinkered the eye against much vital information. The old way of reading the gospels has been found to have the same disadvantages. By cutting them away from their native habitat and putting them in the laboratory of current religious concerns, it has exposed them to infection from anachronistic hopes and anxieties and concealed facts which would illuminate them.

Something of the old way clings to the judgement of Schneemelcher which has been quoted. The gospels are 'confined to the Christian world', but the idea of a Christian world in the first century or two of the Church's existence is a temptation to anachronism. Christianity was a matter of scattered congregations living off the country in a world which belonged to other people. To say that the gospels have their 'origin in the special necessities of preaching and worship' is true enough, but does not do justice to the pluralistic conditions in which that preaching and worship were done, nor does it take the search for origins far enough: Judaism was the matrix from which early Christianity cannot be detached and from which, in Luke's generation, it did not wish to detach itself. It also borrowed here and there from the Hellenistic religions and established itself by contradicting them and so owing them a backhanded debt. There is a further measure of anachronism in looking at the canonical gospels as a unified set. One of the nest of four has long been acknowledged to be a marvellous cuckoo. John's gospel is in some vital respects more akin to the later gnostic Gospel of Truth than to the other three in the canon, and the family resemblance between those three is largely accounted for by the simple fact that Matthew and Luke produced books which are editions of Mark's, to whom they owe the narrative frame on which their character largely depends. These synoptic gospels also have kindred outside the canon of Christian scripture in works like the Protevangelium of James and the Gospel of Thomas.

The gospels are natives of a world in which 'the cultural solidarity of an earlier period . . . has been gradually dissolved into a world-wide megalopolitan civilisation which has no soul of its own'.[18] Popular literature proliferated and 'the range of its content is extended ever more and more to embrace the vagaries unlimited of the spiritual and intellectual nomads for whom it is intended.'[19] Two literary forms mirrored this fragmented and individualised world and spoke to its condition: the novel, which dealt with 'the adventures or experiences of one or more individuals in their private capacities and from the viewpoint of their private interests and emotions'[20] and the aretalogy or biography of the hero or holy man. The two had much in common. The biography or hagiography told the adventures of its historical hero in the same way as the romance told of its fictional hero—and usually embellished it with a good deal of obviously fictional matter: fact and imagination melted into one another in the twilight of a popular syncretistic culture. In a world which had grown too big these stories were a focus and a model for living. The Christians were far from having a monopoly in the field. The staunch pagan Celsus could ask why Jesus of Nazareth was thought so exceptional when there were so many in Palestine and Syria 'who wander about begging both inside and outside temples and frequent both cities and camps on the pretence of prophesying. And any one of them is ready and accustomed to say, "I am the God", or, "a son of God", or "a divine spirit" and "I have come, for the world is already on the point of destruction and you, O men, will perish because of your injustice. But I wish to save you, and you will see me again returning with heavenly power. Blessed is he who has worshipped me now." [21] One of these colourful figures makes a brief appearance in Luke's writings[22] at Acts 8:9f.; Simon, who had convinced a sizeable public in Samaria that he was 'the power of God which is called Great'. Justin the Apologist knew more about him and makes clear (as Luke does not) that 'the great power' was a name for God himself amongst the Samaritans. Simon claimed that he was God, incarnate for the redemption of man (1 Apol 26:3; Dial 120:6). In his own First Apology Justin used the common phenomenon of the holy man or incarnate God to argue the other way from Celsus: with such a gallery of divine heroes there was nothing exceptionally difficult about Christianity. The story of Jesus was 'no stranger than the story of those beings whom you call Sons of Zeus. You know how many of your most reputable authors attribute sons to Zeus. Hermes is his word and his interpreter, the universal master; Asclepius was a doctor too and, having been struck by lightning, ascended into heaven; Dionysus was torn to pieces, Hercules threw himself on the fire to bring an end to his labours.' Justin adds bluntly that the Christian story, though similar to these, is superior. Jesus's birth was much more seemly than that of any son of Zeus, his ascension into heaven a fact while that of Romulus is a bogus fable.[23] Defenders and assailants of Christianity took different views of the divine men, but they both accept them as a familiar part of their world. 'There were Gods who had various adventures—including servitude, suffering and death—like those of men. Almost any God was likely to appear in human form, and consequently a number of historical persons had been supposed to have been deities or *daimones* in disguise.'[24] The figure of Hercules, struggling for mankind and dying tragically, was developing at the same time as the traditions about Jesus.[25] Asclepius became all things to all men, a principle of divine order and a solar deity.

Written lives of two of the inspired men who were revered in the Graeco-Roman world have survived as more than fragments. Aesop, the shrewd slave and inventor of fables, lived in the sixth century B.C. The tradition about him grew in the centuries after his

28

death, fables from elsewhere attaching themselves to it, until in the first century A.D. an Egyptian editor strung them together into a narrative, adding a good many further popular stories.[26] In the first half of the same century Phaedrus, a Hellenised Italian living in Syria,[27] did his fables in Latin verse. Babrius produced a Greek version later in the century. The mongrel provenance of these redactors is typical of the sort of uprooted person who was interested in such a hero. The original narrative on which they worked has striking points of resemblance with Mark's gospel at points where that book is sometimes considered unique. It starts with Aesop as a grown man. His hideous appearance is described—not for its own sake but, as with Socrates, for the spice of contrast it gives to his intellectual elegance. Similarly, Mark describes the Baptist's appearance, not to inform curiosity but to make him a new Elijah. Like Mark's book, the tale is made up of a series of disjointed *pericopae*, little stories which show Aesop's wisdom, sometimes in a deed and few words, sometimes by his telling one of his homely fables. In the middle of the book he receives his freedom. At the end of it he is martyred by the people of Delphi for denouncing their religious chicanery. A plague then falls on the city which consultation with Apollo reveals to be a punishment for the just man's murder. The end of the story shows Aesop to have been something more than a sage: a man close to the gods and a martyr.

The life of Apollonius of Tyana, which Philostratus wrote at some time about A.D. 220, is a longer and more developed specimen.[28] Apollonius lived in the first century A.D., so some of the material in Philostratus's book must come from a time contemporary with the writings of the gospels, even if the writer's appeal to the memoirs of Damis of Nineveh, an eye-witness, is a fiction meant to give an air of authenticity to his work. Here again there are resemblances to the gospels—more to Luke's leisure and polish than Mark's earlier and rougher work. Again the sage's clothing and diet are part of his religious message. The narrative is often disjointed and episodic, a wearisome string of tales to illustrate Apollonius's simple neo-Pythagorean faith, wisdom and miraculous powers to heal, exorcise and raise the dead. Such narrative cohesion as the book has it owes to the journeys of the sage around the eastern Mediterranean. In the end he is tried on trumped-up charges, makes a long defence and is executed. After his death, which is described as 'going up from the earth' he still has power to convert a man to his truth by appearing in a dream. His soul goes marching on.

The help which this Hellenistic material gives to an historical understanding of the Christian gospels is indirect, a matter of background rather than dependence, setting them in the life of a hybrid period of history. Philostratus was a Greek from Memnos who bore the Roman family name of Flavius and wrote, for the Syrian wife of Septimius Severus, the life of a Cappadocian neo-Pythagorean. The traditions about the Greek slave Aesop were gathered together in Greek with a sprinkling of Latin words by an anonymous Egyptian and versified by an Italian living in Syria. The gospel of Mark is written in Greek about a Jewish teacher, exorcist and son of God, probably by a Roman Christian. They all share a world in which syncretism bears witness to the breaking down of those local boundaries which give men an unquestioned security. At the same time they give comfort and an answer to that agoraphobic situation. In the middle of a jumble of ideas the figure of an individual gives a clear focus of interest to enlighten the isolated hearer or community. His biography—fragmentary or complete, factual or fictional or both—brings spiritual sustenance in the attractive form of story to a popular culture where Homer was more popular than Plato, and Plutarch was writing in his *Lives* 'the drama of an individual's success or failure, and the various moral reflections which can be made on these subjects.'[29] A Hellenistic writer, compiling a narrative about a man with a philosophical or religious message, could write like Mark in an episodic fashion which fell short of the best literary standards but put him in touch with middle-brow readers and was quite adequate to convey the central message: and that was what mattered. Books of this kind could be put alongside the Christian gospels in a rough categorisation suitable to an age when the *genre* of a book could be determined in each instance by the writer, when fictions announced themselves as histories and histories could come in verse.

These Hellenistic worthies and their biographers show that the gospels were not unprecedented or entirely singular and that their singularity itself is not surprising. They shared the needs of their time and sought, in similar forms, to answer its longing for wisdom and light. But Christianity's matrix and its closest neighbour was Judaism. The Old Testament scriptures were the basic reading of the young Church, constantly heard and explored in their meetings. They extracted proof-texts or *testimonia* from them. Their forms and structures got into their systems too, giving models of biographical technique to guide them when the time came for them to turn to narrative.

Time and again the writers of the Old Testament went about their theological business by telling stories in which one man plays a leading part. Rather than speculate conceptually about man they told the tale of the one primal and representative man, Adam. The history of their nation was gathered into the destinies of its leaders. Biography follows biography. Sometimes a man's life is told from start to finish, as with Moses, Isaac or Jacob; but the sagas of Abraham and Elijah begin, like Mark's gospel, with the protagonist a grown man. Elijah was bound to attract the interest of the first Christians. They proclaimed the nearness of the end: scripture told them that God would 'send Elijah the prophet before the great and terrible day of the Lord comes, and he will turn the hearts of fathers to their children and the hearts of children to their fathers, lest I come and smite the land with a curse' (Ml 4:5, 6). They were isolated in a world hostile or careless towards their message: so was Elijah. Their message was of one who, like Elijah, had been driven into the wilderness, suffered for his witness and had been taken up to heaven. For Mark, taking Malachi as his starting-point, John the Baptist is Elijah *redivivus*, wearing the same clothes, proclaiming the end and suffering at the hands of royalty. In Luke, where Jesus himself is the prophet of the end, the role of Elijah is taken over by the Christ.

Amongst the Jews contemporary with Jesus and the evangelists theology in the form of biography was by no means a thing of the past—not even of the recent past which had produced Esther, Judith and the stories of the Maccabees. It was kept alive and exploited for practical theological purposes. Adorning and adding to the existing biographical tales in the interests of current concerns was a common literary pursuit, particularly amongst the Jews of the dispersion who were in contact with the Greek histories, romances and aretologies. Josephus and Philo rewrote the stories of the old worthies of their nation with an eye to the cultivated gentile reader. In their hands a patriarch took on some of the character of a Greek sage or hero. The story of *Joseph and Asenath* comes from the mixed culture of Alexandria where Jew met Greek and explained the relation of his religion to paganism by the common medium of the biographical tale. The work is not announced as a fiction. The Christians, soon finding themselves in the mixed culture epitomised by Alexandria, expressed themselves in the same way, as did the stricter and more isolated Dead Sea sectaries who produced the Genesis Apocryphon and the hellenophobic Pharisee who wrote the Book of Jubilees, both amplifying the story of Abraham tendentiously and at some length.[30]

The gospels are not complete bolts from the literary blue. Biographies commending a religious position were common currency, helped by the wide diffusion of the Greek language. To see the wider setting checks the tendency to exaggerate the singularity of the gospels without abolishing it. An unusual power distinguishes them from their surroundings and is evident in the influence over men's minds which they have exerted ever since their composition—and is not completely explained by their canonical status in Christendom.

Some modern critics have pointed to this unusual factor by denying that the gospels are biographies. The claim is obviously untrue but tactically vital: a violent gesture to divert attention from repeated but fruitless attempts to extract scientific historical biography from the gospels and direct it towards their extraordinary theological weight and concentration, which puts the work of Philostratus in the shade. They are not literature for literature's sake but vehicles of an outstandingly intense and immediate theological revelation. The reader of Mark senses it immediately in the lack of relaxation or indulgence, and becomes certain of it when he looks closer and sees that every incident is a summons to recognise the mystery of the divinity of Jesus and to follow him. He is reading a narrative, but a narrative so twisted, blasted and altogether determined by a burning theological heat that narrative, or even didactic narrative, is not an adequate description. The theology is the thing which either strikes and catches the reader or repels him: not merely by its presence, which is not unprecedented, but by the total and relentless demand of its central character which bears down on the reader with disconcerting force. Jesus is presented as Son of God, as the Son of Man[31] who is God's regent in heaven and on earth, who therefore *is* theology. Mark so steadfastly refuses to be concerned with anything else that the reader is not for a moment excused from the summons to change his life and hopes. He launches a concentrated attack in narrative form—and the narrative gains and suffers in consequence. The content and energy of this assault is Christology indissolubly linked to a call to discipleship. Having isolated this outstanding feature of the earliest gospel, the scientific mind naturally looks for its provenance.

The student of the gospels has constantly to remind himself that he is not reading the earliest Christian documents. Even so careful a scholar as F. W. Beare seems to forget it when he gives to a book on the synoptic gospels the title *The Earliest Records of Jesus*. This is seriously misleading and perfectly understandable. The earliest records of Jesus are the letters of Paul which are not the sort of material which a scholar intent on discovering the historical facts about Jesus is glad to find; they furnish so few of them. Even in Paul's ethical teaching Jesus's maxims play a negligible part. As J. L. Houlden has written of the ethical exhortation in Philippians 2, 'It is characteristic of Paul that in commending virtue he should appeal to the *person* and *work* of Christ—not to some saying or deed of his lifetime, but rather to his whole action in becoming a man and dying a death which effected the reconciliation of man to God.'[32] At Romans 1:3 Paul mentions Jesus's descent from David 'according to the flesh'—but only in antithetical contrast to his being 'designated Son of God in power according to the Spirit of holiness in his resurrection from the dead'. At Galatians 4:4 he notes that he was 'born of a woman, born under the law'—but this, besides hardly being very valuable historical information, is only the unavoidable prelude to the death and resurrection which are Paul's gospel. Paradoxically, Jesus only begins to matter to Paul at the moment of his death. Anything that goes before serves that centre of weight and interest. And even this death, the point at which the divine action cuts into history, is not accounted for historically by reference to the preceding trial. Any interest in pure fact is squeezed out of the way by the pressure of Paul's dominating concern for the immediate encounter of God and man in Christ. 'God showed his love for us in that while we were yet sinners Christ died for us' (Rm 5:8). 'We impart a secret and hidden wisdom of God, which God decreed before the ages for our glorification. None of the rulers of this age understood this; for if they had they would not have crucified the Lord of glory' (1 Co 2:6, 8). In this last quotation the possibility that the 'rulers' might be Pilate and the Chief Priests has to compete on equal terms with the possibility that they are spiritual, heavenly actors. Paul's Jesus is an historical figure and it is essential to his theology that he is so, but the terms in which he presents him are mythological: he is the redeemer, the heavenly stranger come down to die an outcast for us men and for our salvation and raised again to the heavenly heights (Ph 2:5–11). He is the transforming symbol in a profound and elaborate symbolic algebra of redemption. Jesus first appears in historical record fully-armed in mythological splendour as the Son of God. The gospel is his death with the resurrection which make it salvific in the present while remaining, for the Christian, a matter of eschatology and hope.

This concentration on the death of Jesus as the mysterious act of divine salvation brings to light a major correspondence with Mark's gospel. There the Jesus who gives his life as a ransom for many is set forth in a narrative so insistently oriented on his death that it might be called a 'paschology' or a 'thanatology' rather than a biography. The resemblance goes deeper in two directions. Both Mark and Paul make a leading point of mystery. The 'secret and hidden wisdom of God' is known only to the initiate who has the spirit by entering existentially into its pattern of dying and rising. The Messianic mystery is a continuous theme of Mark, determining his presentation of parables, miracles and passion. To the ordinary eye it is hidden. When it reveals itself, it is always in a context of death and suffering: Jesus is explicitly called Son of God at the baptism which is a symbolic death, the transfiguration which is immediately followed by teaching about the cross, at his trial and (finally and most resoundingly) at his death. Paul and Mark agree that the gospel is a mystery to which death is the key. They also agree that it involves the reader totally. Paul writes to those who have shared, and still share like himself, in the suffering, death and burial which connect believer and redeemer. In Mark this comes in the repeated call to discipleship to the death which reaches a climax in Chapter 13, connected, in R. H. Lightfoot's view, with the passion narrative which follows it.[33] For Paul this sharing has its definition in baptism. The theoretically sensible inquiry 'are we to continue in sin that grace may abound?' throws him back on his centre: baptism is a new beginning which makes the question anachronistic. 'Do you not know that all of us who have been baptised into Christ Jesus were baptised into his death? We were buried therefore with him by baptism into death, so that as Christ was raised from the dead by the glory of the father, we too might walk in newness of life.' (Rm 6:3f. RSV). This is for Paul the definitive Christian experience where the saving myth is entered by the believer whose death and life are joined by it to his Lord's. There is more than a trace of it in Mark. There is one fact about that book which seems to have been too obvious to be noticed: just as for Paul Christian life begins with baptism, so Mark's life of Jesus begins with his baptism. It need not have been so. Indeed, his successors did not agree that this was the obvious place to begin, and set about things otherwise. But by this bold stroke Mark establishes common ground with his readers at the outset, having the Christ-story begin precisely where the life story of a Christian has its origin, and confronts the initiated reader immediately with the full force of his message of salvation through death. For Mark too baptism has this sombre connotation. At 10:38 Jesus asks his disciples 'Are you able to drink the cup that I drink, or to be baptised with the baptism with which I am baptised?' The cup in Mark denotes suffering and death: the other references to it at the last supper and in the garden leave no doubt of it (14:23f. and 14:36). Baptism, by association, shares its significance. The disciples are being told in imagery that the path to glory goes through suffering. Mark could not have made the point more ominous than by putting the Lord's baptism at the start of his ministry. His book is related to the theological and ideological biographies of Judaism and Hellenism but stands out from them by devoting so much space to the death of his central and redeeming figure. There is a source for these outstanding features in the theology of Paul. Behind Paul we cannot go with certainty in a search for Christ under the strictest standards of history: and that means that Christ first appears in literature (and so is first accessible to us) as a man thoroughly mythologised and theologised. The only sufficient surviving force to account for the weight of Mark's theology is Paul's.

It is now possible to take a further step. In narrative Matthew and Mark are so close that one must depend on the other. It is generally agreed that Matthew depends on Mark. The singularity of Matthew's book then stands out clearly. In answer to the needs of a Church confronted with a host of smaller and trickier issues than Mark's, it supplied a wealth of more detailed ethical instruction. So although its place on the map is very close to Mark's it cannot be quite the same. There is no difficulty in finding a neighbour for Matthew's teaching material. It is like the collections of the sayings of the rabbis—parables, ethical injunctions and proverbs—which became a staple ingredient of the restored Judaism after the fall of Jerusalem. But there is a striking and significant difference. A reader who wants to find all the sayings attributed to Hillel, Akiba or Johannan ben Zakkai, will have to work hard to get them, scattered here and there in Mishnah and Talmud. No such difficulty confronts anyone who wants to find out the sayings of Jesus. He can simply look into Matthew and Luke (in which case he will have no immediate need to look into Mark) where they are laid out in concentrated form. The difference is explained by Matthew's assent to Mark's narrative form which he makes the structure of his own book. He feels obliged to tell Mark's story over again and place his collections of sayings within it so that they are framed by saving history. His place on the map is therefore between Mark and the Tannaitic rabbis.[34]

Luke's debt to Mark and to the teaching material in Matthew establishes his membership in their synoptic family, but again there is something distinctive which asks for further explanation. Luke is not entirely at home with them. They, according to Dibelius[35] are only authors of a very lowly degree, but he 'more than any other of the synoptics shows the strongest literary character'. 'Both in form and material he constantly reached out towards literature as such.' His first four verses announce the fact at the outset by using the polite literary introduction in elaborate syntax which claims to herald the first orderly or properly articulated version of the story of Jesus.[36] Here, for the first time, is a Christian narrative book which can hold its own in the civilised world at large to which it belongs. Further examination will show that it is the hybrid to be expected of a world excited by a wide choice of religions and world-views, with the Jewish scriptural element dominating more than has usually been allowed. But first we have to choose the most useful and appropriate method from the range offered by modern criticism, because the instrument of perception used will determine what is seen at every point.

[1] *The Formation of the Christian Bible,* London 1972, p. 181

[2] H. Chadwick 'Ephesians' in *Peake's Commentary on the Bible,* London 1962, p. 981

[3] Chadwick, op. cit., p. 981

[4] See C. F. D. Moule 'The Problem of the Pastoral Epistles' in the *Bulletin of the John Rylands Library,* 1965. Moule's desire to have both Paul and Luke as their authors results in the suggestion that Paul was too entangled in legal business to find time for writing, so gave Luke the gist and left the rest to him but such intimate acquaintance with Paul is unlikely on grounds of date and his imperfect knowledge of Paul's full doctrine, e.g. of the Law. See also A. Strobel 'Schreiben des Lukas', *New Testament Studies* 1968.

[5] Which suggests that he and the writer of these letters are not the same man.

[6] Jones 'The Epistle to the Hebrews and the Lucan Writings' in *Studies of the Gospels* is a clear study of the family likenesses between the two in which there is more detailed treatment of some of the points noticed here together with further material.

[7] Ibid, p. 125

[8] *The Theology of Acts in its Historical Setting,* London 1970, pp. 21f.

[9] *Ecclesiastical History* iv, 18.5

[10] Chadwick in *Bulletin of the John Rylands Library,* 1965

[11] Ibid., op. cit.

[12] Ibid., op. cit.

[13] F. J. A. Hort *The Ante-Nicene Fathers,* London 1895, p. 7

[14] *1 Clement* 40–44

[15] von Campenhausen *The Formation of the Christian Bible,* p. 70

[16] *Barnabas* 1:7 (trans. M. Staniforth, Penguin, 1968)

[17] In Hennecke *New Testament Apocrypha,* p. 80

[18] B. E. Perry *The Ancient Romances,* University of California Press, 1967, p. 47

[19] Perry, ibid., p 47.

[20] Ibid., p. 63

[21] Origen, *Contra Celsum* 7.9

[22] This is one of many signs that Luke is amongst the earliest Christian writers to see his faith in a context of world civilisation.

[23] *1 Apol* 21

[24] Morton Smith 'Aretalogies, Divine Men, the Gospels and Jesus' in *The Journal of Biblical Literature,* 1971

[25] Marcel Simon *Hercule et le Christianisme,* University of Strasbourg, Paris 1955

[26] Perry *Aesopica,* Urbana, 1952

[27] Perry *Phaedrus and Babrius,* Loeb Classics

[28] Tr. C. P. Jones, ed. G. W. Bowersock, Penguin, 1970. F. C. Baur's contention that this book was a counter-blast to the Christians has long been abandoned for lack of evidence. Nor is there enough hard evidence that Philostratus drew on the Christian gospels. Parallel rather than dependent relation seems most likely.

[29] Rex Warner *The Fall of the Roman Republic,* Penguin, 1958, p. 8

[30] See G. Vermes *Scripture and Tradition in Judaism,* Brill, Leiden 1973

[31] In *Jesus the Jew,* Collins, 1973, G. Vermes has shown that this much debated title was capable of being used by a rabbi as a deprecating way of describing himself. Jesus could have used it in this way. But this does not describe the Markan usage: an apocalyptic title indebted to Daniel 7:13 which denotes the eschatological status of Jesus.

[32] *Paul's Letters from Prison,* Penguin 1970, p. 69

[33] *The Gospel Message of St Mark,* O.U.P., 1950, Ch. IV

[34] They were the teachers or 'traditioners' contemporary with the first Christians and continuing for some four generations who were responsible for the restoration of Judaism after A.D. 70

[35] *From Tradition to Gospel,* London 1971, pp. 3ff.

[36] The use of this convention is not confined to gentile literature. It is used by Jewish authors writing in Greek, notably the grandson of Jesus ben Sira in introducing his translation of his grandfather's work *Ecclesiasticus* and (less coolly and academically) by the writer of the second Book of Maccabees. The preface to the Letter of Aristeas provides a striking parallel to Luke's: 'Since I have collected material for a memorable history of my visit to Eleazar the High Priest of the Jews and because you, Philocrates, as you

lost no opportunity of reminding me, have set great store upon receiving an account of the motives and object of my mission, I have attempted to draw up a clear exposition of the matter for you, for I perceive that you possess a natural love of learning, a quality which is the highest possession of man— to be constantly attempting to add to his stock of knowledge and acquirements whether through the study of history or by actually participating in the events themselves.' After such protestations it is worth remembering that the work which follows is an elaborate fiction.

3
Critical Method

THREE CRITICAL METHODS (source, form and redaction criticism) are currently in use. How are we to know which to use or to which to give priority? The historical basis of Christianity comes into sharp focus with the gospels and insists that the verdict should come from the court of history. The most historical is the best. The method which enters into the most precise, far-ranging and equal dialogue with the historian, not claiming benefit of clergy, will have the best claim. Too often the theologian is evasive. He proclaims that the excellence of his faith lies in its being historical rather than idealistic and invites the historian to inspect it. But, at a point varying with the conservatism of the scholar, he protests that at heart the material is *sui generis,* a unique revelation presented in the allegedly unique form of the canonical gospels, and so at its living centre inaccessible to the historian's tools. It is not on a level with other events—even, according to some, with other divine, saving events recorded in holy scripture. So in practice the canonical material has been given special treatment, the Apocrypha of the New Testament[1] often being regarded as a booby-hatch of tall stories and false doctrines, an optional study sometimes undertaken with a certain marked irreverence. More revealingly still, the fourth gospel, once its independence and majestic theological bias have been recognised, is usually hustled off into quarantine away from the synoptics (where hopes of discovering the historical Jesus are higher, despite Dodd's *Historical Tradition in the Fourth Gospel*) and treated as a special case. The synoptic gospels have become a canon within the canon.

1. *Source Criticism*

Seniority makes this the first method for review. Its classic form is the two-document Hypothesis (Mark and Q). Jameson noticed in 1922 the reason for its popularity: 'It must be admitted that the two-document hypothesis holds a strong position at the present time. It has the support of a majority of critics, and it has met with little serious opposition, partly no doubt owing to the fact that it tends to support rather than detract from the historical validity of the gospel narrative.'[2] It is the desire for historical validity which holds the two documents together. The priority of Mark needs Q because without it the historicity of the mass of teaching common to Matthew and Luke comes under an ominous question mark. Q is the hypothesis necessary to make that question mark disappear. Q needs the priority of Mark because without it Mark would be a writer ready to ignore a tradition available to him and very precious to liberal Christianity: the plain teaching of Jesus without allegorical mystification. The achievement of source criticism is to make virtually everything in the synoptic gospels of sufficient antiquity to boost its authenticity. Painstaking and taxing labours produce welcome results.

Yet at the present it appears in a state of confusion and uncertainty. It depended on the unbiased simplicity of Mark; but Wrede showed[3] that Mark is historically inconsistent with himself at his centre of hiddenness and revelation. Recent work has revealed a powerful thematic theologian, though not a sophisticated *littérateur,* rather than an artless reporter. It depended on the document Q, but recent work has answered the difficulty of drawing its precise bounds at any given point by reducing it to a vague pool of oral tradition. Ropes's judgement of 1934 is still valid: it 'has tended to be modified, refined and complicated to such a degree as, for that reason if no other, to arouse doubts of its validity. There is a simpler, competing possibility, namely that Luke drew these sayings from Matthew, which has never been shown to be impossible.'[4] Frightened, perhaps by Streeter's sarcasm and the weight of opinion, the vast majority of scholars has just not explored that possibility with any thoroughness. Classical source criticism is thus wobbly on both its legs. It is also weak on three other counts: historical setting, verifiability and fulfilment of its own promise.

It refers little if at all to the historical *Sitz im Leben* of the ways of writing theological narratives in the Jewish–Hellenistic world of the first two centuries. Streeter's *The Four Gospels*, like Taylor's recent and posthumous *The Passion Narrative of St Luke* (a Proto-Lukan exercise), ignores it. This is a loud silence. Secondly, the hypothetical documents it invokes are historically invulnerable because uncatchable, incapable of either proof or disproof and so unverifiable. Being beyond historical control is not a virtue. When one hypothetical document shows signs of being unworkable it tends to dissolve into a number of other smaller ones and so to multiply hypotheses. Q itself cannot be disproved because it is not available to us. Thirdly, it fails to fulfil its promise of supporting the historical validity of the gospel narratives. Granted Q, either Matthew or Luke or both have treated it with sovereign freedom. Granted Taylor's historically dependable Proto-Lukan passion narrative, the historical dependability of the other two (or three) must be relatively low. Granted Dodd's historically dependable Johannine Passion narrative, the same applies. A law of swings and roundabouts comes into play which is not even noticed.

2. *Form Criticism*

The bits and pieces which are the ruin of source criticism are the form critic's starting point. He begins by seeing a gospel as a string of pericopae and proceeds to treat these as a picture-restorer does an old painting, removing the Church's varnish and overpainting to reveal the authentic deeds and sayings of Jesus. The work of picture-restorers is disputable but that of form critics even more so. The picture-restorer works on two sets of well-founded knowledge *from outside the picture*: the methods of the master and the methods of his menders. The form critic works on only one such set: knowledge of the methods of the menders which survive in the epistles. His knowledge of Jesus's methods is conjecture from within the picture (or gospel). It will not do to say that the authentic Jesus is distinguished by dissimilarity from Judaism and the Church. He may very well have had much in common with one or both. Even if the critic believes that, despite his imprecise method, he has uncovered the earliest stratum, it is not certain that this is Jesus; though, like Bultmann, he may believe so. The belief could be no more than a hunch, as Jeremias's that Jesus's parables were realistic, the Church's adaptations allegorical and ecclesiastical. On the counts answered by source criticism; for the first, in attention to the historical *Sitz im Leben* it is an advance. The known forms of oral tradition in the ancient world supply its criteria overall, the known teaching of the

Church in particular. The *milieu* of the gospels is thus an imaginatively practical community, using its material rather than just conserving it as the source critics seem to suggest—a much more credible picture of a lively movement. But the study is of pericopae rather than of books so the *Sitz im Leben* of theological narrative writing at the time is still not the central concern it has a right to be. For the second count (verifiability), a form critic's assessment of the history of a pericope is verifiable on one bearing (the Church) but not on the other (Jesus). The latter throws the investigator back on his own preferences (Jesus as realist, zealot, anti-zealot, exponent of through-going or realised eschatology and so on) and so beyond check. At this point the method is open to unnoticed subjectivism. By extracting the pericope from its function in the book, the critic deprives himself of a check on a verifiable bearing which could reduce his guess-work—the tendency of the evangelist. For the third (delivering the goods promised) the method fulfils its promise of giving a more historical view of the early Church, but not its promise of restoring to us the historical Jesus. Its 'New Quest' has fared no better in getting assured and agreed results than the old one.

3. *Redaction Criticism*

Redaction criticism stands on form criticism's shoulders. Where the latter saw evangelists exercising the limited freedom of choosing their pericopae and ordering them, it sees them exercising a decisive freedom on the whole enterprise of writing. It studies their books each with its particular techniques and tendencies, fixing attention on the writers (who have given themselves away by writing) rather than on the misty shapes of Jesus and the Church which stand behind them. A gospel writer is studied in the same way as Paul, although narrative is his form. So: first, the more modest aim of just understanding the book results in greater historical verifiability. The reader, like the critic he reads, has the text before him and can check. The material is not the hypothetical teaching of Jesus or even the less hypothetical teaching of the Church. It is forms, themes and vocabulary which are directly observable and can be studied as directly as another literary critic studies Shakespeare's or Milton's. But in another way the method is less historical and less checkable. How can the reader be sure that the meaning the critic sees is the meaning the writer intended? To put it in a less flummoxing way, how can he be sure that the critic's flight of imagination follows the author's? A mind as ingeniously poetic as Austin Farrer's could well be taking off on its own. Some kind of historical check is needed.

Secondly, the redaction critic is checkable within the narrow field of the gospel concerned and its difference from its synoptic associates (the Synopsis comes into its own here). But he is still, strictly as a redaction critic of the gospels, too bound by the canon to see into its wider world of Jewish–Hellenistic religious narrative and so become thoroughly historical and historically verifiable. We need to know how the work of the evangelists compares with the work of other writers doing similar jobs in the same world at the same time.

Thirdly, the method promised no information about the historical Jesus and delivers none. It is not for that reason unhistorical in the manner of the old Liberal–Protestant attempt to extract eternal principles and throw away their accidental historical wrappings. It simply changes the subject of historical study from Jesus to the (much more accessible) evangelists.

4. *The Next Step*

The trouble with all these methods is that they study the gospels in some measure of isolation, no doubt because most of their exponents are Christians to whom the gospels have a unique importance. A closed field is being investigated by a closed shop. Within that general criticism they vary enough for a rough common-sense order of priority to be drawn up. An understanding of the writer and his book is the obvious place to begin because it is the most accessible. This has to be done in the context of the life of the Church at the time—the perspective opened up by form criticism. Only then should we resort, if we have to, to the most hypothetical method of all—the vanished documents of source criticism. This order is exactly the reverse of the order in which the methods have dominated—an observation which gives the overall history of gospel criticism something of the unhappy character of a slow and bitterly fought retreat from one line of defence to another. It also explains why critics like Strauss and Wrede who were too *avant garde* for their own times are honoured by later generations. Their different strategy, like Kutuzov's in 1812, achieves a more equal encounter by letting the army of scientific historical analysis further into the sacred territory. 'Agree with thine adversary quickly, while thou art with him in the way, lest haply the adversary deliver thee to the judge and the judge deliver thee to the officer and thou be cast into prison' (Mt 5:25; Lk 12:58 where the context is historical as well as ethical).

But to be thoroughly historical we still need to study the gospels in their matrix of contemporary theological story-writing. With this, gospel criticism could come home to history at long last; and so closer to the Lord of history who commands its allegiance and to a new vitality. This means one thing above all: the study of *midrash*, the method by which, in historical fact rather than scholarly conjecture, Jews of various colours from the most chauvinistic Pharisee to the most liberal Hellenist did their history writing. Here, according to Vermes,[5] 'lies the answer to a great many problems confronting the New Testament scholar. Since the Christian *kerygma* was first formulated by Jews for Jews, using Jewish arguments and methods of exposition, it goes without saying that a thorough knowledge of contemporary Jewish exegesis is essential to the understanding, and not just a better understanding, of the message of the New Testament, and, even more, of Jesus.' We have already noticed the mixture of freedom and conservatism by which *midrash* grafts new contingencies to the stock of ancient, authoritative truth. It can be seen happening within the Bible when the chronicler flattens the Books of Kings to suit his own puritan and pedestrian morality, when Ezekiel in his sixteenth chapter tells the whole of Hebrew history concisely and powerfully in terms of the prophetic stock-in-trade of the love story, or when Luke at Acts 7 has Stephen do the same as a prophetic polemic against national disobedience. Two changes of language had their effect on Jewish religion: the adoptions of Aramaic and Greek. Translation was necessary and translation of a still sacred book, as with the New English Bible, was the opportunity for the tendentious modernising interpretations of the Targums and the Septuagint.

In this historical context the synoptic problem could be widened to include John's free *midrash* of the tradition, and find an uncomplicated solution. Overall, Matthew could be seen as a *midrash* on Mark, Luke on both of them, and the Old Testament, as read week by week in the Christian congregations, reinstated as the source which the source critics rejected. In detail, different versions of a parable or an event can be interpreted in midrashic terms. The evangelists resemble the chronicler in sticking to their texts, but within that they indulge in free variations and additions (Matthew's discourses, Luke's parables and both their birth narratives, for

44

instance) for which the Old Testament is a likely source. From there it would be possible to undertake the long overdue task of giving the apocryphal gospels the same serious treatment as the canonical. Streeter *et hoc genus omne* were right in supposing that the evangelists used sources, but *midrash* shows that a source could be anything from a whole written document to a verse within it cultivated as a seed of growth: on which principle the hypothetical documents are likely to prove happily unnecessary. Form criticism is right in revealing the imaginative practicality of the early Church but underestimates the results which *midrash* gets from a text apart from oral tradition. Redaction criticism rightly attends to the writers but needs the control and foundation of an historical situation for redaction—and *midrash* provides it.

It also gives gospel criticism a new lease of life. Like form criticism in its time, it is suspect to mainstream scholars: partly because it is new and therefore relatively unproven, partly out of *esprit de corps* and partly because it is no direct help to a Christianity based more or less exclusively on the authority of the historical Jesus. But it is friendly to a more catholic or pluralistic view which includes the inspired authority of the saints, including the evangelists. It is therefore particularly appropriate to Luke, who does not try to confine revelation to Jesus, the middle of time, but from there explores backward into the Old Testament sagas and forward into Church history. To the Christian reader who gets inspiration from a variety of Christian literature and the work of many exponents of the gospel it should make good sense. It gives new impetus to the doctrine of the inspiration of scripture (how uninspired were Streeter's copyists!) and hinders nobody in his fundamental Christian duty.

[1] i.e. Those early Christian works excluded from the Biblical canon, collected by M. R. James (O.U.P.) and E. Hennecke (two vols., Lutterworth, 1965)

[2] H. G. Jameson, *The Origin of the Synoptic Gospels: A Revision of the Synoptic Problem*. Blackwell, Oxford 1922. p. 7

[3] In *The Messianic Secret*, Clarke, London 1971. (E.T. of *Das Messiasgeheimnis in den Evangelien* 1901)

[4] *The Synoptic Gospels*, Harvard 1934, p. 67

[5] *Cambridge History of the Bible*, 1963–70, ed. P. R. Ackroyd, C. F. Evans, G. W. H. Lampe, I, 8, p. 229

4

Using Scripture

1. *The Infancy Stories and Beyond*
THE BEGINNING OF a book is a good index of its character and quality.
On his first pages a writer makes his initial, and therefore crucial bid
for attention. He contrives to hook his audience. There are different
ways of going about it. The shock of a sudden, uncompromising opening can knock the reader off the perch of his own concerns and grip
him. The first verses of Mark's gospel, with the impact of drums and
trumpets, is an example of this sort of frontal attack. The opposite
way is taken in Luke's ceremonious preface and the extended
stories which follow. Here the reader is wooed rather than bowled
over, treated courteously as an equal rather than aggressively as a
target. But in both instances the object is the same; to cross the
no-man's-land of indifference between author and reader, whether
by stealth or at a rush, and establish an area of engagement. Mark
achieved this participation by making a baptism the climax of his
opening gambit, just as it was the climax of the beginning of the
Christian life for every member of his congregation. Even in the
preface it is clear that Luke works on an area of common interest very
different from Mark's and wider; more civilised, leisured and
literary. In the narrative which follows two features stand out. The
first is the remoteness of the point of its beginning from the point of
its central interest: only after eighty-five verses is Jesus, the subject
of the book, born. In this way a sense of continuity and of rhythmic
unfolding is achieved which is enhanced by the second feature: in
style and content Luke's first two chapters are so packed with Old
Testament language, reference and themes that a reader coming to
the book freshly might easily suspect that he is hearing something

46

from the old stories of the Jews—from Judges, Samuel or Genesis. An examination of these distinguishing marks of Luke's prologue will establish with some precision the kind of literature to which he aspires.

'Very deep is the well of the past, fathomless'. Luke begins, not with the cross, not with the baptism of Jesus, not even with his birth nor with the birth of his immediate predecessor John the Baptist, but with the promise to the Baptist's father. The setting at the centre of Jewry, with the entire nation present, together with the hitherto unprecedented reach backwards in time, are symptomatic of the conscious bid for historical continuity which marked Luke's generation of Christians. The stories which follow exploit it. The first character to come forward is Zechariah, a priest serving the old dispensation with customary ritual and surrounded by 'the whole multitude of the people' in the temple at Jerusalem.

An interest in the birth and childhood of great men was common in the Judaism of the turn of the eras.[1] Josephus in his Jewish Antiquities shows a marked tendency to embroider the details of those which he finds in the scriptures and to add to them out of his own imagination or the traditions of the rabbis—who enjoyed and cultivated the same interest. To the account of the birth and childhood of Moses in Exodus he adds a wealth of circumstantial detail. Before the birth God appears to his father in a dream and tells of the child's future: 'I am watching over the common welfare of you all and thine own renown. This child, whose birth has filled the Egyptians with such dread . . . shall escape those who are watching to destroy him, and, reared in marvellous wise, he shall deliver the Hebrew race from their bondage in Egypt and be remembered, so long as the universe shall endure, not by Hebrews alone but even by alien nations; that favour do I bestow upon thee and upon thy posterity. Furthermore, he shall have a brother so blessed as to hold my priesthood, he and his descendants, throughout all ages.'[2] The resemblance of this to the prophetic canticles in Luke 1 and 2 needs no advertisement. Moses's birth is providentially easy. Pharaoh's daughter is supplied with a name, Thermutis (also in Jubilees 47, 5 as 'Tharmuth'). She is amazed at the size and beauty of the child. Josephus, with his civilised Greek audience in mind, warms to this theme with the sentimentality of a nineteenth-century biographer of Christ. 'Persons meeting him as he was borne along the highway turned, attracted by the child's appearance, and neglected their serious affairs to gaze at leisure upon him: indeed childish charm so perfect and pure as his held the beholders spell-bound.'[3] Pharaoh, playing with the child, puts his crown on his head, 'but Moses tore it off and flung it to the ground, in mere childishness, and trampled it underfoot.'[4] The long narrative of Moses's defeat of Egypt's Ethiopian enemies (Ant 2, 238ff.) is an invention attributed by Thackeray to the Jewish colony in Alexandria, working on Numbers 12:1 ('Moses . . . had married a Cushite woman') with the same creative skill as they deployed on Genesis 41:45 to produce *Joseph and Asenath.* Josephus elaborates the birth of Samson in a similar way, dwelling on the excellence of the parents, adding to the indications of his future destiny and (as with Moses) giving an etymology of his name. He also adds, apparently for the sake of sheer story-telling, the motif of Manoah's jealousy at his wife's encounter with the angel who is 'in the likeness of a comely and tall youth'—a suspiciously Greek young man.[5] Texts from the less liberal sects of Judaism also supply details of the birth of heroes which were lacking in scripture. 1 Enoch 106 (according to Charles a fragment of a Book of Noah) tells of Noah's birth with the obligatory description of his luminous beauty and prophecy of his future. The Qumran Genesis Apocryphon has a version of the same legend. In Jubilees 2 the childhood of Abraham and his break with the idolatrous worship of his people (not found in Genesis) are told at length as an expression of the writer's own intransigent anti-hellenism.

All these examples are instances of the sheer vitality of story-telling and of the common human drive to track down the origin or *arché* of any matter of vital concern. They share a heightening of supernatural elements and circumstantial details, an interest in names, and are by writers intent on showing that some new style of life has an ancient pedigree: whether it be Josephus the hellenist giving Moses the attributes of a Greek or Roman sage and general, or the writer of Jubilees insisting with bold anachronism, that the patriarchs obeyed the Torah. Josephus believed that the highest Jewish and Graeco-Roman achievements had something in common long before he and others set about explaining each to the other; the writer of Jubilees that, for all its comparative novelty, Pharisaism was the primeval religion of the patriarchs. The disciplined freedom of Jewish *midrash*, combining a devout attention to ancient scripture with a conviction of its contemporary relevance, provided the literary technique. Luke's first two chapters are an exercise in the same *genre*. They are pervaded by the vital sense of a new beginning in a time-honoured setting, a young plant growing out of rich and ancient soil. Here is a revival of old Jewish historical narrative designed, like a Victorian gothic-revival Church, to show that something new is the heir of a religion hallowed by antiquity.

Vocabulary and phraseology are its most apparent and obvious means. There is no need to posit other sources when Luke's Greek bible provides such a host of parallels as to suggest that it is the source. Luke's habit of giving a more or less precise date at the outset of his story, and thereafter when there is a fresh beginning, is a biblical custom. Joshua, Judges, Ruth, 2 Samuel and 1 Maccabees begin with rough dates (e.g. 'after the death of Saul' 2 S 1). Hosea, Amos and Jeremiah are more precisely fixed. Awareness of historical time does not necessarily indicate a debt to the Greek historians, to whom Luke's relation is problematical. The Septuagint, to which his relation is close and certain, provides plenty of precedent. In the subsequent narrative septuagintal words and phrases are as thick on the ground as autumn leaves. There is scarcely a verse which is uncoloured by them. 'Of the daughters . . .' (1:5) and 'of the house of . . .' are characteristic ways of describing people. Luke is usually careful (a certain carelessness and inconsistency in detail is one of his faults) to use the septuagintal 'Hierousalem' (Ἰερουσαλήμ) of the Holy City instead of the 'Hierosoluma' (Ἱεροσόλυμα) preferred by the other synoptics. 'The people' (λαός), the common septuagintal designation of the people of God, is rare in Mark (3 times), common in Matthew (14 times) and very common in Luke (37 times). A selection of other instances has been put at Appendix A.

The most cursory glance at Luke's first two chapters reveals that substantial portions of them are in verse. The songs of Elizabeth or Mary (1:46–55), of Zechariah (1:68–79) and of Simeon (2:29–32) are psalms in the Old Testament manner which are still used as such in the offices of the Church. The Revised Standard Version rightly prints some further passages as verse: Gabriel's words to Zechariah at 1:14–17 and to Mary at 1:32, 33, 35, the song of the angels at 2:14 and Simeon's prophecy to Mary at 2:34, 35. But it is possible to go further still and discern the psalmodic pattern in the other instances listed in Appendix B.

It is not difficult to compose psalms in the Old Testament manner. The metrics are so tolerant that the form is virtually a rhythmic and antiphonal prose. To suggest that Luke wrote these is not to posit any very exalted skill on his part. They are certainly from the same hand which wrote the whole of the first two chapters, for like the prose in them they are so packed with Old Testament references as to be collages or mosaics of scriptural texts.[6] To find a man with a head full of the Septuagint we need look no further than Luke himself. His claim to authorship is vindicated by the fact that these songs express themes which are integral to his whole work: God's classical action of raising the low and bringing down the lofty, his visiting of his people in fulfilment of ancient prophecy, the joy which this evokes, the use of $\sigma\omega\tau\dot{\eta}\rho$ (saviour) and $\sigma\omega\tau\eta\rho\dot{\iota}\alpha$ (salvation) which is peculiar to Luke amongst the synoptics, the two references to Abraham and the glimpse of revelation to the gentiles which foreshadows the Acts. A further observation argues for Lukan authorship. In the Old Testament, psalms are by no means confined to the book of that name. Many of the oracles of the prophets and the sayings of the wise are in this form. Above all the books of history, Luke's models and tutors, are punctuated by bursts of song which serve, as in these chapters of his, to make explicit the theology latent in the narrative. Such are the songs of Moses at Exodus 15 and Deuteronomy 33, of Deborah in Judges 5, of Jonah in the belly of the whale, of the three martyrs in the furnace and the prayer of Azariah which were both added to the Book of Daniel, the oracles of Balaam in Numbers 23 and 25 and the last words of David in 2 Samuel 22 and 23. Apocryphal narrative books, nearer in time to Luke than the canonical ones, still use the form. Jubilees has psalms of blessing in the midst of an extensive *midrash* of Genesis, Tobit culminates in the old man's song of praise and Judith in her psalm of triumph. Psalms are so at home in narrative for the Jewish historians that they often take on its historical colour and themselves become historical by retelling the story or prophesying the course of future events.

Luke's psalms show that he is indebted to his Bible for more than a generous sprinkling of words and phrases, a golden varnish to give a patina of antiquity. He owes to it a form, so thoroughly exploited that little of the direct speech in his first two chapters is unshaped by it. As a composer of psalms he is not alone in his time. The discoveries at Qumran, particularly the Hymns Scroll, establish that the writing of psalms was going on in the time of Jesus. Philippians 2:1–11 and other New Testament examples show that it was a customary exercise in the early Christian Church. Luke is, however, peculiar in two respects: he more than the other synoptic evangelists makes use of it in the midst of narrative and in doing so revives a favourite technique of Old Testament historical writing.[7]

Historical psalms are not the only stock-in-trade of ancient Jewish historiography which Luke deploys. The opening scene of Zechariah ministering in the temple with all the people praying outside is a grand tableau of the whole of Israel gathered at its national shrine, the house of its God, strongly reminiscent of the scene at Solomon's dedication of the same temple in the presence of the whole assembly of Israel at 1 Kings 8. Luke's opening scene has the double effect of bringing the fundamental pattern of the old dispensation before the reader, and of raising expectation of some new and momentous event in this long history. Those binding themes of the Deuteronomic history, God, people, Jerusalem, temple and prayer, also give unity to Luke's prologue. The literary form of the great set-piece or tableau which dramatises the themes is common to them both.

In the use of another literary convention, Luke stands out from his synoptic colleagues: women are given prominent roles in the prologue and more attention in the gospel as a whole. Possibly Luke is taking his cue from the women at the empty tomb in Mark, and the four questionable ladies in Matthew's genealogy, Tamar, Rahab the harlot, Ruth the gentile, and the adulterous wife of Uriah. Too often this noticeable feature of Luke's work has been the cue for sentimental conjecture about Luke's (or Jesus's) courteous interest in ladies. More to the point is the wealth of Old Testament precedent for it and its theological function. In the histories of salvation, women often come to the fore as participants in the historical action of God: Sarah and Hagar, Miriam, Deborah, the wife of Jael the Kenite, Hannah and the Queen of Sheba. Delilah and Jezebel are powerful examples of women on the wrong side. According to Weinfeld, the significance and status of women was advanced by the Deuteronomic school: 'In contrast to the earlier biblical sources, in which no mention is made of women and according to which the male participants must even separate themselves from their women before the (covenant) ceremony (Ex 19:15), the author of Deuteronomy makes a particular point of mentioning that women, as well as men, participate (29:11, 18; cf. 31:12). The tendency to give women increasing importance continued. In such later histories as Ruth, Esther, Judith[8] and *Joseph and Asenath*, women take the lead. Similarly in Christianity Luke and the Pastoral Epistles show women coming into more prominence as the religion grows and settles. There is a balance of forces here, if not an unresolved contradiction. On the one hand women are given greater social and theological importance in the laws and stories of the later material in the Old Testament. 'The book of Proverbs exhorts the child to obey the teaching of his mother as well as his father (Pr 1:8; 6:20) and regards her as contributing equally to the child's education (Pr 6:20; 10:1; 15:20; 19:26; 23:22–25; 30:17).'[9] The good wife of Proverbs 31:10–31 is a formidable manageress, buying land, giving to the poor and keeping a firm grip over a large household: a prototype, perhaps, of the women of Luke 8:2f. who ministered to Jesus out of their substance. Yet, on the other hand, a prime benefit of her capable activities is the glory which they reflect upon her husband whose superiority is not challenged. This continued subordination gives the theological force to God's action in raising up women in his cause. Greater glory is reflected on him by the triumphs of his servants amongst the weaker sex.

Other *motifs* of Luke which are more than mere stylistic colouring are taken from the Old Testament. Jerusalem is the geographical magnet which determines the movement and the action of the whole two-volume work up till Paul's departure for Rome, and particularly of Luke 1 and 2. The action starts there, in the temple which is the navel of Luke's traditionally Jewish world—destroyed when he wrote, but still alive in his bible and historical meditation. In Deuteronomy it is 'the city that the Lord has chosen' and the 'house for the name of the Lord'. In the prophecy of Zechariah it is the place to which God will return in election and comfort (Zc 1:17 etc.)—aptly fulfilled in Luke by his own Zechariah being the first to hear of the Messianic visitation. At 1:26 the scene is transported to faraway Nazareth in Galilee. But the pull of Jerusalem shapes everything which follows. At 1:39 Mary goes to see Elizabeth in 'a city of Judah' somewhere between Nazareth and Jerusalem. She returns to Galilee, but only to leave on her next journey which is to Bethlehem in Judea, the city of David—more important than Elizabeth's anonymous city and less than Jerusalem: Luke probably thought of it as being situated between the two. At 2:22 the great thing happens: the Son of God comes to his father's house to be greeted by two aged exemplars of Jewish piety and expectation. Thereafter the link is forged. Jesus and Jerusalem are never (in the prologue) apart for long. 'His parents went to Jerusalem every year at the feast of the Passover' (2:41), visits which reach their climax with the pilgrimage when his parents miss him and find him 'in the temple, sitting in the midst of the doctors, both hearing them and asking them questions'. The geographical pattern of the prologue is a series of deepening stabs towards the Holy City, eventually reaching their goal in the temple where the tale began. In this way Luke establishes the first firm pillar of his whole architecture. His gospel will end in the same place as it began and a large section will be a journey towards it. Although the prologue is a unit it is not isolated but an integral part of a grand scheme. In it Luke takes the pains appropriate to the beginning of his design to do everything according to the old ways, and so tie his Christian history to the whole course of the salvation history of God's people.[10] It is a particularly luxuriant and concentrated example of a studied technique used throughout the work.

Prophecy and its fulfilment give to the prologue, as to the whole gospel, its underlying dramatic drive and tension. In the first place the ancient hopes, spoken of old 'by the mouth of his holy prophets'[11] and the promise to Abraham long ago (1:55, 73), wake up in the dawn of their fulfilment. Secondly, prophecy of the future of John, Jesus, the people of God and all God's world, is uttered by the main characters, human or angelic, who stand around the holy family. The present of the prologue is thus a peak from which can be seen the realisation of the hopes of the past and the light, deliverance and pains of the future. The same double perspective will open out from the mount of transfiguration and the table of the last supper. This pattern is present in Mark and Matthew, as in all the documents of primitive Christianity. But in Mark it is not tidily systematic, in Matthew systematic but obtrusive and obvious. Luke's achievement is so to have absorbed it that it is an integral and inseparable part of his narrative. Prophecies spoken by the tale's *dramatis personae* are fulfilled within its course. In this he stands out from his fellow evangelists and joins the tradition of Old Testament historiography. By the end of his two-volume work, Luke has recorded the fulfilment of all the prophecies he has raised except the second coming of Christ and the destruction of Jerusalem which is all but an inevitable formality after the rejection of the Jews in the last scene of Acts— the reader knows about it, it has been prophetically described at Luke 21:20–24 and Luke achieves his dramatic effect by saying no more.

God's judgement and mercy always form the classic prophetic message, worked out in the annihilation of the achievements of disobedient human pride and the rebuilding of a new life in obedient humility. So God makes history. Luke is loyal to this pattern of the reversal of fortunes, proclaiming it loudly in the Magnificat and making it the structure of his story. Its lighter side predominates in the first two chapters. The barren and the unmarried women become joyful mothers of children. Shepherds on the hills are the Christ's first visitors, not Matthew's impressive eastern Magi, and in Jerusalem the family is received and celebrated in the temple by a man and a woman who are not members of its hierarchy—even lowly ones like Zechariah. Obscure Nazareth and little Bethlehem are scenes of momentous events. The darker side is a matter of prophecy to be realised later. Simeon forecasts falling as well as rising, contradiction and the sword piercing the mother's soul. The Lord of history who takes the initiative in these first chapters by his angels and his spirit is the same up-ender of destinies who brought prosperity out of trouble for Jacob, Joseph, Moses, the Judges, David, Esther, Judith, Tobit and Asenath.

Luke's monotheism and its consequences are fundamental to the structure of his first two chapters. The great psalms, Magnificat, Benedictus, Gloria and Nunc Dimittis, are all addressed to the God who redeems his people, keeping his promise by initiating a new era in history. He is 'the Most High' (1:32, 35, 76) a divine title used seven times in Luke–Acts, once by Mark and in Hebrews, and not elsewhere in the New Testament. The angelic visitations by which this transcendent deity touches his world set the story in motion. Luke's angel is real, not the dream figure which appeared to Matthew's Joseph. He has a name ('Gabriel' from the Book of Daniel, which shares with Luke and later Old Testament writings a predilection for the title 'Most High'). He comes and goes with complete physicality, like his colleague Raphael in Tobit. Angels get five mentions in Mark, nineteen in Matthew and twenty-three in Luke. Hebrews and Revelation are the only other New Testament instances of such thorough and systematic treatment. At Luke 12:8f. angels are added as God's entourage (absent in the parallel Mt 10:33), they rejoice over the repentant sinner at Luke 15:10, carry Lazarus into Abraham's bosom at Luke 16:22, one appears to comfort Jesus in his agony at Luke 22:43 (accepting the authenticity of the verse with Harnack, Streeter and Creed), they are referred to on the Emmaus road at Luke 24:23 ('a vision of angels' could reflect the speaker's scepticism—they may not be real). In Acts they work hard. An angel delivers the apostles from prison by opening the doors (Ac 5:19), tells Philip to go south (Ac 8:26), appears in vision to Cornelius (Ac 10:30), wakes up Peter in prison by slapping him on the side and then leads him out (Ac 12:7–10), kills Herod Antipas (Ac 12:23) and stands by Paul in the night and storm at sea (Ac 27:23).

The Most High also affects human history by raising up men to carry out his plan. Prophets are among them. John the Baptist is celebrated by his father at Luke 1:76 as the future 'prophet of the Most High': a role which passes to Jesus in the body of the book and may even refer to him here, since salvation in the house of David has already been announced in this psalm at 1:69—and Zechariah's 'house' is Levi. Zechariah represents the ancient priesthood, set apart to represent the people to God in the temple cult. Caesar Augustus, like Cyrus in Second Isaiah, assists the divine purpose. The shepherds, though poor people, recall Moses pursuing the same trade when God called him (Ex 3:1), together with the divine, royal and prophetic associations of the trade in the Old Testament. Mary is in the line of the women who had furthered God's purposes of old. Simeon and Anna exemplify devout Jewish expectation, open and ready for God to act. Jesus himself is presented under titles which describe pre-eminence amongst men but subordination to God. His name already recalls the Jesus (Joshua) of the Old Testament who led the people into the promised land. He is 'Son of the Most High', by no means an exclusive notion in the Old Testament where the Sons of God include angels, kings and the just and wise—in *Joseph and Asenath* Joseph is a son of God. Jesus is the heir to David's throne (Lk 1:32) and, connected with this, the Christ (Lk 2:11). Mark and Matthew had both used 'Christ' as a title prefixed by the definite article, but also without it as a kind of proper name, as Paul had done. This latter usage disappears in Luke, leaving 'the Christ' to stand out as a designation of God-given authority which preserves the more traditional and biblical sense (see Lk 3:15 etc.) A possible exception to this is Luke 2:11—'a saviour who is Christ Lord', But 'Christ' could here be the adjective 'anointed', common in the Septuagint, or perhaps a mistaken transcription of the 'Lord's Christ' (χριστὸς κυρίου becoming χριστὸς κύριος), a phrase which is used by Luke at 2:26. He is a saviour, usually a description of God in the scriptures, but used of men at Nehemiah 9:27 ('thou didst give them saviours who saved them from the hands of their enemies': compare Lk 1:71 'salvation from our enemies, and from the hand of all that hate us') and at Obadiah 21 ('Saviours shall go up to mount Zion': compare Lk 2:22). 'Lord' is another title applied to God and to men. Luke's Christology reaches its highest point with Jesus's begetting by the Holy Spirit, a doctrine inherited from Matthew which goes further than his overall tendency to see Jesus in the horizontal line as God's agent, his preference for a Christology of ascent rather than descent. But discontinuity is as essential to story-telling as continuity, particularly in a theological context, and Luke is not the man to philosophise this into a high doctrine like John's. There is no trace of any notion of Jesus's pre-existence.

The details of the plot, its twists and incidents, express Luke's deliberately conservative theology. They are not mere archaic fancy-dress but outcrops of the same ancient rock which underlies and shapes the whole landscape. The Old Testament assists the development of the story which is founded on it.

The opening note of dating, which we have seen to be a feature of Jewish historiography, introduces Zechariah and Elizabeth in terms which connect them with the nation's remote past and age-old worship, founded by Aaron and reformed by David's division into classes. Their characters and situation (1:6 and 7) are derived from Old Testament narrative and spirituality. They are 'righteous before the Lord' like Noah ('And the Lord said to Noah . . . Thee have I seen righteous before me' (Gn 7:1).

By 'walking in all the commandments and ordinances of the Lord blameless' they sum up in septuagintal phrase, the Jewish devotion exemplified by Psalm 119 and recall Abraham at Genesis 26:5. The whole of this section resembles in style and vocabulary the description of Samson's parents at Judges 13:2: 'There was a certain man of Zorah, of the family of the Danites, whose name was Manoah, and his wife was barren and bare not.' This is reinforced by another reference to Abraham and Sarah whose childlessness ('she had no child' Gn 11:30), like that of Elizabeth and Zechariah, was aggravated by their age ('old and well-stricken in years' Gn 18:11). The rich Old Testament content of verses 8–11, the ideal tableau of Israel, has already been noted. The arrival of the angel Gabriel is dictated by prophecy. 'Behold I send my messenger (angel/ἄγγελος) and he shall prepare my way before me, and the Lord whom ye seek shall suddenly come to his temple; the messenger of the covenant in whom you delight, behold, he is coming, says the Lord of hosts' (Ml 3:1), combining with Daniel 9:21 'while I was speaking in prayer, the man Gabriel, whom I had seen in the vision at the beginning, came to me in swift flight at the time of the evening sacrifice.'[12] John's derivation from Samson, the last of the judges before Israel was given an anointed king, appears again in Gabriel's command that 'he shall drink no wine nor strong drink'. Samson's mother was given the same instruction in much the same words (Jg 13). Malachi is drawn on again for Gabriel's words about John's mission of preparation by repentance. The last three verses of Malachi read 'remember the law of my servant Moses, the statutes and ordinances that I commanded him at Horeb for all Israel [Zechariah and Elizabeth have done so and all Israel is present in the temple court]. Behold I will send you Elijah the prophet before the great and terrible day of the Lord comes. And he will turn the hearts of fathers to their children and the hearts of children to their fathers, lest I come and smite the land with a curse.' Zechariah's doubting rejoinder 'how shall I know this?' is an exact verbal parallel to Abraham's at Genesis 15:8: 'how shall I know?' His dumbness takes us back to Daniel who turned his face to the ground 'and was dumb' after being addressed by the angel (Dn 10:15). The episode concludes with Elizabeth's grateful relief: 'thus has the Lord done to me in the days when he looked upon me, to take away my reproach among men', resembling Rachel's at Genesis 30:23 when she bears Joseph. The word ὄνειδος (reproach) is used in both. The verbal resemblances to the old stories are symptoms of a larger debt. The plot and action, a childless old couple, promised a son by a divine messenger and doubting the happy possibility, come from Luke's Bible.

To the modern mind it seems that such a wealth of scriptural reference on the part of Luke suggests an incredible ingenuity and erudition. But Luke did not have a modern mind. In particular, his education was not spread over the wide spectrum of subjects which make up our school curricula. It was concentrated on the one subject of scripture, the devout man's study day and night in which he became expert and informed beyond most modern biblical scholars, whose attention (at least in the formative years of youth) has been claimed by other disciplines. John Bunyan, self-educated in the same concentrated field, is the best familiar parallel. His writings display the same debt of style, plot and detailed incident to his Bible as Luke's; and incidentally owe to Luke the basic image of life as a voyage to a city.

Luke's Old Testament sources in this section are not chosen at random. John the Baptist is the figure whom Christian tradition regarded as penultimate, immediately preceding the ultimate figure of the Christ. The author's mind homes on the forerunners and penultimate figures in the Old Testament, typology serving his greater concern with history. The last two prophets, Zechariah and Malachi, represent the latest biblical promises of God's visitation of his people. Samson is the last of the Judges and followed by Kings. Abraham is literally the father of Israel (Jacob). The original Simeon was Jacob's second son. The major source behind Luke's birth narratives is the account of the birth of Samuel in 1 Samuel 1 and 2. Like Elizabeth, Hannah suffered from barrenness and its reproach, like Zechariah she received the promise of a son in the temple, like Elizabeth she breaks into song:

> My heart exults in the Lord,
>   my strength is exalted in the Lord.
> My mouth derides my enemies,
>   because I rejoice in thy salvation . . .
> Those who were full have hired themselves out for bread,
>   but those who were hungry have ceased to hunger . . .
> He raises up the poor from the dust;
>   he lifts the needy from the ash-heap . . .
>
> (1 Samuel 2 RSV)

There can be no doubt that Hannah's song is the model and source for the Magnificat. But why Samuel? The answer comes from his place in the Old Testament story. He is the bridge connecting the era of the judges and the kings, the precursor of Saul and David and their anointer. With the anointing of David, Samuel's mission reaches its climax and he disappears from the narrative, his death being noted some time later and after he has been virtually forgotten (1 S 25:1). This is very similar to Luke's treatment of John, whose career culminates in the baptism of Jesus and whose death is also laconically reported long after he has left the story. According to Mark and Matthew, Elijah, not Samuel, is the type for John. Luke preserves a carefully qualified version of this tradition in 1:17 ('in the spirit and power of Elijah'), but the fact that his Bible gave him no account of the birth of Elijah may have turned his attention to the other prophetic kingmaker. Thereafter he is chary of tendencies to make John into Elijah-come-again, omitting his tell-tale clothing at Mark 1:6. John is Samuel come-again, with traits of Samson.

It is well known that Luke's prologue is in the form of a diptych or picture of two panels which relate to one another. The circumstances of the birth of Jesus match those of the birth of John with telling differences. It follows that, having constructed the foretelling of John's birth on Old Testament lines, his major work of building with scriptural materials is done for a while. Now he need only make such alterations to the basic formula as will show Jesus's destined superiority, like David's over Samuel. The plot is the same: the birth of a son, together with his name, is promised by Gabriel to someone who seems outside the possibility of child-bearing. So the Old Testament remains as fundamental to the annunciation to Mary as to the annunciation to Zechariah.

This time Gabriel visits a virgin—a reference to the famous Septuagint version of Isaiah 7:14 which Matthew quotes overtly ('Behold a virgin shall conceive and bear a son'), characteristically woven by Luke into the texture of the narrative. She is 'of the house of David', a phrase borrowed from the prophet Zechariah (Zc 12:7, 8, 10, 12; 13:1), denoting an ancestry which qualified her to be the mother of the Christ (see the promises at Ps 132:11; Is 9:7, 16:5 etc.). Gabriel has a courteous and deferential greeting for Mary such as he did not have for Zechariah the priest, beginning with the Greek pun χαῖρε, κεχαριτωμένη and then breaking into Old Testament speech, 'the Lord is with you' being precisely the greeting of the angel to Gideon at Judges 6:12. 'You have found favour with God' is an exact echo of Genesis 6:8 (Noah); 'you will conceive in your womb and bear a son and shall call his name . . .'; of Genesis 16:11 (Rebecca—'The angel of the Lord said to her, Behold you are with child and will bear a son and shall call his name Ishmael'). Gabriel's prophecy of the destiny of Jesus derives from Isaiah 9:6f.:

> For to us a child is born
> To us a son is given . . .
> Upon the throne of David, and over his kingdom . . .
> From this time forth and for evermore.

Like Zechariah, Mary questions the possibility of the promise, so the angel explains how it will come about in the biblical language which is his native tongue. 'The Holy Spirit will come upon you as upon the judges and kings of old (see Jg 3:10; 6:34; 1 S 10:6; 16:13), 'the power of the Most High will overshadow you' as it overshadowed the tabernacle at Exodus 40:35—the verb ἐπισκιάζω in both instances. Gabriel's final word, 'with God nothing shall be impossible' (οὐκ ἀδυνατήσει παρὰ τοῦ φεοῦ πᾶν ῥῆμα) is a slight modification of its source at Genesis 18:14 where Abraham is asked 'Surely nothing is impossible with God?' (μὴ δυνατήσει παρὰ τῷ θεῷ ῥῆμα). Mary's devout reply uses the Septuagintalism 'behold' (ἰδού), refers to herself as the Lord's handmaid (δούλη), like Hannah (1 S 1:11), Judith and Esther, and in 'be it unto me according to your word' (γένοιτό μοι κατὰ τὸ ῥῆμά σου) uses a common septuagintal phrase which occurs at Joshua 2:21; Judges 11:10; 2 Kings 14:25 and elsewhere.

Having recounted his two annunciations, Luke brings together his two expectant mothers. Mary goes up to 'one of the cities of Judah' just as David had on the way to his coronation (2 S 2:1). Septuagintal phraseology is maintained throughout. For its pervasive presence in Elizabeth's songs the reader is referred to Creed's commentary *ad loc.* and at pp. 303ff. The only narrative incident is the leaping of John in his mother's womb. It is realistic, as every pregnant woman knows, but it is also biblical, recalling Genesis 25:22 where Jacob and Esau struggle in Rebecca's womb. In both instances the phenomenon is prophetic.

It now remains for Luke to tell of the birth of John and Jesus. In doing so he does not allow the Septuagint to dictate the course of events as totally as he has up to now. It still provides a host of references and details, but he emerges as a storyteller in his own right. He has warmed to his task and now gives rein to his own talents. The Septuagint's contribution is still, however, sizeable and worth noting. The scene of John the Baptist's birth inherits the biblical view of the importance of a child's name, the phrase 'wrote saying' at 2:63 is a Septuagintalism which creeps in despite Zechariah's dumbness (see 2 K 10:6) and the note that the hearers of the events 'laid them up in their hearts' is an echo of 1 Samuel 21:12, 'and David laid up the words in his heart'. A similar phrase recurs at 2:51. Zechariah's song, like the others, is a collage of scriptural texts and ends with the thoroughly biblical note of growth as at Judges 13:24 (Samson again) and 1 Samuel 2:26 (Samuel again). For the census, which is the major incident in the first part of the story of the birth of Jesus, Luke uses a garbled version of recent secular history (see Appendix C). The manger (φάτνη) of 2:7 could be a reference to Isaiah 1:3:

> The ox knows its owner,
> and the ass its master's crib (φάτνη)
> But Israel does not know,
> my people does not understand.

Certainly in later Christian iconography, using the Gospel of Pseudo-Matthew, this verse became so firmly attached to Luke's account that the ordinary reader expects to find the animals there; and the reference in it to Israel's failure to recognise its Lord's visitation raises a theme which is of major importance to Luke. In the Old Testament the inn or lodging (κατάλυμα) is associated with the presence of God among his people—'Thou hast led in thy steadfast love the people whom thou hast redeemed, thou hast guided them to thy holy lodging' (Ex 15:13). At 2 Samuel 7:6 Nathan is told to speak to David about the building of a temple for the Lord, reminding him that up till now God has not dwelt in a house but 'in a lodging and a tent' (LXX: ἐν καταλύματι καὶ ἐν σκηνῇ). Jeremiah 14:8 in the Septuagint version is equally suggestive:

> O Lord, hope of Israel,
>> its saviour in time of trouble,
> Why shouldst thou be like a stranger in the land,
>> like a wayfarer turning aside into a lodging?

For the reader of the Septuagint the word κατάλυμα had connotations of the divine presence in Israel, not in the grandeur of the temple but in obscurity and humility. This field of meaning is particularly apt to Luke's birth of God's son in a provincial town: and he caps it by having Jesus born outside the lodging. As with the manger, this is a matter of resonance, a field of reference rather than a single precise quotation. Sceptics may wave it aside. But the same applies to the shepherds at Bethlehem, whose Old Testament associations are not so easily brushed away. As Creed remarks, 'David himself was a shepherd, and a pastoral scene is fully in harmony with the Old Testament associations of Bethlehem.'[13] Moses too was a shepherd when God revealed himself to him in the burning bush. The patriarchs were shepherds and the word is a widely attested title for a king—as for God as 'shepherd of Israel'. But the setting near Bethlehem gives the Davidic reference the lead. David was keeping the sheep of his father Jesse the Bethlehemite when Samuel anointed him (1 S 16). According to the prophecy of Micah 5:2 a ruler of Israel would come from there:

> But you, O Bethlehem Ephrata,
>> who are little to be among the clans of Judah,
> from you shall come forth for me
>> one who is to be ruler in Israel,
> whose origin is from of old,
>> from ancient days.

61

In Matthew's infancy narrative (2:5, 6) this text is quoted outright, with proper acknowledgement. Again Luke, the more sophisticated narrator, mixes it into the fabric of his story: another indication that his more advanced achievement is later than Matthew's book and likely to be dependent upon it.[14] The sign spoken of by the angel at 2:12 is explained by Creed as 'a token which shall at once serve to identify the child and to confirm the angel's words'. Even the best of commentators can flag. This is not adequate. Luke is using 'sign' in the prophetic sense, and indeed quoting from the most appropriate instance of the usage: 'Therefore the Lord himself shall give you a sign (ὑμῖν σημεῖον precisely as at Luke 2:12) Behold a virgin shall conceive and bear a son' (Is 7:14). It is hard to believe that Luke did not have in mind this particular sign of the virgin's child: again, overtly quoted by Matthew but fed by Luke into his narrative action—and so concealed. 'Mary kept all these things, pondering them in her heart' like the people who heard about John's birth at 1:66 and like David again (1 S 21:12).

The next two incidents are based on scriptural law and custom. For Jesus's circumcision, as for John's, Luke compresses the two separate customs of naming and circumcision: a sign that his scriptural learning may not be equalled by familiarity with current Jewish ceremonies, for the effect gained is of concentrated Jewishness though at variance with likely practice.[15] The presentation in the temple is another doubling of two ceremonies, the sanctifying of the first-born (Ex 13:1–2) and the redemption-cum-sin-offering of Leviticus 12:6. In Leviticus 12 the two rites are separated by sixty-six days. The presentation of Samuel in the temple (1 S 1:24) is in the background of the scene. Simeon and Anna are ideal types of Old Testament piety and expectation, Simeon being endowed, like the old worthies, with the spirit. It can hardly be a coincidence that his namesake in the Joseph stories was kept waiting in Egypt until the arrival of the child Benjamin. Luke's Simeon is waiting for the comforting of Israel (Jacob) which would fulfil Isaiah's promise, 'Comfort ye, comfort ye my people, saith your God' (40:1). His song is the usual mosaic of Old Testament words and phrases with the latter chapters of Isaiah, particularly 49 and 52, making the major contribution. The fall and rising of many in Israel appears to be a free version of the 'stone' text at Isaiah 28:16—a passage so familiar to Christians (see Romans 9:33 and Luke 20:17 with synoptic parallels etc.) that it would be easy for Luke to produce a variation on it. Simeon's prophecy is a further example of the prologue's integrity with the whole of Luke's grand scheme. He prophesies the course of events right through the gospel and beyond it to the end of Acts. In vision he sees, like Moses on Pisgah, the scope of future blessing. Anna is his female counterpart, a convinced widow like Judith (Jdt 16:22) and Naomi, a member of a class well known in the Church of Luke's day (1 Tm 5:5).

The last incident of the boy Jesus in the temple shows Luke's growing confidence as a narrator. At the beginning he stuck to his Bible like a navigator hugging the coast. And it suited his purpose to do so, since this made unmistakably clear that his Christian story is all of a piece with the old salvation histories. Style, plot, dialogue and virtually every single detail were scriptural. As the tale gathers momentum so the spirit of story-telling comes upon him and gives him his freedom. This is first noticeable in the scene of John's naming, which has no exact parallel in the Old Testament. The stories of Jesus's birth and first coming to the temple are stiff with Old Testament allusion and imbued with the spirit of the scriptures but are not totally determined by them. They are 'originals' in a traditional style. With Jesus's second visit to the temple we have a tableau firmly set in the old dispensation. The time is passover. Jesus is a prodigy and paradigm of Jewish youth, attending to the instruction of the teachers of the law, joining in their theological discussions with answers so intelligent that it is clear that a new master has entered the ancient discipline. Other features of the story increase the sense that the Christian future is starting to gain on the Jewish past. There are prophetic hints of the great passover at the end of the gospel (Luke mentions no other in the interim) when again Jesus taught in the temple and again was lost to his people for three days. Jesus is, for the first time, seen to belong to a wider world than his family circle: to the things of his father and to the centre of the life of the nation. This aspect recalls Mark 3:31–35 and suggests strongly that Luke is using it as a source. There too Jesus is absorbed in debate when his relations (mother and brothers) come looking for him. There too he answers that he has another duty and another allegiance (towards the disciples who do God's will). The incidents are the same in function and similar in detail. The return of Jesus to Nazareth is an act of pious obedience, which witnesses to a higher valuation of family life than Mark's fierce negative. Overall, the balance has shifted, almost imperceptibly in the hands of a skilled and smooth storyteller, from the old dispensation to the new: we are not clear of the old religion (that waits until the very end of Acts) but now, with prophecy already fulfilled, the new beginning in Christ has taken the initiative. The influence of the Old Testament wanes from the total to the allusive, from determining every incident to providing an hospitable frame of reference. The same movement can be seen in a synopsis of the prologue. Jesus starts behind John, then gains on him until the precursor and even the family are forgotten and Jesus stands alone in the setting of his destiny.

1 }		(1:5–25)	Annunciation of John
2 }		(1:26–38)	Annunciation of Jesus
3	(1+2)	(1:39–56)	Meeting of mothers
4 }		(1:57–80)	Birth and naming of John
5 }		(2:1–21)	Birth and naming of Jesus
6		(2:22–40)	Jesus in the Temple I (with parents)
7		(2:41–52)	Jesus in the Temple II (with the teachers)

The fact that there are seven incidents (a Jewish week) may not be due to conscious artifice on Luke's part, but is scarcely a coincidence. The structure shows a clever and much used device of Luke's. Great and momentous matters emerge gradually, catching the reader's attention by prophetic hints before they happen. He is aware of the divisions between times, the distinction between one era, its predecessor and its successor. In this conscious and sophisticated sense of the past, rather than in a modern attention to hard facts, lies his claim to be called an historian, skilled in the ancient Jewish discipline of weaving skeins of prophecy and fulfilment from one event to another.

Within this theological and apologetic context it makes excellent sense that Luke's first pages have the character of the ancient stories of salvation stamped upon them by his conviction that the new order is continuous with the old. They have strong resemblances to the story books of the Jewish dispersion, Tobit, Esther and Judith, which carry into the rest of the gospel and Acts. Theology comes in the form of a tale in which the poor and meek are exalted, the great and proud brought low. Psalms of praise by the chief characters bring it into the open (Tb 13, Jdt 16:1–17). Speeches are long and frequent in Judith. Soliloquies admit the reader to the minds of the actors in Tobit and Esther. Both are used by Luke. All three books begin with elaborate dating, particularly precise in Judith. Like the wealth of names and places they serve to give a realistic secular setting for God's saving acts rather than to gratify modern historical curiosity. Literary versatility is shown in the use of the distinctive styles appropriate to royal edicts, orations and psalms.

Tobit is set among the humble and devout, the old man himself 'looking for the consolation of Israel' like Luke's Simeon and also recollecting the scriptures: 'I remembered the prophecy of Amos, how he said, Your feasts shall be turned into mourning and all your festivities into lamentation. And I wept.' (Tb 2:6). He is given to acts of mercy, including hospitality (Tb 2:2). Jerusalem is the centre of cultic observance: 'I alone went often to Jerusalem for the feasts, as it is ordained for all Israel by an everlasting decree' (Tb 1:6). The angel Raphael is sent in answer to his prayers and accompanies his son Tobias *incognito* on the long journey. Like Luke's Gabriel he is physically real (but he refuses to eat and drink: Tb 12:19), like the mysterious companion on the Emmaus road he reveals his identity at the end and departs. Angels, intervening in the domestic scene rather than keeping to their native apocalyptic air, are as integral to Luke's scheme as the journeys and dinners which are settings in Tobit too.

In Tobit the defeat of the oppressor is represented by the routing of a demon. In Judith and Esther it plays a larger part, these two formidable handmaids of the Lord accomplishing the destruction of the Assyrian general Holofernes and the arrogant courtier Haman. Judith, described as 'blessed above all women' (Jdt 13:18 cf. Lk 1:42) is particularly congenial to Luke in being wealthy and a widow as well as female. The conversion of the gentile Achior to faith in the Most High is a splendid precedent for Acts. The story of Esther moves around banquets at which the most telling conversations and actions take place. The battle of Bethulia in Judith shows narration for its own sake indulged to the full with a wealth of circumstantial detail. The only thing like it in the New Testament is Luke's account of Paul's sea voyage to Rome.

If the Old Testament is less dominant after Luke's first two scenes and first two chapters (though still creatively present) it is because the link with the old dispensation has been forged and the graft made. A less pedestrian and freer use of *midrash* is in order and will be maintained for the rest of the book. After Chapter 2 a Christian source will give him his narrative framework: Mark's gospel. Matthew will provide him with a wealth of teaching matter. The Septuagint will have competitors for his attention. But it is never put aside, continually bears on Luke's work and at great moments such as the beginning of Jesus's public ministry (4:16–30), the great turning point of 9:51, and the Lord's last words to his apostles and his nation (23:28–31) its voice rings out loud and clear. It is always as valuable a source to him as Mark and Matthew. In the prologue it is undoubtedly the major source, with Matthew's infancy stories having the minor, if seminal, influence.[16] One thing at least is clear: the midrashic use of the Old Testament gives so satisfactory an account of the origin of Luke 1 and 2 that there is no need to posit Christian sources—still less sources from the circle of John the Baptist. Examination of some further instances points to the conclusion that Luke's hypothetical 'special source', Proto-Luke or L, may well not be hypothetical at all and could have been staring the critics in the face all the time. There are strong indications that it is the Old Testament, called in by hints from Mark and Matthew and deployed with the same learned versatility and freedom as we have noticed in the first two chapters.

2. *Some Turning Points*

The scene in the synagogue at Nazareth (Lk 4:16–30) marks the beginning of Jesus's ministry with clear notes of prophecy fulfilled and made. Jesus reads Isaiah 61:1, 2 and proclaims that it is fulfilled 'today'. The sceptical reaction is answered scripturally by reference to Elijah and Elisha who point towards the gentile converts of Acts. The anger provoked by this second dose of biblical teaching boils over into an attempted lynching which is a foretaste of things to come in the greater hill-city of Jerusalem. The scripture plays so determinative a part in the drama that it is, together with Jesus who reads and enacts it, the leading actor. Examination of sources confirms this impression. Verses 17–20 and 25–27 are the clear and major additions Luke makes to Mark's more meagre account and the Septuagint is their source.

The beginning of the Church's ministry is made with a similar addition of scriptural force to Mark's version at Luke 5:1–11. The stupendous catch of fish is a miracle of material provision and, as such, paralleled in the gospels only by the feedings of multitudes. But there are examples of the same kind in the Old Testament, notably the never-ending supply of meal and oil which Elijah managed for the widow at Zarephath (1 K 17), Elisha's similar benefaction on the destitute wife of a prophet (2 K 4:1–7), his saving of the noxious stew during a famine (2 K 4:38–41) and his feeding of a hundred men with twenty loaves of barley, despite the scepticism of his servant—and with left-overs (2 K 4:42–44), which is an obvious source for the gospel feedings. This kind of miracle, unlike the exorcisms beloved by Mark, is a decidedly Old Testament *genre*. In this instance Mark's calling of fishermen to discipleship, which is Luke's Christian source, dictates that the material should be fish. The climax and point of the scene comes with Jesus's word to Peter. In Mark (addressed to Andrew too) it ran 'Come ye after me and I will make you fishers of men'. Luke subjects it to a characteristic and septuagintal revision: 'Fear not, from henceforth thou shalt take men alive' (RV using footnote). 'Fear not' and 'from henceforth' are Septuagintalisms much used by Luke. 'Take alive' translates Luke's ζωγρῶν, a verb used in the Septuagint to denote rescue from peril of death, not the capture of animals—and so as inappropriate to fishing as it is appropriate to the Christian mission which it initiates.[17]

The next great departure is at 9:51–62 when Jesus sets out on his momentous long journey to Jerusalem. 'And it came to pass, when the days were well-nigh come that he should be received up, he steadfastly set his face to go to Jerusalem, and sent messengers before his face.' The sentence is a compact mosaic of pregnant Old Testament references and owes its solemn effect to them. 'The construction of ἐγένετο (it came to pass) with ἐν τῳ (when) and the infinitive followed by καὶ (αὐτὸς) and a verb in the indicative, which is almost peculiar to Luke in the New Testament, is characteristic of the narrative style of the LXX.'[18] Receiving up (sc. into heaven) recalls Elijah, Enoch (Si 49:14) and, in post-biblical Jewish legend, Moses, as well as anticipating Jesus's own ascension. 'Set his face' is a septuagintal phrase often coloured by prophetic hostility or doom. 'Hazael King of Syria went up and fought against Gath and took it: and Hazael set his face to go up to Jerusalem' (2 K 12:17). 'The Lord God will help me; therefore I have not been confounded: therefore have I set my face like a flint' (Is 50:7). 'Son of man, set thy face towards Jerusalem and drop [or, pour out] thy word toward the sanctuaries and prophesy against the land of Israel' (Ezk 21:2). Here the phrase looks forward to Jesus's prophetic warnings of A.D. 70 and his denunciations of Jerusalem, which play a greater part in Luke than in the previous gospels. Jesus 'sent messengers [= angels] before his face' just as God sent his angel before Moses and Israel in Exodus. This high density of Old Testament quotation is followed by further examples as the narrative goes on. Two stories about Elijah are used. At 2 Kings 1:10 the prophet called down fire from heaven to consume the messengers sent by the king of Samaria (an echo of the heavenly fire on Mount Carmel) and at 1 Kings 19:19 he met Elisha, who was ploughing, cast his mantle on him and then gave him leave to say good-bye to his household before following him. At Luke 9:52–56 Jesus refuses James's and John's suggestion that he call fire from heaven to consume Samaritans. At Luke 9:61–62, appended to Matthew's two would-be disciples, is a third who wants to say good-bye to his household but is refused with a proverb about ploughing: 'No man, having put his hand to the plough, and looking back, is fit . . .' In both instances Luke is modifying the scriptures he uses in order to show, by contradiction, that an Elijah greater than Elijah has come. The mission of seventy follows. It draws on Deuteronomy 1:21–25 and Numbers 11:16ff., Moses's spies sent to 'search the land for us and bring us word again of the way by which we must go up and the cities into which we shall come' being doubled with the seventy elders whom God made his colleagues and deputies. Jesus 'appointed seventy others and sent them two and two before his face [septuagintal phrase] into every city and place whither he himself was about to come' (Lk 10:1). Seventy was also the number of the world's nations in Genesis 10 and, in current legend,[19] of the translators of Luke's Greek Bible. These incidents mark the beginning of the most grandiose of Luke's Old Testament exercises, his Christian version of Deuteronomy which extends to 18:14 and will be examined in Chapter 7.

The last of the great turning points is more diffused: the last supper, passion and resurrection. Mark provides most of the material but the Old Testament makes telling points which have often been attributed to 'Proto-Luke'. At the last supper, Jesus, like Moses, takes leave of his people by recalling the past and ordaining the future. The added promise of eating and drinking 'at my table in my kingdom' recalls Psalm 23:5 ('thou preparest a table before me') and the Israelites who 'beheld God and did eat and drink' at Exodus 24:11. The further addition of dialogue between Jesus and Peter at Luke 22:31–33 is of scriptural origin. At 2 Samuel 15:20–21 David told Ittai the Gittite to go back: 'Return thou and take thy brethren; mercy and truth be with thee.' Ittai answered, 'Surely in what place my lord the king shall be, whether for death or life, even there also will thy servant be.' Luke has Jesus say, 'when once thou hast turned again, stablish thy brethren', and Peter rejoin, 'Lord, with thee I am ready to go both to prison and death.' The differences are explained by Luke's dominant interest in repentance and a prophecy of Peter's imprisonment in Acts. This is followed by a retrospective and prospective utterance to mark the change of times at 22:35–38, in the middle of which the Septuagint speaks out: 'That which is written of me must be fulfilled in me, And he was reckoned with transgressors (Is 53:12), for that which concerneth me hath fulfilment.' When Jesus is arrested Luke gives him the additional words, 'Ye stretched not forth your hands against me: but this is your hour and the power of darkness' (Lk 22:53). The first phase is strongly biblical; so is the momentous use of 'hour' and of darkness as a symbol of oppression and loss. On the way to the cross Jesus utters his last prophecy at 23:27–31. It is to 'the daughters of Jerusalem', a phrase common in prophecy, quotes Hosea 10:8 ('They shall say to the mountains, Cover us; and to the hills, Fall on us'). That may well be coloured by the compassionate lamentation of the people of Jerusalem at Zechariah 12:10, and refers to Ezekiel 20:47, 'I will kindle a fire in thee and it shall devour every green tree in thee and every dry tree' while making a characteristic historical distinction between green and dry. The saying about wombs and breasts at verse 29 is an echo of Luke 11:27 and shares with it the shape of a verse in the Hebrew metrics used in prophetic oracles. When Jesus dies the loud cry of Mark becomes biblically articulate, 'Into Thy hands I commend my spirit' (Ps 31:5). The two men at the empty tomb say that Jesus's resurrection is fulfilment of his own prophecy: a motif which is absent in Mark, introduced by Matthew with a brief 'as he said', and expanded by Luke into two verses (Lk 24:6f.) in accordance with his emphasis on prophecy and its fulfilment. There is a likeness between the walk to Emmaus and Tobit. The *dénouement* of the tale hangs on scripture. The two men are rebuked for being 'slow of heart to believe in all that the prophets have spoken' (24:25) and then given a lesson in the christological interpretation of the entire Old Testament—'in all the scriptures the things pertaining to himself'. When Jesus has vanished they recall the warming of heart, which this exposition of the sacred texts had effected in them. The second appearance, to the eleven, also becomes a scripture lesson. 'Then opened he their mind that they might understand the scriptures' (Lk 24:45). Jesus's very last words, 'clothed with power from on high', use the Old Testament image of people being clothed with righteousness, strength, salvation or some other God-given virtue. He is then 'carried up into heaven' like Elijah.

3. 'Today'

The word 'today' (σήμερον—RV sometimes 'this day') was used once by Mark (14:30, prophecy of Peter's Denial), eight times by Matthew and eleven times by Luke, of which eight, excluding doubtful texts, are peculiar to him. The eight are:

2:11	'There is born to you this day . . . a saviour'
4:21	'Today hath this scripture been fulfilled'
5:26	'We have seen strange things today'
13:32f.	'I cast out devils and perform cures today and tomorrow and the third day I am perfected. Howbeit I must go on my way today and tomorrow and the day following, for it cannot be that a prophet perish out of Jerusalem'
19:5	'Today I must abide at thy house'
19:9	'Today is salvation come to this house'
22:61	'Before the cock crow this day'
23:43	'Today shalt thou be with me in paradise'

22:61 may be discounted because it is an echo of the solitary Marcan usage, but the two doubtful instances might be admitted on the grounds of Luke's deliberate use of the word:

3:22	'Thou art my son, this day have I begotten thee' (Ps 2:7)
24:21	'it is now today the third day since these things . . . '
	The first could have been suppressed in the interests of christological orthodoxy, the second for less ponderous syntax.

13:32f. is the most elaborate and derived from Exodus 19:10 where God promises that the people will hear his voice and commands preparation with 'Go unto the people, and sanctify them *today and tomorrow* and let them wash their garments and be ready against *the third day*, for the third day the Lord will come down in the sight of all the people . . .' It is set in the middle of Jesus's ministry and so matched by 2:11, 3:22 and 4:21 which mark the three points of its beginning (birth, baptism and manifesto at Nazareth) and 22:61 and 23:43 which mark its last day—to which might be added the 'that very day' of 23:12, when Pilate and Herod are reconciled, as an equivalent of 'today'. This leaves 19:5 and 19:9 which both belong to the story of Zacchaeus and 5:26 which Luke adds to the healing of a paralytic.

'Today' is used in the Old Testament, particularly the narrative books, to signal momentous occasions too numerous to list, and comes up repeatedly and solemnly in Deuteronomy which is artificially set on the one great day of Moses's leave-taking, a day of memory and expectation as Israel waits on the threshold of the promised land. Luke follows the usage, the single word performing the same function as the quotations and references noticed in the previous section. It is a landmark or trigonometrical point borrowed from his scriptures and placed at high points in his narrative to emphasise, in a typically historical way, their importance.[20]

4. Some Stories Only in Luke

The resurrection of the widow's only son at Nain (Lk 7:11–17) is not found elsewhere. The wonder is heightened by Jesus performing the miracle by touching the bier (7:14) rather than taking the corpse's hand (Mk 5:41; Lk 8:54). He uses the same words as at Mark 5:41, 'Damsel/young man, I say unto thee, Arise', though in his version of Jairus's daughter Luke omits 'I say unto thee'—an indication that Jairus's daughter is a shadowy source for his widow's son. But it is not a sufficient one. For that we have to go to the Old Testament. 1 Kings 17:8–24 tells of Elijah's encounter at Zarephath, 'at the gate of the city' (as Lk 7:12) with a widow whom he asked for sustenance. When she declared her destitution Elijah provided the miraculous meal—tub and oil-jar. Her son (her only son, it seems, as at Luke 7:12) died. Elijah took him into a room and revived him by stretching on him three times. Then he took him and gave him to his mother, like Jesus at Luke 7:15. She recognised that he was 'a man of God and the word of the Lord in thy mouth is truth'. Similarly, the miracle at Nain results in recognition of Jesus as 'a great prophet risen among us' (Lk 7:16), which can only be the Elijah whose return Malachi promised (Ml 4:5). A similar story is told of Elisha at 2 Kings 4 with increased drama and detail, but Luke does not seem to refer to it. The Elijah version is senior and sufficient—he has already shown his familiarity with it in Jesus's speech at Nazareth (Lk 4:26). Next in importance to the Old Testament's contribution is his own. The woman and her son make a neat pair with the man Jairus and his daughter (compare Zechariah and Mary, Simeon and Anna, the bent woman and Zacchaeus as daughter and son of Abraham respectively). Like the mourners over Jairus's daughter in Luke's addition to Mark's narrative, the widow is told 'weep not'—so are the daughters of Jerusalem at Luke 23:28. Jesus's compassion is emphasised (compare the good Samaritan and the prodigal son) and so is monotheism: the people 'feared' and 'glorified God' (two stock Lukan-biblical reactions), and said, 'God hath visited his people', in fulfilment of Zechariah's prophecy in the first chapter.

The story of Zacchaeus at Luke 19:1–10 is packed with Luke's characteristic language and moral theology. It is about money and repentance, its main character being a member of that rogues'-gallery-become-a-communion-of-saints which gives humanity and excitement to his gospel. He is 'little of stature': Luke, who favours the under-privileged, is the only evangelist to talk of stature in an historical frame (here and at 2:52) as well as a didactic one (Lk 12:25; Mt 6:17). 'He sought to see Jesus', like Herod at Luke 9:9: one of many instances of the evangelist's ability to get inside the skins of his characters. 'He made haste', like the shepherds at Luke 2:16: (σπεύδω is a verb used only by Luke and 2 Peter in the New Testament but common enough in the Septuagint). He 'received Jesus joyfully', ὑποδέχομαι being a word found in Tobit, Judith and Maccabees but used only by Luke and James in the New Testament and χαίρω (excluding the greeting χαίρε) being a common septuagintal verb used not at all by Mark, only thrice by Matthew and eighteen times in Luke–Acts. He is a 'son of Abraham' as the bent woman of Luke 13 is a 'daughter of Abraham'.[21]

Luke's stock-in-trade mark the telling of the tale. The shape of the story, dictated by repentance, is a central crisis flanked by 'before' and 'after', a pattern displayed by Luke's own parables (as by his grand scheme) in contrast to Mark's one-for-one allegories and to Matthew's eschatological parables with crises at the end rather than in the middle. The crowds preventing access to Jesus derives from the healing of the paralytic at Mark 2:4 and is also found when Mark 3:31 ('his mother and brothers, standing without, sent unto him') is edited into his 8:19 ('they could not come at him for the crowd'). The vocabulary is Luke's. To his reading of the Septuagint he owes the solemn 'and behold' (καὶ ἰδοῦ). 'Today' occurs twice. Salvation (σωτηρία) and cognates are common in the Septuagint but occur only in Luke amongst the evangelists, and in the New Testament predominantly in the later writings. The use of καταλύω (19:7) in the meaning of 'lodge' rather than 'destroy' occurs in the Septuagint but only in Luke in the New Testament:[22] here, the lodging of 2:7, and the addition of 'and lodge' to Mark at Luke 9:12. Other Lukan words are 'because' (καθότι only in Luke–Acts but also in the Septuagint), 'goods' (ὑπάρχοντα—Matthew thrice, Luke eight times), 'poor' (πτωχός—Mark and Matthew five times each,

Luke ten times), sinful ($\dot{\alpha}\mu\alpha\rho\tau\omega\lambda\dot{o}s$) as an adjective qualifying 'man' is only in Luke. The sycamore which Zacchaeus climbs recalls the (biblical) sycamine tree substituted for Matthew's mountain at Luke 17:6: both are peculiar to Luke. The use of 'the Lord' of Jesus is common in Luke–Acts.

In spite of all this it would be a logical jump to attribute the whole story to Luke's fertile imagination. It is only in Luke, it is covered with his fingerprints, but that does not prove that it originated with him—only that he wrote it in this version and that it evoked his particular powers in rich profusion. There may still be contributions from elsewhere. No human imagination works *ex nihilo*. Besides, we know that Luke used three major sources: Mark, Q or Matthew, and his old scriptures in 'all' of which he found 'the things concerning' Jesus (Lk 24:27). Can none of them stake any claim here?

The story is set in the third and final block of Markan matter in Luke's gospel. Luke has reached that puzzling point in Mark (10:46) where it is recorded of Jesus and his disciples that 'they come to Jericho and as he went out from Jericho' meets blind Bartimaeus. The modern critic wonders why Mark mentions Jericho at all.[23] The less detached ancient editor wonders what happened there. Scripture records (2 K 2) that it was visited by Elijah and Elisha *en route* to the great events of Elijah's exodus and ascension: an excellent reason for Luke's retention of Mark's mysterious mention of Jericho, thus explaining 19:1, but giving no great help with the rest of the story. However scripture has more and greater things to say about Jericho. Joshua 2 and 6 tell how the first Jesus ($'I\eta\sigma o\hat{v}s$ = Joshua) came and conquered there on his way to the promised land. The coincidence of names rings a loud bell. The other leading part in the old story is Rahab's. This enlightened whore enjoyed a good press from the early Christian writers, the epistle to the Hebrews praising her faith (11:31) and James her works (2:25). Matthew included her, with other ladies of dubious reputation, in his genealogy of Jesus. She does not appear in Luke, which is very surprising in an evangelist so favourable to women, sinners and hospitality. But her absence is more apparent than real. Zacchaeus has a remarkable family resemblance to her, pursuing in the same city an equally sinful trade when it is visited by another Jesus to whom he gives lodging (Jos 2:2; Lk 19:7). But why should a female harlot be changed into a male publican? Conzelmann has noticed that 'it is a feature of Luke's account that the typological meaning of passages is brought out at a later point without any

73

express reference to the earlier passage',[24] but not that this prophetic bridge-building includes the Old Testament which provides a host of examples (e.g. Lk 1 and 2; 9:51–56; 2 K 1:9–16; 9:57–62; 1 K 19:19–20). As for the change of sex, Luke has already had Jesus hospitably received by a sinful woman at 7:36–59. This sinful man makes a pair like Simeon and Anna. As a 'Son of Abraham' he is also the counterpart of the bent woman of Luke 13:10–17 who is a 'daughter of Abraham'.[25] Harlots and tax collectors are in fact paired at Matthew 21:31f. and 'go into the kingdom of heaven before you'. Luke used either Matthew or Q: if the former, he certainly knew this saying and the whole passage in which it occurs (Mt 21:23–33), if the latter he very probably did.[26] He shows his knowledge of Matthew's saying about publicans and harlots by, far from ignoring such congenial material, making it into two dramatic incidents—just as he had made Mark's laconic saying about fishers of men into a tableau at Luke 5:1–11. These two incidents are the sinful woman at 7:36–50 (Mk 14:3–9 much changed) and the present story. But Matthew's pairings of publicans and harlots takes him further still. To a mind soaked in the Septuagint the mention of harlots entering the kingdom will bring to mind the great saved harlot of the Old Testament—Rahab. Her male counterpart and fellow citizen of Jericho cannot but be a publican.

So each of Luke's known sources has played a part. Mark takes him to Jericho but tells him of no incident in that city. The Septuagint in its Book of Jesus supplies the void handsomely, presenting Luke with the attractive figure of Rahab of Jericho, venerated by his Christian contemporaries. But he has already told at length of just such a figure at 7:36–50. Matthew (or Q) tells him that the publican is the harlot's pair. Although he has already given his version of Mark's call of Levi, he is ready to have a second and more fully depicted publican—Levi is very sketchy—in the manner of his amplification of Matthew's centurion into Cornelius. It is inevitable that such an allusive and wide-ranging use of sources should be more laborious in its critical unravelling than in its original making —and result in a passage full of his own vocabulary and shaped by his own techniques.

Was Luke so ingenious? The officious critic comes after the creative writer, explaining references of which he was not always consciously aware. It is not suggested that Luke looked up all these references as he wrote his tale. In a world of few books, read aloud and midrashically pondered, there would be no need. The books in question here are Mark, Matthew or Q, and the Greek Old Testament scriptures, all of which were his sources for the story of God's Christ. He knew them thoroughly—even, in a sense, backwards. Reference sparked off reference in a well-stocked mind, excited by a devout and derivative creativity.

5. *Parables Peculiar to Luke*

These have posed no problem of sources to most critics. Their direct morality, narrative beauty and absence of allegorical mystification have ensured that they are usually attributed to the best possible source, Jesus himself.[27] But even if that is granted—and it ought really to wait upon an assessment of the Lukan characteristics which proliferate in them—it still allows for Jesus himself, whose humanity precluded total creation *ex nihilo*, to have spun them out of ideas known to him as a scripture-learned Jew.

The Prodigal Son is the longest, and perhaps the best, of them. Deuteronomy 21:15–17 defends the right of inheritance of the first-born son, even if his mother was a hated wife, against a younger son, even if his mother was a beloved wife. At 21:18–21 a 'stubborn and rebellious son' who is 'a riotous liver and a drunkard' is to be stoned. For all the Deuteronomist's strictness, in their legend and narrative the ancient Jews cherished the sneaking distrust of older brothers and the fondness for the younger (even when a rebel), which is common in folk-lore and fairy-tales. Cain and Abel were the first two brothers of mankind. God respected the offering of the younger but not the older. Jacob, the original Israel, was a younger son, like his father Isaac, and supplanted the older Esau by God's favour, assisted by his own unprincipled intelligence. His youngest son Joseph had God-given ideas of his own superiority which God-driven history vindicated. In his prosperity he showed warm affection for Benjamin, the youngest brother of all, born to Jacob during Joseph's exile. From Benjamin Saul, the first king, was descended, to be succeeded by David, the youngest son of Jesse the Bethlehemite. Two deliverers of Israel, Gideon and Judas Maccabaeus, were younger sons. Galatians 4:21–31, appealing to Ishmael and Isaac, shows that the lesson was not lost on Christianity, the junior Jewish heresy struggling for its rights and superiority. The theme emerges first in the gospels with Matthew's tale of two brothers at 21:28–32, the setting of work in a vineyard referring to Mark 12:1–12 which follows immediately upon it. Matthew is, to say the least, a great respecter of the law, and so prefers the Deuteronomic view to the insubordinations of the stories. The first, or elder, says he will not work but then 'repents himself' and does; the second, or younger, *vice-versa*. Luke is a devotee of the stories, and so is happy to reverse Matthew (while cherishing his *motif* of repentance) to fit their predilection for younger brothers.

The tale begins with the father dividing his goods (favourite word of Luke) between his two sons, flouting the sound advice of ben Sirach (Si 33:19–23) that the father who parts his goods before his death, whether to relations or friends, puts himself in jeopardy. The younger son leaves for a far country and plunges into the riotous living condemned by Deuteronomy, only to become a victim of a famine such as was endemic in the days of Jacob, Elijah and Elisha. He joins himself to a citizen of that country, like Ruth amid the alien corn, to become a swineherd—abhorrent parody of patriarchal shepherding. Hunger makes him think, like the Israelite prisoners-of-war in Solomon's prayer at 1 Kings 8:47ff.: 'if they shall bethink themselves in the land whither they are carried away captive, and turn again and make supplication unto thee . . . saying, We have sinned and have done perversely . . . if they return unto thee . . . then hear thou their prayer.' Similarly Hosea's prodigal wife said to herself in her abandonment, 'I will go and return to my first husband; for then it was better with me than now' (Ho 2:7). He meditates upon the good luck of the hired servants ($\mu\iota\sigma\theta\iota\iota$—only here in the New Testament) whom his father, like ben Sirach, kept. Like Pharaoh who told Moses, 'I have sinned against the Lord your God and against you' (Ex 10:16), he will say 'I have sinned against heaven and before thy sight.' While he is still far off his father runs to meet him, just as Joseph got his chariot ready to meet his father Israel coming to Egypt, falls on his neck and kisses him—the classic expression of reunion in Genesis.[28] The clothing and ornaments which his father showers upon him shine with biblical ceremony, recollecting the clothing of the ragged high priest Joshua at Zechariah 3:3–5 and God's clothing of foundling Israel with shoes, fine linen and silk at Ezekiel 16:10. The ring is the symbol of authority given to Joseph by Pharaoh (Gn 41:42) and transferred by Ahasuerus from Haman to Mordecai (Es 8:2). The fatted calf is a gastronomic honour bestowed by Abraham on his angelic visitors (Gn 18:7) and by the witch of Endor on Saul (1 S 28:24). 'Eat, drink and be merry' is the doomed festivity of Ecclesiastes 2:24 and the rich fool at Luke 12:19, revived for the happier day when the father, like Jacob, finds that the son who was 'dead' is alive. The elder brother, out in the fields like Esau (Gn 25:29), hears music such as enlivened ben Sirach's dinner parties (Si 32). He quotes part of Proverbs 29:3: 'Whoso loveth wisdom rejoiceth his father, but he that keepeth company with harlots wasteth his substance.' The tale ends with more reference to the Joseph saga of the son lost in a far country and restored, which has influenced it all along.

Luke's interests abound throughout. The setting is in the affluent middle class. The classic Lukan shape is clear: a central crisis preceded by its making and followed by its *dénouement*—the overall shape of Luke–Acts in miniature. It expresses Luke's unfailing delight in the reversal of fortunes and provides the frame for a grand instance of his great doctrine of repentance. Two momentous journeys are made. Soliloquy lets the reader into the mind of the anti-hero. The father is moved with compassion like the good Samaritan and Jesus at Nain. Septuagintalisms abound, to which may be added the elder brother's Jonah-like resentment at the repentance of the wicked, and come mostly from the narrative books Luke loves. Matthew has made a seminal contribution to the tale.

The shorter tale of the Good Samaritan competes with the Prodigal Son in universal popularity and shares its shape together with the modest affluence of its eponymous character and his journeying. It too has grown out of a Matthean stock and is heavily indebted to the Old Testament. Matthew (22:34ff.) was content to follow Mark in answering the lawyer's question with the summary of the law from Deuteronomy 6:5, combined with Leviticus 19:18, and leave it at that. By his own lights one could not do better. Luke adds the Deuteronomic aphorism that the obedient will 'live',[29] then develops the theme of love of neighbour, which he has already made the dominant doctrine of his abbreviation of the Sermon on the Mount. He begins characteristically with dialogue which gives the recitation of the law (realistically and appropriately) to the lawyer, and then bursts into a story which draws heavily on 2 Chronicles 28: the record of a three-cornered struggle between Syria, Judah and Israel (including Samaria). The Syrians, allied with Israel, massacred the men of Judah; but the Syrians' intention to make slaves of the captives was resisted by the Israelites as the foreign army advanced on Samaria. Four of them, 'heads of the children of Ephraim (i.e. Samaritans) took the captives, and with the spoil clothed all that were naked among them and arrayed them, and shod them and gave them to eat and drink, and anointed them, and carried all the feeble among them upon asses. and brought them to Jericho, the city of palm trees, unto their brethren: then they returned to Samaria' (28:15). The incident supplies Luke with plot, location, characters and detail for his story. The failure of the priest and the Levite to help heightens the practical compassion of the Samaritan schismatic. These indifferent clergymen stand midway between Zechariah's faithful performance of priestly duty and the wickedness of the chief priests at Jesus's trial and death. Contrast between a Samaritan and orthodox Jews will recur in another peculiarly Lukan episode, the ten lepers of 17:11–19. Inns and innkeepers (πανδοχεῖον and πανδοχεύς) were more common in the Graeco-Roman world at large than in Palestine[30]—a touch of Hellenism within a decidedly Old Testament picture to match the music in the Prodigal Son.

The Unjust Steward presents an immoral character as a good example in the manner of the Reluctant Friend (Lk 11:5ff.) and the Unjust Judge (Lk 18:2ff.). It follows upon the Prodigal Son which did precisely the same—a fact which points to its not being the embarrassing bolt from the blue which some critics have supposed— and takes further the same doctrine of repentance in the interests of self-preservation which Luke's Jewish nation so tragically ignored. This resourceful villain would be at home in no other gospel: and here he is very much at home. The story has the classic shape of a central crisis, the entirely secular audit, flanked by 'before' and 'after' and provoking the anti-hero's soliloquy. The setting is again the affluent bourgeois household. Money, that favourite theme of Luke's, plays a leading part. The great difficulty, which remains and cannot be dissipated, is the use of the bad man to make a good point. This does not make the steward a singular phenomenon in Luke. It makes Luke's whole rogues' gallery a singular phenomenon in the synoptic gospels, so posing a problem of source. Leading characters in the Old Testament have given similar offence by being included in salvation-history: Jacob and his dirty tricks, Rahab the prostitute, David and his adultery. 2 Kings 7 is an interesting and little known example of the rewards of low cunning, perhaps the only biblical story to stand with the Unjust Steward. The puritanical chronicler eschewed it. When Samaria was under siege by the Syrians and its inhabitants starving, four Samaritan lepers (Luke, incidentally, has the only Samaritan leper in the New

Testament) sitting in the gate decided that they had nothing to lose: 'Why sit we here until we die? If we say, we will enter into the city, then the famine is in the city and we shall die there: and if we sit still here, we die also.' They decided on an expedition to the Syrians who might save them alive ($\zeta\omega\gamma\rho\epsilon\hat{\iota}\nu$ again) and could only kill them at worst. To their astonishment they found the Syrians' camp deserted. Unknown to them, God had frightened them away with military sound-effects. The lepers took full advantage of the situation, eating, drinking, looting at will and prudently hiding their best spoil for later. After a while they rebuked themselves for not spreading the news: 'this is a day of good news ($\epsilon\dot{\upsilon}\alpha\gamma\gamma\acute{\epsilon}\lambda\iota\alpha$/gospels) and we hold our peace.' They ran back and told the King of Samaria who thought it was a Syrian ruse until a patrol convinced him otherwise. The enterprising Samaritan lepers share the unjust steward's tactics of 'when surrounded, advance!'—the gambler's last throw in an apparently doomed situation. Again the Old Testament provides the only adequate accessible solution to the problem of the source of a peculiarly Lukan parable. And again there is a Hellenistic touch: 'I cannot dig' is a Greek proverb found in Aristophanes *The Birds* 1432.

The major influence of the Old Testament on these three Lukan parables suggests a further line of thought.[31] Strictly speaking they are not parables at all. In Mark parables are allegories, the sower and the vineyard (Mk 4:1–20; 12:1–12) being the chief examples which Matthew and Luke agree also to label as such. Matthew adds some of his own, the wheat and tares at 13:23–30, the marriage feast at 22:1–14, being examples labelled as 'parables'. Luke has no quarrel with this view of parable, only reviving also the ancient scriptural usage of applying the word to simple proverbs such as found in his favourite books of Samuel and Kings (Lk 4:23; 5:36; 6:39). By legitimate extension he also uses it of proverbs which have grown into little moral stories (the Rich Fool at 12:16, the Fig Tree at 13:6 and the Unjust Judge at 18:1). The renaissance of salty biblical wisdom is a feature of his gospel. But the three stories which have been examined are best called stories rather than parables: and this not out of pedantry but in the interest of their character being appreciated. Still less, incidentally, should they be used as normative, authentic parables of Jesus in defiance of Mark's (and very likely Matthew's) priority to them. They are stories in the Old Testament tradition. Like the tale told by Nathan to David at 2 Samuel 12:1–6 (also not called parable) they catch the reader by sheer narrative skill rather than the fascination of allegory which is not necessarily excluded but takes a lower place. They belong securely in a book which is itself a renaissance of Old Testament story-telling.

[1] Perrot 'Les Récits d'Enfance' *Recherches des Sciences Religieuses* 1967.

[2] *Ant.* II, 215, 216

[3] *Ant.* II, 231

[4] *Ant.* II, 233

[5] *Ant.* V, 276ff.

[6] See the first of the 'Additional Notes' in Creed's commentary for a synoptic presentation of the Magnificat and Benedictus with their Old Testament sources.

[7] John, however, could be said to do something very similar to Luke if the Jerusalem Bible is correct (and it appears to be so) in printing much of the discourses of Jesus as verse.

[8] Judith resembles the women of Luke 8:2–3 in being wealthy and other Lukan ladies (2:37; 7:12; 18:3) in being a widow. She is also 'blessed above all women' (Jdt 13:18) like Mary at Luke 1:42 who is 'blessed among women'.

[9] Weinfeld *Deuteronomy and the Deuteronomic School*, p. 305

[10] Laos (the people) is, in Luke–Acts, a word ordinarily reserved for the Jewish nation, used thirty-seven times in the gospel, compared with thrice in Mark and fourteen times in Matthew (one of many indications of a line of development Mark–Matthew–Luke, without recourse to 'Q'). In Luke's psalms the people are the recipients of God's promised deliverance (1:17, 21; 2:10, 31, 32).

[11] Cf. 2 Kings 17:23 'as he had spoken by all his servants the prophets'.

[12] There were two sacrifices of incense in the temple: Philo *de Victimis* 3 Luke does not particularise the evening.

[13] Creed, p. 31

[14] For an exploration of the neglected possibility that Luke knew Matthew's birth stories and used material from them, see chapter IV

[15] See Creed and Strack Billerbeck *ad loc*.

[16] See Chapter IV pp. 122–127

[17] See R. Pesch 'Le Logion des Pêcheurs' in *L'Evangile de Luc*, Paris 1973, p. 242

[18] C. F. Evans 'The Central Section of St Luke's Gospel' in *Studies in the Gospels* ed. Nineham, Blackwell 1955, p. 37. RV translations added in brackets.

[19] See *The Epistle of Aristeas* in R. H. Charles's *Apocrypha and Pseudepigrapha of the O.T.*, Oxford 1913, Vol. II.

[20] I am indebted to an unpublished note by the Rt Revd Kenneth Woollcombe for a clear and perceptive tabulation of Luke's usages of 'today'.

[21] See Nils A. Dahl 'The Story of Abraham in Luke–Acts' in *Studies in Luke–Acts* ed. Keck and Martyn, London 1968, for a definitive treatment of this theme.

[22] But Mark uses the noun 'lodging' at 14:14

[23] E.g. D. E. Nineham (*St Mark*, London 1963, p. 285) who suggests that 'Bartimaeus of Jericho' may have been 'a figure well known in the early church as one who had *followed Jesus on the way*', the name of the town being stuck in tradition to the name of the man.

[24] In *The Theology of St Luke*, London 1960 (E.T. of *Die Mitte der Zeit*), p. 75, footnote 4.

[25] Zacchaeus is also related to Levi, the converted and hospitable tax collector of Mark 2:13–17 and Luke 5:27–32. Similarly Cornelius in Acts is the centurion of Matthew 8:5–13 and Luke 7:1–10 writ large.

[26] The parable of two sons which occurs in it is a source for his tale of two sons, usually called 'the Prodigal Son'.

[27] As in J. Jeremias *The Parables of Jesus*

[28] 33:4 (Esau and Jacob), 45:14 (Joseph and Benjamin), 46:29 (Joseph and Israel). See also Raguel and Tobias at Tobit 7:6

[29] See also Leviticus 18:5: 'keep my statutes and my judgements: which if a man do, he shall live in them.'

[30] Billerbeck and Dalman say they were taken over by the Jews as 'loan-words' though absent from Josephus and Philo. See Arndt and Gingrich *Lexicon*.

[31] Rather provocatively opened up in my 'The Sower, the Vineyard, and the Place of Allegory in the Interpretation of Mark's Parables' in *Journal of Theological Studies*, October 1973, with rejoinders in October 1974.

5

Using Mark

LUKE IS THE only evangelist to take the reader into his confidence by declaring his hand at the outset of his work, making two clear admissions about his method. The first is that he acknowledges himself to be an editor. 'Many have taken in hand to draw up a narrative concerning those matters which have been fulfilled among us.' He has a legacy of Christian material which he has subjected to a painstaking study—'traced the course of all things accurately from the first.' Luke's second admission reveals the grand motive and principle of his editing: 'to write unto thee in order'. The adverb καθεξῆς lets the reader into Luke's reason for writing and his way of going about it. At Luke 8:1 and Acts 18:23 he uses it of Jesus and Paul travelling from place to place, at Acts 3:24 of a succession of prophecy beginning with Samuel which foretold the events he narrates, and at Acts 11:4 of Peter telling in orderly succession the events which led him to support the admission of the gentiles. Its meaning emerges as 'in succession', 'connectedly' or 'in historical order'. It testifies to Luke's enthusiasm for temporal succession as his vehicle for theology, a conviction inherited from the Old Testament and, above all, from the Deuteronomic historian whose Succession Narrative, well so called, deployed it on an equally epic scale. This gives an answer to the obvious question of what is, for Luke, the *cantus firmus* and content of historical succession. For a modern historian it could be economic or social forces, but for the Old Testament historian and for Luke it can only be the force of God's will for mankind worked out in prophecy and its fulfilment. It is from this familiar point of view that he works on the existing Christian sources which he has to hand; and one of these is the gospel according to Mark. The great benefit of Luke's first verses is that they excuse the critical reader from having to infer or invent motives for Luke's literary labour—and just how perplexing and taxing that can be is clear enough in recent attempts to understand what Mark was trying to do. Instead we have it from the horse's mouth and can approach his redaction of Mark in the confidence that we are not foisting ideas upon him. He is out to make Mark more historically consecutive. Our previous findings made it likely that he owes both this intention and the techniques for its execution to his biblical heritage.

Most readers of Mark will agree that something of the sort was needed. Incident is piled upon incident with no more apparent connection than a mere 'and' or 'and suddenly'. The method certainly has power, and is appropriate to Mark's approach, governed by the idea of a divine invasion of human life working violently against the grain of all human aspirations. But if it impresses the reader it also disorients and tires him. If there are connections in many stretches of Mark's book they strain the poetic ingenuity even of Austin Farrer to uncover. The ordinary reader is soon lost. And he is in ancient and respectable company, for both Matthew and Luke decided that Mark needed radical attention in order to make sense to their communities and, as a result of their success, Mark subsequently fell out of esteem and practically out of use in the Church. An example of the difficulty of Mark is the baffling exchange about bread in the boat at Mark 8:14–21. Matthew laboured hard to make Mark's subsidiary point about the leaven of the Pharisees into the whole point, thus abolishing Mark's absolute emphasis on the incomprehension of the disciples: 'then understood they' (Mt 16:11). Strong editing yields the ethical sense which Matthew requires. Luke cuts the story altogether, only salvaging the essence of Matthew's interpretation of it by putting 'beware ye of the leaven of the Pharisees *which is hypocrisy*' (a further ethical definition) in a collection of sayings about the all-seeing and all-caring eye of providence (12:1). Both subsequent evangelists in their different ways edit against the provocative interruptions and dislocations of the Markan tale and in the interests of homogeneous sense. No doubt Mark was expressing a warm conviction in this passage, but just what it was eluded Matthew and Luke and seems to be a secret which he and his community have carried with them to their graves.[1]

Fortunately Mark's delight in interruption (rapid cutting, in cinematic terms) has its limits; and so does his jolting and episodic style. In two very important respects, Mark gives coherence to his work and writes 'in order'. He has an overall plan, shaped like an hourglass. The central revelation of Peter's confession and the transfiguration bind together the threads already spun and direct them towards the coming end. On either side of it are events centred on Galilee and events centred on Jerusalem. Luke takes over this overall scheme, making it even more explicit with his famous turning point at 9:51, couched in septuagintal terms, 'When the days drew near for him to be received up, he set his face steadfastly to go to Jerusalem.' Bound into this scheme of Mark's is a rudimentary[2] pattern of prophecy and fulfilment. Three times Jesus foretells his passion and in a number of proleptic hints the shadow of the gallows falls across the story, giving the narrative a drive which has led to the book being called a passion narrative with an extended prologue. Matthew and Luke are perfectors. They stand on Mark's shoulders and are related to him as masters to an innovator, improving at leisure the raw force of a first attempt. To edit an existing document is both to pay a great compliment to its value and to insist that it is not entirely satisfactory as it stands—the twin convictions of every exercise in *midrash*. Mark had a sense of history: he was the first Christian writer to put the gospel into narrative form from start to finish and without remainder. But he does not measure up to the high standards which Luke has learnt from the Deuteronomic historian: the handling of prophecy and fulfilment over long distances, the leisurely use of grand tableaux and speeches, retrospective and prophetic, and the continual and overt sense of succession and development in time which links one event to another. There is still a great deal to put 'in order', much carelessness about succession (or failure to make it clear) in Mark, which calls for the skills of a Luke who stands at the peak of the growth of historiography in the New Testament.

Luke, as the next chapter will try to show more fully, is indebted to Matthew for some of his more sensitive historical awareness. We have already seen, in Matthew's overt scriptural citations, a sense of time more exact than Mark's but less mature than Luke's ability to weave them into the fabric of the tale where they are almost hidden. Matthew 11:2–19 is an attempt at historical distinction which defines John the Baptist's temporal position on the bearings of law and prophets, Christ and Church. Luke 16:16 alters Matthew's verses 12 and 13 to take in a wider historical sweep and divide it more clearly: first the age of law and prophets, then John as caesura or link, followed by the preaching of the gospel. Matthew's final tableau (28:16–20) provides a connection, missing in Mark, between Jesus and the Church. Luke spins it out, not only with two scenes involving the risen founder and his disciples, but also on into Acts. The same line of development has been seen more extensively in the increasingly remote points at which each writer begins his story, soundings into the past going deeper and deeper with the passage of time. Matthew provides a genealogy which traces Christ's descent back to Abraham: an exercise in historical authorisation of the gospel unattempted by Mark. Luke goes further, indeed as far as possible, and writes a genealogy which goes back to Adam. A further effect of this *recherche du temps perdu* thus comes to light. It makes for a wider setting of the gospel: in national history by Matthew's pedigree and in the whole biblical human history by his own. History is no longer just the work-bench on which God fashions salvation. It is beginning to be seen as itself the thing which he is making and within which he is revealed.

1. *Luke's Edition of the Beginning of Jesus's Ministry in Mark*
Luke's overall strategy can be seen in a diagram of two columns.

Part I

Mark 1:14–45	*Luke 4:1—5:16*
1) Jesus enters Galilee—'the time is fulfilled' etc	1) Jesus returns to Galilee—his preaching not given.
2) Calls Simon, James and John 'fishers of men'.	2) Manifesto in the synagogue at Nazareth, lynching attempted.
3) Demoniac cured in synagogue at Capernaum.	3) Demoniac cured in synagogue at Capernaum.
4) Healing of Simon's mother-in-law and others.	4) Healing of Simon's mother-in-law and others.
5) Goes out to pray before dawn, found by Simon and those with him, moves on through Galilee.	5) Goes out at dawn, found by crowd, moves on through Judea.
6) Leper cleansed—Jesus withdraws.[3]	6) Call of Simon, James and John, miraculous catch, 'fishers of men'.
	7) Leper cleansed—Jesus withdraws to pray.[3]

Incident 3 is the place at which Luke begins editing Mark in a continuous and consecutive fashion, but it is clear that his first incident corresponds to Mark's and is drawn from it. His second incident appears from the diagram to have no Markan parallel, but it takes as its theme the preaching of Jesus in Mark's first incident which Luke omitted from his own. 'The time is fulfilled, and the kingdom of God is at hand: repent ye and believe in the gospel' (Mk 1:15) is precisely the point of the Nazareth manifesto, midrashically developed into the fuller, septuagintal speech, overtly recalling stories about Elijah and Elisha from 1 Kings 17 and 2 Kings 5, which Luke gives to Jesus for his first announcement of the gospel. The element of opposition is not to be found in Mark 1:15 but derives from another passage in Mark—6:1–6, also set in a synagogue and containing the crucial proverb about the prophet in his own country which Luke retails and, characteristically, dramatises in the attempt to kill Jesus. The Markan material evokes, in Luke's version, memories of the hostile treatment of the prophets of old such as Elijah and Jeremiah, and pre-echoes of the fate of the apostles when their turn comes to preach the gospel to the Jews. The other remarkable feature of Luke's version is his sixth section, the call of the three and their miraculous catch. Mark 1:16–20 (Mark's incident 2 in the diagram) is its origin. Again a proverbial utterance in Mark, 'I will make you fishers of men' is, like the proverb of the prophet at home, spun into drama and becomes a story: heavily dependent, as we have seen, on the Septuagint.

Luke's second and sixth incidents are thus both made according to the same techniques. A hint in the form of a proverb from Mark is nurtured by Luke's narrative skill into a story which owes a debt to the Deuteronomic historian. More obviously, these two incidents form Luke's contribution to the telling of Christian origins. The first is a dramatic tableau of the beginning of Jesus's own ministry, the second of the beginning of the ministry of his disciples and successors. The place of each in the epic plan of salvation history is made clear by its retrospective and prospective notes. In both scenes the course of events to come is prophetically indicated: Jesus's death at the hands of his countrymen and the world-wide mission of his followers. Luke teases out Mark's laconic brevity into rich scenes fully staged.

In Mark Jesus's preaching is immediately and mysteriously followed by the call of the disciples, but Luke spaces them out and puts three incidents between which show in action the restoration proclaimed in the manifesto. They come from Mark and retain their original order. This spacious architecture, with the two tableaux carrying the structure-like pillars, involves Luke in a slip. Jesus heals Simon's mother-in-law without the reader having any idea of who Simon is or how he is connected to Jesus, as he would have if

Mark's order were intact. He is more careful in the next incident (his incident 5). Jesus is tracked down by the crowd instead of Mark's 'Simon and those that were with him'. The crowd is still there at the beginning of his sixth section which starts with a reminiscence of the setting of the parable of the sower at Mark 4:1: the crowd on the shore and Jesus teaching them from the boat. But no detail of the teaching is given and at verse 4 Luke is back again to Mark 1:14–45 for his grand editing of its second incident. The fishing which started as a proverbial summons in Mark became an eschatological parable in Matthew (Mt 13:47–50—the drag-net) which Luke does not retail but works into a story. Each step in this development is highly characteristic of the evangelist concerned: the summons, the parable of judgement, the historical tableau. The two mentions of the crowd which we have noticed, one in Luke's fifth incident and one in his sixth, are deliberate and common with him. They give an impression, at the end and climax of the whole section, of the public and secular setting of the gospel. The crowd seeks Jesus (an apologetic stroke) and is a witness to the miracle which marks the beginning of the Church's history. These things are not done in a corner (Ac 26:26). Luke has controlled the long crescendo which leads up to this with patient care. His master-move was to separate Mark's first two incidents, which follow one another so suddenly as to obscure the momentous widening of scope which they contain— from the solitary master to the beginning of the Christian community. Like a gardener separating seedlings Luke spaces them out so that each can grow and the difference between them be clear. The historian, working in order, insists that first Jesus should explain himself and set to work, then call a nucleus of followers. How, after all, could anyone follow him without knowing what he is about—as the disciples seem to do in Mark? The Deuteronomic historian has taught Luke the value of spacious development and how to link and control it.

More than this, the block of incidents which we have been looking at is not complete in itself. Previous hints come to fulfilment in it. The Jesus who reads the book in the synagogue is the adult development of the boy who sat among the doctors. He preaches the redeeming visitation prophesied in the canticles and its reception fulfils old Simeon's gloomy forebodings. The block also contains some seeds of later events. The whole scene at Nazareth is the prototype of similar scenes in Acts where Christians will preach the gospel and meet with a hostile, even violent response. The admission of the gentiles, which Luke is at such pains to keep out of his gospel because it belongs 'in order' in Acts, is prophesied in the speech at Nazareth by references to the widow of Sidonian Zarephath and Naaman the Syrian. There is a near-passion as the people cast him forth out of the city and lead him to the brow of the hill to throw him down, a hint of the resurrection in 'but he passing through the midst of them went his way'. As a prototype of Acts, the marvellous catch prophesies the Church's putting out from the home waters of Judaism into the deep of the wider world. Peter's repentance at 5:8 is the first occurrence of a major theme. For Luke each decisive advance of the Church and the gospel begins with Peter repenting: here, at the passion (22:32) and at the admission of the gentile Cornelius (Ac 10).

Luke is throughout revising Mark from the point of view of the historian. He takes trouble to connect the events he describes with Israel's past, makes the order of their present happening clearer and more coherent than Mark had cared to do, and discerns within them hints of the future. Matthew before him had found Mark's account of the opening of Jesus's ministry unsatisfactory and had dealt with it in his own characteristic way. In the Sermon on the Mount, a longer manifesto than Luke's, he establishes Jesus's message at the outset. The emphasis is on ethics, for Matthew is more of a moralist than an historian, and as a result the flow of the narrative is massively interrupted. The tableau of Matthew's sermon is static, contributing to the tale only the note of the crowds' astonishment at his authority at 7:28. There is little of the strong organic linking of discourse and narrative which means so much to Luke. Yet within the Sermon on the Mount there is frequent reference to the ethical régime which has operated up till now and the different requirements which Jesus brings into force, particularly from 5:17 to 48. The end of the sermon brings eschatological forces to bear on ethics (7:15–27). Between these two comes instruction on present conduct (6:1—7:13). It is clear from this presentation in order of past, present and future reference that Matthew has a sense of history, no doubt evoked by the bitter and perplexing arguments with the old synagogue which forced him to historical reflection to find the authority which is bound up with history. He makes more of history than Mark, but less than Luke. In discussing the historical problem of the relations of the old Jewish dispensation and the new Christian one he resorts to both stark contrast ('It was said . . . but I say unto you') and proprietary agreement ('Think not that I have come to abolish the law and the prophets; I have come not to abolish but to fulfil them.') Notoriously he does not resolve the inconsistency, leaving his readers perplexed whether he is more the traditional Jew or the Christian. He lacks the historical sophistication to sort out the problem of continuity and discontinuity. But he poses it and he sees the Church's life between the legacy of the past and the day of judgement in the future. In retrospect he can be seen as the essential mid-point of development between Mark and Luke in the early Church's search for its past.

The plan of the rest of Luke's ordering of Mark's account of the beginning of the ministry is:

Part II

Mark 1:40—3:19	*Luke 5:12—6:19*
1) Leper healed	1) Leper healed
2) Paralytic healed	2) Paralytic healed
3) Call of Levi	{ 3) Call of Levi
4) Fasting debate	{ 4) Fasting debate at Levi's table
5) Cornfield debate	5) Cornfield debate
6) Withered hand healed	6) Withered hand healed
7) Multitudes healed	7) Twelve chosen on the mountain
8) Twelve chosen	8) Descent to the plain Multitudes healed

The reduction of Mark's narrative to a plan shows that it has a pattern. Two miracles are followed by the call of one man, two debates about eating are followed by two more instances of miraculous healing and the choosing of twelve men. Luke's love of the pattern of widening scope makes him value the development inherent in this: from the summoning of one disciple to the appointment of the twelve. While he leaves most of Mark's order as it stands, his editorial work at incidents 3, 4, 7 and 8 is designed to make the development clearer.

He joins the third and fourth incidents into one. The link needed to do so is already there in Mark: Levi is a publican and the debate is sparked off by Jesus and his disciples 'sitting at meat in his house' with 'many publicans and sinners'. Luke reads the 'his' as referring to Levi, though in Mark it could just as well refer to Jesus. Mark's note about the fasting of John's disciples and the Pharisees is easily made part of tne conversation at verse 33 so that there need be no change of scene. The unity is further strengthened by the exploitation of two favourite themes of Luke's which are germinally present in Mark: the dinner table and the repentance of sinners. Mark's simple meal becomes a 'great feast' at which the discussion takes place. There may be a shadow of Plato's *Symposium* here, but more precisely appropriate to Luke's own world are the long-winded dinner debates of the Jewish–Hellenistic *Letter of Aristeas*, the fellowship meals referred to in *Joseph and Asenath*, or the sumptuous feast of Artaxerxes in *Esther*. This is the first of a series of conversations at table, to be followed by the scene in the house of Simon the Pharisee (7:36–50), the healing of dropsy at table in Chapter 14 and the dinner parables which follow it, the Last Supper and the meal at Emmaus—and on through the Church's common meals in Acts to the breakfast on the doomed ship at Acts 27:33–38. The second theme, of repentance, is brought out by Luke's addition to Mark at the end of verse 32 ('to repentance'). Levi is the first of Luke's great gallery of penitent sinners, often people of means. He is an obvious prototype of Zacchaeus (19:1–10) and belongs with the parables of repentance in chapter 15 and 16:1–13, the woman at Simon's dinner party and the crucified criminal. The whole of the debate is integrated around the story of Levi's call, repentance and hospitality.

At the end of this block Luke reverses Mark's order by having the twelve chosen before the mutitudes are healed. Again a pattern of widening scope is achieved by the editing: Jesus is alone on the mountain at 6:12, surrounds himself with the twelve at 6:13–16, then comes down with them to the plain to be with 'a great multitude of his disciples and a great number of the people' amongst whom he does therapeutic miracles. Luke takes particular pains over the choosing of the twelve, amplifying Mark's simple note of place ('and he goeth up into the mountain', Mk 3:13) into 'and it came to pass in those days that he went up into the mountain to pray; and he continued all night in prayer to God, and when it was day . . .' (Lk 6:12f.). Since the great prophetic tableau of the miraculous catch, Jesus's followers have been as hazy and indistinct as they are in the parallel passages in Mark which Luke has edited only lightly. They are part of the discussion in the fasting debate and present in the cornfield, but it is not even clear whether they include those called on the lake. Now it is, to Mark's mind as well as to Luke's, high time that their connection with Jesus should be more strongly defined—and Luke does so more clearly than his source by the momentous introduction (6:12 quoted above) and the crescendo of scope. Geography is also used to define the story. Mark had Jesus choose the twelve on 'the mountain' immediately after healing the multitudes by 'the sea'. Luke emphasises the mountain as the scene of Jesus's nocturnal prayer as well as his choice of the twelve, then has him come down with them to the plain (6:17) where (rather than somewhere by the sea) he heals the crowds before preaching a version of Matthew's Sermon on the Mount. It is typical of both evangelists that the one should have Jesus preach from the divinely authoritative mountain and the other in the secular and populous setting of the plain. In using both mountain and plain Luke echoes the great Sinai scenes in Exodus with their movement of Moses between God on the mountain and the people on the plain.

So before he leaves Mark to take up Matthew and his teaching material (a switch probably suggested by the mountain at Luke 6:12 and Mark 3:13) he has refined the drama into a connected and steady development which reaches its high point just before the sermon. By 6:20 Jesus has announced his own mission and put it into action, summoned the three first disciples, received the first penitent sinner at the first table scene, surrounded himself with the college of the apostles (called apostles here in Matthew and Luke but not Mark if the textual variant at Mark 3:14 is dismissed), stood on mountain and plain as well as by the sea, and now is surrounded by the twelve, a great multitude of his disciples and great number of the people.

2. Luke's Edition of the Ministry in Mark (Mark 14: 3–10 and 4:1—6:44; Luke 7:36—9:17)

Luke's editing of Mark began with a major transposition of Mark's rejection at Nazareth (Mk 6:1–6), much amplified from other sources and rewritten, to the outset of Jesus's ministry. The same happens at the beginning of this second block. Luke's editorial energy is high when he makes fresh starts. The story of Jesus's anointing by a woman is brought forward from its Markan place just before the passion (Mk 14:3–19), edited into a radical change of character and put after the debate about John the Baptist which is the last item in Luke's preceding block of Matthean material. The placing is far from arbitrary and makes such excellent sense that the reader need not notice the switch from Matthew back to Mark. The end of the discussion about John in Matthew is 'The Son of Man came eating and drinking and ye say, Behold, a gluttonous man and a wine-bibber, a friend of publicans and sinners. And wisdom is justified by her works', which Luke copies, only changing 'works' into 'children'.[4] He warms enthusiastically to references such as this in his sources to table fellowship with sinners. His powers are stimulated and, being the powers of a story-teller, look for an incident to make the Matthean teaching concrete in drama. Knowing Mark well, he does not have to look far. He has already used the meal after Levi's call. The meal at Bethany in the house of Simon the Leper remains to actualise the Son of Man's eating and drinking. Simon the Leper becomes Simon the Pharisee, continuing Luke's added reference, in his edition of Matthew's debate about John, to the Pharisees who 'rejected for themselves the counsel of God' in contrast to the publicans who 'justified God' (Lk 7:29, 30). They provide a dramatic foil for the doctrine of forgiveness. The woman becomes a sinner, embodying the sinners who are the Son of Man's friends (Mk 2:16; Mt 11:19; Lk 7:34). Matthew, who expands Mark's doctrine of forgiveness, provides the necessary stage of development for Luke's treatment of the theme, which is the fullest of all. So to Matthew Luke goes, more probably in memory than in exact reference, and amplifies Mark's anointing story by telling a parable of two debtors (Mt 18:23–35). It is thus given a characteristically dramatic setting but is so tightly compressed as to alter its shape (no question of forgiveness of one debtor by another, the Matthean crux). Luke's financial knowledge is brought to bear on Matthew's fantastic sums. The ministering women of Luke 8:1–3 are a natural development into plurality of the one woman who has just ministered to Jesus.

High-handed editing of Mark continues. Strictly speaking the Beelzebub argument should follow the appointment of the twelve and healings of the multitude which ended the first Markan block used by Luke. It does not—probably because the transposition of the anointing scene has taken Luke's eye off Mark's order and left him free to choose where to start again. Again, a table will make things clear:

Part I

Mark 3:20—4:34	*Luke 8:4–21*
1) Beelzebub	(used in Lk 11)
2) True kindred	(3 below)
3) Sower—parable and interpretation	1) Sower—parable and interpretation
4) Light and other sayings about parables	2) Light and other sayings about parables
5) Secret growth	
6) Mustard seed	(used at 13:18)
7) Note about parables	3) True kindred

92

Luke has just told of the relatively civilised discussion at Simon the Pharisee's table, admitting the reader to a much gentler world than Mark's. It would spoil the effect to plunge from this polite confrontation into the boiling sea of hostility of Mark's incidents 1 and 2. Besides, his extended use of Matthew between his two Markan blocks (Lk 4:1—6:19 and 8:4—9:50) has interrupted, and so deflated the violent contrast between the choice of the twelve and the enmity of so-called friends, family and scribes. He is temperamentally ill-disposed towards Mark's violent suddenness of contrast; his editing has deprived the Beelzebub argument of its *raison d'être ici*,[5] so he looks ahead for more attractive and appropriate material. He finds it in the parable of the sower and feels tolerably happy with Mark again at last.

Here is a parable of response which can serve to recapitulate the various responses to Jesus which he has narrated in the non-Markan incidents preceding: the centurion's faith, the doubt of John's disciples and the obduracy of 'this generation', his contrast between Simon's disapproval and the sinner's faith. 'A parable of response'— so it seems to the modern reader, so it seemed to Luke and so it reads in his gospel. In Mark's it is that and something more: a provocative clue to 'the mystery of the kingdom of God' (changed to the plural and weaker 'mysteries' by Matthew and Luke) which drives a wedge between the unresponsive and their salvation 'lest haply they should turn again and it be forgiven them' (Mk 4:12). This clause is omitted by both Matthew and Luke, leaving Mark's other and lesser explanation at verse 15, that Satan is responsible, for Luke to emphasise with 'that they may not believe and be saved'. For Mark the parable is an instrument of division because he used the word in the septuagintal sense of enigma and 'dark saying'[6]—a sense to which Matthew and Luke agree without pressing it beyond the limits of understanding as he does. His ferocious doctrine was as indigestible to them as to the modern exegetes who wrestle with the passage. Matthew resorts to extending the quotation from Isaiah until it explains the lack of receptivity more by the dullness and blindness of the audience rather than the darkness of the message. He returns to the problem with his parable of wheat and tares which attributes opposition and obduracy to Satan and points to the last judgement for the resolution. The eschatological moralist is at work on the gospel of dark secrets. Luke's interest like Matthew's is in the attitudes of the listeners, but he does it in the parable itself rather than by Matthew's long quotation, embellishing the last two verses with notes which add a sense of time and psychology: 'as they go on their way', '(no fruit) to perfection', 'in an honest and good heart' and 'with patience'. He omits Mark's climactic 'thirtyfold, sixtyfold and an hundredfold'. The interest has shifted from the mystery of resurrection in the teeth of loss to the practice of virtue. The dark saying has been humanised and historicised.

The figure of the light follows. In Mark it is a statement of his stark central contrast between hiddenness and revelation. Matthew adds 'and it shineth unto all that are in the house' in his version at 5:15, thus institutionalising by an ecclesiastical setting. Luke in turn sets it in a larger world with 'that they which enter in may see the light', his open community contrasting with Matthew's more closed Church. From its Markan centre of divine revelation the scope of the saying ripples out to include first the Church and then the unchristian world in a characteristically expanding development. This is followed by an abbreviation of Mark's saying about hearing and the omission of the seed growing secretly and the mustard seed (to be used in its Matthean version at Luke 13:18–19), and of Mark's saying about parables (Mk 4: 33–4) with its unwelcome distinction between Jesus's teaching to the disciples and to the world outside. The incident about true kindred, put aside at the outset, can now be brought in as dramatic historicisation of the whole theme of teaching and response. An event takes the place of Mark's repetitious little parables. The motive behind Luke's *midrash* of Mark in this section, with Matthew mediating between the two of them, is now clear enough. Where Mark was content to posit his mysterious doctrine of revelation and division and to repeat it again and again, Luke focuses on the theme of human response and tells it in a much clearer and more concise narrative development.

From the stilling of the storm to the feeding of five thousand, Luke follows Mark in order with two substantial omissions: one because of previous use, the other a virtually complete ditching.

Part II

Mark 4:35—6:44	*Luke 8:22—9:17*
1) Stilling the storm	1) Stilling the storm
2) Gerasene demoniac	2) Gerasene demoniac
3) Jairus's daughter and bleeding woman	3) Jairus's daughter and bleeding woman
4) Rejection in synagogue	(already used at 4:16–30)
5) Mission of 12	4) Mission of 12
6) Herod on Jesus	5) Herod on Jesus—'seeks to see him'

| 7) Death of John | (omitted save brief note at 9:9) |
| 8) Return of 12 and feeding of 5000 in desert | 6) Return of 12 and feeding of 5000 at Bethsaida |

Luke omits Mark's horrifying account of John's death. Matthew had already reduced it to about half its length. It interrupts the narrative, but Mark uses the interruption to give time for the twelve to go and come back. Besides, the story fits his concentration on martyrdom and death, providing an ominous prophecy of Jesus's fate. It is not so welcome in Luke's more settled world where rulers and governors, if not exactly models of piety, play a more constructive part in the history of salvation and are pillars of the structure in which the Church lives in comparative peace. But one element in Mark's story is valuable to Luke. Mark's Herod is a weak and sensual man, captivated by his step-daughter's dance but 'exceedingly sorry' at its gruesome outcome. Luke has a penchant for morally ambivalent characters like this. In his hands the Herods become complex participants in the story. Herod Antipas was 'much perplexed' (his addition at Lk 9:7) 'sought to see Jesus' (his addition at Lk 9:9: a prophetic note fulfilled when he does so in the peculiarly Lukan trial at Lk 23:8–12), reported as wanting to kill him and described as 'that fox' at 13:31f. Herod Agrippa I persecutes the Church and finally reaches a nasty end at Acts 12:1–3 and 20–23. The Herods flit on and off the scene in various increasingly unsatisfactory states of mind until their downfall—an interesting example of Luke's developing continuity.

Another reason for ditching this Markan narrative is that Luke has run himself into a difficulty apparently shared by the writer (or final redactor) of John's gospel:[7] how to make much of John as Christ's forerunner and yet keep him in a subordinate position? Luke has compounded the problem by giving so much space to John in his first chapters and adding to his teaching as given by Matthew. After that he has to go into reverse. John plays a negligible role, if any, in Jesus's baptism, where his role in Mark had already embarrassed Matthew. His attributes of Elijah, the once and future prophet, have passed to Jesus in the Nain story (Lk 7:11–18). To include Mark's tale of his death would spoil this editorial work by bringing John out of the obscurity into which Luke has so carefully manoeuvred him in the interests of a clearer historical succession. The evangelist's attitude to the two main characters in this story, Herod and John, seals its fate.

For the rest of the section Mark is followed in order though there are transpositions of order within two of the incidents. In the Gerasene demoniac Mark described the lunatic's behaviour at the outset. Luke leaves part of the description there but moves the rest until after he has met Jesus, making his 8:29 an awkward and lengthy parenthesis. This seems to be an example of unnecessary and unsuccessful editing. So does the end of the story. Mark has the cured lunatic ask to be with Jesus while Jesus is entering the boat. Luke says that Jesus 'entered into a boat and returned' but then has to go back on himself in the conversation between Jesus and the cured man. The same phenomenon recurs in the feeding of five thousand. Mark keeps the number till the end as a climax. Luke brings it in earlier, which looks sensible but again involves him in an awkward parenthesis at 9:14.

Luke's creative powers are at a low ebb in this section, repeating Mark for the most part but making minor adjustments which look like mere titivations and are not always improvements. Frequent little touches of editing give the disciples a less negative part in the proceedings than in Mark. In the storm on the lake, Matthew had already changed their querulous 'Carest thou not that we perish?' to a stylised 'Save Lord, we perish!' Luke follows his example with 'Master, master, we perish!' Matthew had altered Mark's 'feared exceedingly' of the disciples into the more reverent 'marvelled'. Luke does the same. In the healing of the bleeding woman Mark has the disciples answer Jesus's 'Who touched me?' with a rude rejoinder, 'thou seest the multitudes thronging thee, and sayest thou, Who touched me?' Matthew omitted this exchange. Luke makes it less offensive ('Master, the multitudes press thee and crush') and gives Peter the lead. He dislikes Mark's roughness but values his note of the public scene, amplifying it by having the healed woman declare her cure 'in the presence of all the people'. Mark's account of the sending of the twelve is also embellished in their interest. They are given power as well as authority[8] over unclean spirits and, as in Matthew, are also to cure diseases. Further, they are sent to 'preach the kingdom of God and to heal the sick'—a concise pre-echo of things to come in Acts. Such touches, usually derived from Matthew, strengthen the ties between Jesus and his followers and so forge a stronger historical continuity.

3. *The Great Omission and the Gospel's Axis*

At the end of the feeding of the five thousand which closes this section we stand in the presence of the most arresting feature of

Luke's editing of Mark, the Great Omission or wholesale ditching of the material between Mark 6:45 and 8:26. It is a source of understandable distress to those who would like the evangelists to be faithful retailers of the tradition available to them. Exculpating hypotheses of early editions of Mark without this section have been called in. But Matthew had no such edition and Luke's interpolation of Bethsaida as the scene of the feeding of five thousand, a place which is mentioned by Mark within the material of Luke's omission in the next incident of Jesus walking on the water, betrays a knowledge of the material he abandons at its very first verse, so making such theories doubtful. Creed found them unnecessary: 'as we have no other weighty grounds for supposing that Luke used Mark in a form essentially different from that which we possess, it is reasonable to consider motives which, on the hypothesis that Luke knew the present form of Mark, may be supposed to have influenced him in making the omission.'[9] Amongst such motives Creed suggests economy, the avoidance of doublets and obscurities and respect for the gentiles. Though it is unlikely that one motive will cover all the material, it is still possible to sympathise with those who feel that Creed's case is not sufficient. A powerful and dominant motive is needed for such powerful and dominant editing. It is clever editing too. The jump from the feeding of the five thousand to Peter's confession gives the reader no sense of hiatus, and what more appropriate to a gospel containing the Emmaus story than that the Christ should be recognised immediately after the breaking of bread?

The Markan material omitted by Luke is:

1) 6:45   Jesus walks on the sea
2) 6:53   Healings at Gennesaret
3) 7:1   Controversy about Jewish defilement laws
4) 7:24   Syro-phoenician's daughter healed in district of Tyre and Sidon
5) 7:31   Deaf man healed in Decapolis
6) 8:1   Feeding of 4000
7) 8:11   Pharisees seek a sign
8) 8:14   Argument in the boat about bread and leaven
9) 8:22–6 Healing of blind man at Bethsaida

The block is a unity, the first incident occurring on a sea voyage to Bethsaida (which is presumably reached at the end of the voyage) and the last taking place in Bethsaida. The intervening material is thus a circular tour cutting into gentile territory in the middle. This geographical unity is an important factor in understanding the phenomena of the omission. If we can discover a leading motive which requires the excision of a central feature of the whole block and of central incidents within it, and if we can then find subsidiary motives for the omission of other things, then any remainder can be accounted for by attraction—it goes because the rest goes. Creed's argument of economy is reinforced by the repetitious nature of some of the material such as the reiterated sea journey and feeding miracle. But this can have force only when we have found a strong reason why Luke should have economised at this particular point.

Creed's argument is at its weakest when he pleads respect for the gentiles as the reason for the omission of the Syro-phoenician woman: 'It could not fail to be a stumbling block to the evangelist and his gentile public'. The bantering petition of the woman would surely be congenial to the evangelist who alone has the importunate friend and the importunate widow—no ground for offence or disapproval there. Creed is up against the received opinion, which he endorses, that Luke's is the gentile gospel. Nineham aptly calls the section Mark 7:24—8:26 'Jesus's "Gentile Mission"'.[10] How could the gentile evangelist have made this, of all sections, the victim of omission? The answer is that Luke's is the least gentile gospel of all the synoptics, and that this is because as an historian he insists that the gentile mission was the great business of the Church in his second volume, not realised by its founder though he prophesied it. Simeon foresaw that God's salvation would be 'a light to lighten the gentiles' but the fulfilment is kept for the climax of the first part of Acts. The miraculous catch and the mission of the seventy hint it—but no more than that. 'For everything there is a season, and a time for every matter under the sun' (Qo 3:1). Nothing else explains Luke's curious treatment of Matthew's centurion at 7:1–10, building him up into a model of God-fearing piety but laboriously keeping him off-stage so that he does not meet Jesus. The 'time of the gentiles' (Lk 21:24) is not yet. Here is the reason, weighty because integral to his historical scheme, for Luke's Great Omission. He leaves Mark at the point where the gentile journey begins and resumes him when it is over, Bethsaida being the geographical marker in both instances. Gentile excursions are, very precisely, another story.

This grand principle most obviously demands the excision of the two miracles at the centre of the section. The Syro-phoenician woman is a gentile in gentile territory, the deaf stammerer lives in

98

the middle of the 'predominantly gentile district of Decapolis'.[11] The omission of these two incidents takes with it the surrounding material, geographically tied to them in a well-defined, and so easily detachable, unit. But since things are rarely done for one simple reason, it is worth noticing possible motives, reinforcing the leading one, which might also have been effective.

The walking on the sea is something of a repetition of the stilling of the storm (Mk 4:35–41; Lk 8:22–25), which makes it dispensable —a reason secondary to the decisive one that it marks the outset of the gentile journey. The healings at Gennesaret add little to the tale and are told in a general way which makes them dispensable too. Matthew had already abbreviated Mark severely here.

The omission of the controversy about Jewish defilement laws is usually put down to its containing much detail about Jewish customs irrelevant to Luke's gentile readers. The omissions in his version of Matthew's Sermon on the Mount show a similar unconcern on Luke's part with the rituals of pharisaic piety. But again historical reasons are likely to have weighed more heavily with Luke. Jesus lived as a Jew among Jews. So did the Church until the intervention of the spirit brought in the gentiles and demanded a conservatively statesmanlike (and not unbiblical or un-Jewish[12] version of Jewish dietary laws. Even then it is a striking feature of the letter sent to the gentile churches by the Jerusalem council that it says nothing about circumcision although the issue had been raised (Ac 15:5); and immediately after it Paul circumcises Timothy 'because of the Jews' (Ac 16:3)—an incredible action by the writer of Galatians, but entirely appropriate to Luke's own eirenical and law-abiding temperament. Luke tended to conservatism about those Jewish laws which stood written in his own holy scripture[13]— and so was not positively anxious to include criticism even of the pettifogging and oral developments of it which are the subject of this discussion. Here again there is a development from Mark to Luke through Matthew. Mark's Jesus drove a coach and horses through the sabbath law (see Mk 2:23—3:6). 'Mark leaves the two positions (*sc.* old and new) starkly side by side: Matthew attempts to paper over the cracks.'[14] Luke, happily distant from the sweat and inconsistencies of Matthew's interscribal controversies, can take a more peacefully conservative view.

The feeding of four thousand is dispensable by virtue of being a doublet of the feeding of five thousand. It is not accurate to say with Creed that 'Luke clearly avoids doublets' (p. lxi): he has a resounding pair of his own in his two mssions which frame the gospel's centre of transfiguration and setting out for Jerusalem—just as Mark's two feedings frame his gentile excursion. Mark is thus for Luke a source for this feature of architectural design: the use of a pair of doublets as pillars holding up an exalted central pinnacle. Having decided to jettison Mark's gentile journey he is also ready to abandon at least one of its sustaining pillars.

Two debates follow in Mark, one with the Pharisees about a sign, the other with the disciples about bread and leaven. The first is retailed by Matthew in a form expanded by weather lore and the sign of Jonah (Mt 16:1-4). Luke will use this Matthean version later, so it is not in the strictest sense omitted. The second, as we have seen (p. 83) is so obscure a passage that its meaning seems to be one of the secrets which Mark and his community have taken with them to their graves. Matthew did his best with it, softening and cutting the Lord's rebuke to his disciples and taking 'the leaven of the Pharisees' as the central meaning (though it is not obviously so in Mark) which the disciples understand. Luke will follow suit at Luke 12:1 'Beware of the leaven of the Pharisees which is hypocrisy' —a much reduced version, following Matthew in preferring moralism to Mark's mysterious intransigence but lacking the warmth of his attack on the Pharisees. Again this may not count as a straight omission and again we notice Luke's debt to Matthew who had modified the stupidity of the disciples enough to enable him, in his turn, to make them a still stronger link between the time of Jesus and the time of the Church—a function which could hardly be fulfilled by Mark's numskulls.

It is hard to find a good intrinsic reason for the last omission, the blind man at Bethsaida. Creed observes that it 'is effected with apparent difficulty, and for this reason may not have commended itself to Luke'.[15] This is likely in view of Luke's belief in Jesus's effortless magic powers (Lk 8:46), but not decisive. Having already made such substantial omissions of Mark's material, Luke is free to decide when to pick him up again. Should it be here with the blind man or at the next incident with Peter's confession? He is sufficiently acquainted with Mark to know that there is another blind man in store later in Mark's tale (Mk 10:46-52). Othe men's doublets will always look dispensable-by-half to their editors. The determining factor in Luke's choice of place to rejoin Mark must now be the last Markan incident he retailed: the feeding of five thousand— what will best follow that? A miracle following upon a miracle is the kind of massive accumulation which Mark likes but does not suit Luke's concern for development. Matthew before him had omitted the blind man at Bethsaida. His own continual interest in linking the witness of the apostles to the mission of Jesus makes him prefer an incident which will fasten that historical continuum. Peter's confession serves both these needs. As we have seen, what more congenial to the teller of the walk to Emmaus than that the Christ should be recognised after the breaking of bread? Luke's Great Omission, motivated by his historical conviction that the mission to the gentiles is not yet, does not spoil the narrative connection which he nurtures but improves it.

The continuation of Luke's story vindicates his strategy. There are two focal complexes at the centre of Mark's gospel, the gentile journey and the transfiguration with the events on either side of it. Like most of Mark's readers, and possibly like Mark himself, Luke has decided that the second of these is the more important. Having acted drastically on this decision by omitting the first altogether, he redresses the balance by stressing the second. Mark had already strengthened the transfiguration by a doublet, similarly deployed. The mission of the twelve (supplied by Mark) and his own mission of seventy give Luke a stronger architecture of which the chief pillars are: mission of twelve, passion prediction, transfiguration, passion prediction, mission of seventy. Its threefold centre is Markan, its extensions backwards and forwards half Markan and half his own second version of the Markan first half: which is to say that Mark's mission of twelve is the primary source for Luke's mission of seventy. But the architecture is not static—how could it be in historical narrative? The scope widens from the twelve to the seventy, who receive a more detailed charge and whose success is more resoundingly celebrated. The main feature of Luke's editing is clear. It gives him a single, central axis to his gospel. After it the Christ has been recognised, seen in glory and set onto the road to Jerusalem. A momentous turning point has swung the action into a new phase—as in Mark, but more so.

This centre of the story of Jesus is also a milestone in the story of the Church and the two are connected yet again by the pair of missions, for when in Acts Luke writes his Church history it will emerge as a tale of triumphant missionary journeys. The centre of Luke's gospel makes clear that these are no new departure but continuous with that which the Christ commanded and approved at the centre of his work. The mission of the seventy in particular has a prophetic character by virtue of the reference of the number to Genesis 10 where the nations of the world come to the same total (in both cases seventy-two in some versions), and by virtue of the instructions given by Jesus—which amount to a guide to missionary strategy and etiquette for the early Church. Like the miraculous catch the whole incident is a prophetic sketch for Acts. Concern for the validity of the Church's witness informs Luke's editing of the centre of Mark's transfiguration complex. Peter's rebuke to Jesus after the first prediction of the passion is omitted together with the rebuke he gets in return. The taking up of the cross is described as the disciple's daily, and so continuous, task. At the transfiguration Luke adds that 'when they ("Peter and they that were with him") were fully awake they saw his glory' and that 'they entered into the cloud' out of which the voice speaks. They thus enter into and share the divine mystery like Moses of old who 'entered the cloud' on Sinai (Ex 24:18): a typically retrospective and prospective note which marks the enhanced significance of the scene, Peter as leader of the Church to come being granted the privilege of Moses as leader of the people before. Since Moses has previously been Jesus's antetype, this shows that in using scripture, Luke is more interested in the resonances of prophetic history than in exact typology.

To have increased the apostolic role so decidedly raises the possibility of forestalling Acts—which Luke's historical sense forbids. After the transfiguration he has the three apostles tell 'no man in those days any of the things which they had seen'. That will come later. The disciples' failure with the epileptic boy is retailed from Mark with no alleviation and the second prediction of the passion labours Mark's 'But they understood not the saying and were afraid to ask him' by adding that 'it was concealed from them, that they should not perceive it'—which may exculpate them in some measure (they were not meant to understand) but also makes clear that salvation history has lessons yet to teach them. The last two sections in this Markan block also show misunderstanding on the part of the disciples. They argue about who is greatest and are answered by Jesus with the little child, they react chauvinistically to the unchristian exorcist and Jesus corrects them. Abbreviation of both incidents diminishes their force, but they stand and make their point: Luke's treatment of the disciples is not monochrome and allows for later development.

4. Luke's Edition of Mark's Passion: Part i—Prelude

At 18:15 Luke is resuming Mark after his longest space without him: the eight chapters and more of the so-called 'Central Section' which combines Matthean material with his own and is throughout didactic rather than narrative. In spite of the occasional historical notes ('as they went on their way' at 10:38, 'as he went from there' at 11:53, 'he went on his way' at 13:22 and so on) the wealth of teaching overpowers any sense of temporal or spatial development. Some of it is framed in incidents such as Martha and Mary, the Bent Woman, the Ten Lepers, but most is loose from any determinative historical setting and comes straight as parables, stories, maxims and exhortation. In other words Luke has here been the Christian moralistic story-teller indebted to Matthew and Deuteronomy. When he picks up Mark again he works as follows:

Mark 10:13—13:37	*Luke 18: 15—21: 38*
1) 10:13 Children	1) 18:15 Children
2) 10:17 Rich man and riches	2) 18:18 Rich man and riches
3) 10:32 Third passion prediction	3) 18:31 Third passion prediction
4) 10:35 Sons of Zebedee	
5) 10:46 Jericho blind man	4) 18:35 Jericho blind man
	5) 19:1 Zacchaeus
	6) 19:11 Pounds parable
6) 11:1 Jerusalem entered	7) 19:29 Jerusalem entered
	8) 19:41 Lament over Jerusalem
7) 11:12 Fig Tree—1	
8) 11:15 Temple purged	9) 19:45 Temple purged
9) 11:20 Fig Tree—2	
10) 11:27 Authority	10) 20:1 Authority
11) 12:1 Vineyard parable	11) 20:9 Vineyard parable
12) 12:13 Questions: tribute	12) 20:20 Questions: tribute
resurrection	resurrection
1st commandment	
David's son	David's son
13) 12:38 Beware of scribes	13) 20:45 Beware of scribes
14) 12:41 Widow's mites	14) 21:1 Widow's mites
15) 13:1 Temple's doom	15) 21:5 Temple's doom
16) 13:3 Discourse on Mount of Olives	16) 21:7 Discourse in Temple

The first six incidents in the table form a transition between the didactic and the narrative, the historical aspect increasing its dominance until it comes triumphantly to the fore with the entry into Jerusalem and then governing the rest of the gospel. Picking up Mark does not mean a sudden jolt from the morally general to the historically particular. Indeed it takes the critical eye to notice that Luke *has* resumed Mark at Luke 18:15, so well does the incident of the welcoming of little children develop the rejection/acceptance theme of the parable of the Pharisee and the Publican. Mark's next step is the story of the rich man followed by teaching about riches: obviously congenial and welcome to Luke who retails it faithfully. Although both the children and the rich man are narrative incidents, probably paired in contrast, the morals matter more than the history. They could, apparently, be at some other point in the gospel, since they are without strong organic function in the overall narrative development and so do nothing to change the manner to which the reader has got accustomed in the central section. But the third passion prediction makes the difference, recalling attention to the unfolding of events by means of prophecy. Coming near Jericho for the healing of the blind man marks a geographical development: this is the last city before Jerusalem. Mark makes mysteriously little of the location. Jesus comes there and leaves immediately, healing the blind man on the way out. Luke reverses this, having the blind man healed on the way in and making Jericho the scene of his Zacchaeus story (see p. 72ff.). The sense of Jesus reaching a particular point in his journey is enhanced by this vivid incident which takes Mark as a starting point but develops into something of Luke's own. The theme of riches which it raises calls to mind Matthew's great parable about the use of money (the talents, Mt 25:14–30). Luke takes advantage of his temporary absence from Matthew to retail it quite out of its context in Matthew's order—with particular pains to place it precisely in his own overall scheme. It is prefaced by the note that Jesus told it 'because he was nigh to Jerusalem and because they supposed that the Kingdom of God was immediately to appear' and concluded with 'and when he had thus spoken he went on before, going up to Jerusalem'. Still more historicising of Matthew's moral parable is achieved by the allusion to Archelaus (Josephus, *Ant.* 17.11.1), the Herodian prince who went to Rome to be given office and found Jews lobbying against him. Luke's editing attaches his material more closely to his history. The treatment of the disciples fits with this. The rivalry caused by the sons of Zebedee is omitted, the second and didactic part being reserved for use at the Last Supper. If this exonerates them the laboured note of their failure to understand the third prophecy of the passion does the reverse and adds to the tension of the story. They will only understand when events have run their full course.

With the entry into Jerusalem the change from moral instruction to historical narrative is complete. Mark is followed closely, edited in ways which make the historical significance of his story more precise and resonant. 19:37 gives an additional note of place ('as he was now drawing nigh, even at the descent of the mount of Olives') and a motive for the acclamation which refers back to many previous incidents ('the whole multitude of the disciples began to rejoice and praise God with a loud voice for all the mighty works which they had seen'). The words of acclamation are altered to make an echo of the angels' Christmas song—omitting peace *on earth* as inappropriate to this contentious point in the drama. The shouting stones of Jesus's riposte to the Pharisees activate a more remotely historic echo and a dark prophecy: 'You have devised shame to your house by cutting off many peoples: you have forfeited your life. For the stone will cry out from the wall and the beam from the woodwork respond' (Hab 2:10). Luke's historicising tendency reaches its climax with the prophecy uttered by Jesus when he at last sees the city and immediately before he enters it (Lk 19:41–44). It is cast in resounding septuagintal language which recalls the previous destruction of the city by the Babylonians while describing the events of A.D. 70 with a precision only found elsewhere in the New Testament at Luke 21:20–24. Most important of all, this speech fastens a link between Jesus's doom and the doom of city and nation which is a salient feature of Luke's passion narrative and sets it in the epic sweep of international events. Christ's *via dolorosa* is a fateful turning on the longer path of the nation's road to ruin. The Roman destruction is a direct consequence of failure to know 'in this day . . . the things which belong unto peace . . . They shall not leave thee one stone upon another, because thou knewest not the time of thy visitation' (Lk 19:42–44).

The speech has been a stepping outside of Mark's account in order to see, from a prophetic watch-tower, the longer perspectives of history and the causal links between distinct events. Returning to Mark, Luke is faced with three incidents: the fig tree cursed, the temple purged, the fig tree withered away. They are symbolic happenings in which the catastrophe of A.D. 70 is anticipated. He prefers to deal with this by the more direct means of the oracles which we have just noticed. The fig tree is omitted altogether, having been already dealt with at 13:6 as a parable with a more expansive sense of time: the vine-dresser will dig round it and dung it to give it a second chance to bear fruit (historical allegory of the Church's mission to Israel following upon its founder's)—a further instance of the way in which sayings and events were interchangeable to the evangelists. The purging of the temple is much abbreviated. Like Matthew, Luke omits 'for all the nations', knowing that this destiny was never achieved by the temple but transferred to the Church. On the other hand Luke, more of an historian and less of a symbolist than Mark, gives the temple an enhanced place in present events. At 19:47 he adds that Jesus 'was teaching daily in the temple'. It becomes the scene of his utterances in the momentous days before his death—the place where as a youth he was found about his Father's business, hearing and questioning the teachers of the law. This is reiterated at Luke 21:37-38: 'and every day he was teaching in the temple, and every night he went out and lodged in the mount that is called the Mount of Olives. And the people came early in the morning to him in the temple to hear him.' Most decisively, the long eschatological prophecy from Mark 13 is given there instead of on the Mount of Olives.

The same theme is added to the setting of the next incident, the debate about authority (Lk 20:1-8). 'By what authority doest thou these things?' In Mark 'these things' must be the cursing of the fig tree and the purging of the temple. But Luke has preceded the question with a note that Jesus was 'teaching the people in the temple and preaching the gospel' so the question refers to these activities which present a new and saving possibility to the nation at its traditional centre: the crux of Luke's two-volume scheme. Next comes Mark's great allegory of the whole sweep of salvation history, the parable of the vineyard. It is obviously welcome to Luke and will have helped to form his perspective before he wrote. A few characteristic retouchings are all that is needed. The owner goes away 'for a long time'; the last of the servants sent and rejected is noted to be the third; as in Matthew the allegorical tailoring to history is improved by having the son killed after he is thrown out; in reaction the authorities try to arrest him 'in that very hour': all of which sharpen the sense of time. God, like the unjust steward and the rich fool, muses 'What shall I do?' The threat in the parable evokes the horrified 'God forbid!' of the people. Jesus 'looked upon them' as he will at Peter (Lk 22:61).

A quartet of little disputes follows in Mark: about tribute, the permanence of marriage, the great commandment, and the status of the Christ. Luke omits the third because he has dealt with it already. The first two are slightly historicised: the question of tribute by the added 'so as to deliver him to the rule and to the authority of the governor' at Luke 20:20, the question of the much married woman by the embellishments in Luke 20:35 and 36 which make it into a discussion of the bigger and more historical matter of resurrection and human destiny. The riddle about David's son is left as it is with the more precise reference added 'in the book of Psalms' (Luke 24:44 shows that Luke thought of his scriptures as divided into law, prophets and psalms), instead of 'in the spirit'. In spite of his famous interest in the spirit, Luke's scriptural scholarship is here given the upper hand.

The Widow's Mites is told without significant alteration. The prophecy of the temple's destruction is, in Mark and Matthew, uttered by Jesus as he leaves it. Luke changes this so that Jesus can still be in the temple for the apocalyptic discourse which follows. Instead of Mark's 'What manner of stones and what manner of buildings!' Luke has 'adorned with goodly stones and offerings'. It is a more refined and stylish way of speaking, paralleled in 2 Maccabees 9:16 where Antiochus promised 'that he would adorn with the finest offerings' the temple which he had formerly plundered.

The apocalyptic discourse follows. In Mark it has an impressively lonely prominence as Jesus's most extended uninterrupted utterance. In Matthew and Luke it loses much of this impact by sharing the stage with other long speeches dealing with more everyday concerns. Further, in Luke's hands the whole thing is earthed and made less gnomic by a number of editorial strokes. In the first place he makes a speech delivered in private to the disciples into one delivered in the public setting of the temple court to a general 'they' (Lk 21:7). Overall, Luke's version achieves an historicised eschatology with a moral conclusion. The historicising is achieved by the addition of a number of little notes of time. The false prophets say 'the time is at hand' (Lk 21:8), a delusion already corrected in the preface to the Parable of the Pounds. 'First' is added at Luke 21:9. Luke 21:11f. cancels Mark's sonorously vague 'these things are the beginning of travail' and substitutes his own more precise and pedestrian 'but before all these things'. First comes the persecutions of the Christians, then the universal calamities. The prophecies of persecution are themselves made to fit more accurately the trials to come in Acts. The disciples will be delivered to prisons as well as synagogues (Lk 21:12). They will be given 'a mouth and wisdom which all your adversaries will not be able to withstand or gainsay' (Lk 21:15), a prophecy which is exactly fulfilled in Stephen when 'they could not withstand the wisdom and the spirit with which he spoke' (Ac 6:10). The promise of safety—'not a hair of your head shall perish' (Lk 21:18) will be recalled in Paul's assurance to his shipmates at Acts 27:34 'not a hair is to perish from the head of any of you'. In verses 20–24 Luke's regard for history comes into its own. Mark has spoken obscurely of an 'abomination of desolation standing where he ought not (let the reader understand)' followed by advice to flee from this vague terror. Luke drags it all into the light of known history. The desolation is Jerusalem's, following upon a siege. The terror is the Roman campaign in Judea, history and prophecy coming together in verse 24, which is Luke's addition and strongly septuagintal in content and language: 'They shall fall by the edge of the sword, and shall be led captive into all the nations: and Jerusalem shall be trodden down of the Gentiles until the times of the Gentiles shall be fulfilled'. Actuality achieves a greater intelligibility and sense without diluting the horror to come. Luke even adds a terror of his own at 21:25, though characteristically it adds to Mark's prophecy of disruption in the heavens a foretelling of crisis and disorder on earth: 'upon the earth distress of nations, in perplexity for the roaring of the billows; men fainting for fear, and for expectation of the things which are coming on the world'. This cosmic anxiety is penultimate to the coming of the Son of Man which brings redemption near: redemption being the end of a long temporal process and not something finally and exclusively achieved in the death of Christ.

There are clear signs that Luke has tried to bring some schematic order to the swirling menaces of Mark 13. The outlines of an overall plan in three phases emerge: first the persecution of the disciples, then A.D. 70 and a subsequent period of famines, plagues and wars reaching a climax of dread with the shaking of earth and heaven which brings in the coming of redemption with the Son of Man. For all this an irreducible vagueness clings, understandably enough, to the welter of heated prediction. The meaning of Luke 21:29–33 is far from precisely clear: what things will have been accomplished before this generation passes? Luke does not answer the question but passes at verse 34 into the safer realm of moral advice.

Come what may the reader should keep faith and a clear head, eschewing those temptations of the well-to-do, worry and over-indulgence. Mark 13 has been historicised and, in the last verses, moralised. But there is no sign of any reduction of eschatological belief, only that for Luke it is set in history more firmly and distinctly than for Mark.

4. *Luke's Edition of Mark's Passion: Part ii—The Process*

As Luke moves into the dramatic process of the passion his previous use of Mark's anointing at Bethany (Lk 7:36–50) proves an advantage. In Mark there is a threefold pattern of: the plot—anointing at Bethany—the plot continued. Luke can have a continuous account of the plot and follow it with the preparation of the passover and the meal itself. The last of these gets greater impact from the omission of the scene at Bethany and evokes Luke's full powers, becoming one of those momentous tableaux which gather the threads of his story and move it into a new phase. Time past and time-to-come converge at the supper table where the present business is to establish the Church by giving it a focal rite, a divine authority bound into a charter of service, and an eschatological destiny.

In Mark no sooner has the company sat down to table than Jesus, with a characteristic and disturbing suddenness, speaks of his betrayal. Luke postpones this. Only after the institution of the eucharist is Judas spoken of, and without Mark's terrible 'good were it for that man if he had not been born'. The meal begins with Jesus describing it as something to which he has looked forward passionately (the septuagintal 'with desire I have desired') and which will be fulfilled for him in the future. The supper is thus given its threefold temporal frame at the outset. It is a present fulfilment of the past (Luke emphasises that it is a passover, with all the historical memory implied) directed towards a fulfilment in the future. The latter comes from Mark 14:25 ('Verily I say unto you, I will no more drink of the fruit of the vine until that day when I drink it new in the kingdom of God'), but Luke uses it twice: of the whole passover (Lk 22:16) as well as over the cup (Lk 22:18). The bread too is given a temporal reference not found in the other gospels (but see 1 Co 11:24) with 'this do in remembrance of me' (Lk 22:19).[16] By this element of memory the meal, as it will be continued in the Church, is stamped with history like the old passover in which it originates.

After the ceremony comes the prophecy of betrayal, leading into a debate among the disciples about 'which of them it was that should do this thing', and then into the dispute about greatness. This last has come from Mark 10:41; a substantial shift which enhances its importance while drawing some of its sting by putting it in the constructive setting of the founding of the Church and making it the occasion for the rule of service—typically expounded by Luke in terms of the dinner party (Lk 22:27). Having been given its ethic the infant Church is set in its historical frame. 'Ye are they which have continued with me in my temptations' (past) 'and I appoint unto you a kingdom . . . ' (present and future) 'and ye shall sit on thrones judging the twelve tribes of Israel' (future—from Mt 19:28). Attention is then turned to the more immediate historical process with the words to Peter, 'Simon, Simon, behold, Satan asked to have you that he might sift you as wheat.' When retailing Jesus's first prophecy of his death and resurrection, Luke had omitted 'Get thee behind me Satan' for obvious enough reasons of respect and discrimination. He now presents the relation of Peter to Satan, but in a quite different way. Peter is not Satan, who has become incarnate in Judas (Lk 22:3), but a target for his activities, fended off by Jesus's prayer. The gloom of Mark's prophecy of denial is lightened by the promise that beyond it he will turn again and strengthen the brethren. The abject apostate will become the pillar of Acts, for Jesus has already prayed for him. Matthew has lent a hand here, his image of Peter as the Church's foundation rock being echoed in Luke's 'support your brethren', στήρισον (support) having connotations of rock and stone (Is 50:7 LXX: 'The Lord became my helper, therefore I was not ashamed, but set my face ὡς στερεὰν πέτραν and I know that I shall never be ashamed). The denial is held in the hopeful scope of God's great plan.

It only remains to give the Church a strategy for the future at Luke 22:35–38. This is done in terms of historical distinction. The first mission was carried out in peaceful and propitious conditions. The disciples had little but enough and were well received. Now the conditions of the Lord's passion apply to his followers. By implication they too will be 'reckoned with transgressors', as indeed will happen time and again in Acts. The injunction that each man should have a sword recalls Nehemiah 4:18 'each of the builders had his sword girded at his side while he built'. Like the rebuilding of Jerusalem the building of the Church will go forward through adversity. The two swords (22:38) are a riddle. Luke knows from Mark that there was one sword, used by Peter at the arrest, but this does not explain the other. Jesus's 'it is enough' (ἱκανόν ἐστιν) is a formula used at Deuteronomy 3:26 to break off a discussion—significantly in the great farewell discourse of Moses in which the old Israel was given its charter as the Church is now.

After the meal the company moves to the Mount of Olives, no mention being made of Gethsemane: perhaps because, like Golgotha which is omitted at 23:33, Luke has no use for the curious name, perhaps for narrative economy which is a factor in the editing of the events here. Instead of Jesus praying twice and three times coming to rouse the disciples there is one prayer and one call to wake up. Abandoning the repetition also dilutes the ferocity of Mark's animus against the disciples. The hard-hearted refusal to be awake to what is happening becomes an understandable exhaustion by grief.[17] The cosmetic editing of Mark's material relating to the apostolic eye-witnesses is part of Luke's struggle for continuity. Continuity is also the motive for the healing of the slave's ear: Luke will be at pains to show that the saving and reconciling work of the ministry is maintained through the passion. Further, in Creed's view (ad loc.), 'Suffer ye thus far' (Lk 22:51) means 'let events take their course'. Luke's historical sense reasserts itself powerfully at the end of the passage (Lk 22:53). 'Ye stretched not forth your hands against me' has the resonance of the septuagintal language to which Luke always resorts at solemn moments. 'This is your hour and the power of darkness' fixes the moment with a sombre strength which lets Luke omit the flight of the disciples without diluting the terror of the scene, and adds to the substitution of satanic for apostolic culpability already found in Luke 22:3 and 31.

Mark's version of the legal process against Jesus is thoroughly revised by Luke in the interests of a clearer narrative and better historical plausibility. A nightmare becomes an ordered legal procedure moving by inexorable stages. Rearrangement is necessary to achieve it. In tabular form for the first part:

Mark 14:53—15:1	Luke 22:54—23:1
1) Jesus examined by the council, false witnesses, sentence of death	1) Peter's denial
2) Jesus mocked and struck by some of the council	2) Jesus mocked and struck by his guards
3) Peter denies him	3) Examination in morning: no clear verdict or sentence
4) Going to Pilate	4) Going to Pilate

The chief and deliberate casualty of Luke's strategic editing is the

trial before the Council which is but a brief examination: two
questions and two gnomic answers. This means that the legal
weight is transferred to the proper authority with whom Luke
knows it belongs—Pilate. Two trials become one with little remainder. The unlikely physical violence of the clergy (Mk 14:65) is
all given to the guards. Peter's denial remains as the major incident of
the series: an indication that Luke's tendency to exculpate the
Church's fathers does not drift into a banality which would relax
the tension of the drama. Mark's version of the denial is retailed
faithfully with the addition of 'the Lord turned and looked upon
Peter' and 'bitterly' to 'wept'[18] (Lk 22:62). Both heighten the
impact, the latter following Matthew whom Luke has also imitated
in adding the guards' 'Who is he that struck thee?' to give point to
Mark's unexplained 'Prophesy!'

The trial before Pilate begins with something lacking in Mark
as in Matthew, the bringing of charges (Lk 23:2). They show a
shrewd awareness of the threats to *Pax Romana*, but they are false.
Jesus has not been perverting the nation but trying to lead it to peace
and godly order (Lk 19:42 etc.). He did not forbid but enjoined the
paying of tribute to Caesar (Lk 20:20–26). He has never called
himself 'Christ a King'. But the charges are explicit, nevertheless,
and join the trial more firmly to the ministry. Pilate rejects them
and the Jewish leaders answer back in Lukan retrospective terms:
'He stirreth up the people, teaching throughout all Judea and
beginning from Galilee even unto this place'—a perverted résumé
of the story so far. The mention of Galilee introduces the strange
incident of Jesus's appearance before Herod: judicially pointless
in its outcome, but theologically and morally effective in the
reconciliation effected between the two enemies, gentile and Jew
(see pp. 16ff.). The trial before Pilate is resumed, not with the
historically unlikely custom of releasing a prisoner at passover
(Luke does not mention it, which makes his treatment of Barabbas
at 23:18f. and 25 entirely obscure—a characteristic carelessness)
but with a second attempt by Pilate to dismiss the case having
found the charges empty, though nothing is said of precisely how
he came to this conclusion. A third and final declaration by Pilate
of Jesus's innocence follows, tied into Luke's unsatisfactory version
of the Barabbas tradition. Mark's assertion that Pilate had Jesus
flogged before sending him to execution is changed into something
less barbaric: Pilate unsuccessfully suggests flogging as an alternative
sentence. 'But their [*sc.* the Jewish authorities'] voices prevailed,

and Pilate gave sentence that what they asked for [crucifixion— Lk 23:21] should be done' (Lk 23:24). Jesus is 'delivered up to their will, and when they led him away . . .' Luke deliberately alters Mark to make Pilate more, and the Jewish leaders less, sympathetic. This redistribution of the guilt as apportioned in Mark had been begun by Matthew with Pilate's wife's dream and his own hand-washing on the one side, and the terrible cry 'His blood be on us and on our children' on the other. Luke's suggestion, with Pilate's three declarations of innocence and the impression he gives that the Jews took Jesus away and crucified him (in the interests of his grand theme of the rejection of the Jews) is as serious and disingenuous as it is deliberate. At Acts 2:22–23 the same suggestion is made, 'Men of Israel . . . this Jesus . . . you crucified and killed by the hands of lawless men': with the slight refinement that the Romans were mere instruments of a Jewish deed. At Acts 7:52f. even this concession is absent: 'They killed those who announced beforehand the coming of the Righteous One, whom you have now betrayed and murdered, you who received the law as delivered by angels and did not keep it' (RSV).

Simon of Cyrene provides a small but telling example of mid-rashic development in historical writing. In Mark and Matthew there is no note of his place in the procession. Luke assigns him a subordinate place 'after Jesus'. In John he disappears and the synoptic tradition is contradicted by Jesus bearing the cross himself —as befits the one who alone can bear the sin of the world (Jn 1:29, and compare Jn 12:14 where Jesus finds the ass for himself). The prophecy to the daughters of Jerusalem (septuagintal phrase) is packed with septuagintal reference (with Ho 10:8 and Ezk 20:47 to the fore) and cast in the phrase and form of traditional biblical prophecy. It is placed at the most solemn and telling moment possible, immediately before the execution of the prophet and son in whom God has visited his people. Nothing matters more to Luke than the pattern of prophecy and fulfilment which the Deuteronomic historian has taught him to be the stuff of history.

In telling the crucifixion, Luke leaves scarcely a single incident in the same place as it occupied in Mark. A diagram is needed again, the second column of figures indicating the place in the Lukan order to which a Markan incident has been transposed:

Mark 15:22-41		Luke 23:33-49
1) Arrive at Golgotha	(1)	1) Arrive at place called The Skull
2) Offer of wine/myrrh	(8)	2) Crucifixion
3) Crucifixion	(2)	3) Malefactors right and left
4) Casting lots	(5)	4) *'Father forgive'*
5) Third hour	(*)	5) Casting lots
6) Title 'King of Jews'	(9)	6) *People watching*
7) Thieves right and left	(3)	7) 'Saved others' jest ('Come down' omitted)
8) Temple jest	(*)	8) Vinegar and 'Save thyself' jest
9) 'Saved others—come down' jest	(7 & 8)	9) Title
10) Thieves mock	(10	10) Two malefactors *contrasted*
11) Darkness at sixth hour	(11)	11) Darkness at sixth hour
12) Cry of forsakenness—Elijah	(*)	12) Temple veil
13) Vinegar	(8)	13) Loud cry
14) Loud cry	(13)	14) *'Father into thy hands'*
15) Temple veil	(12)	15) Death
16) Death	(15)	16) Centurion
17) Centurion	(16)	17) People watch
18) Women	(19)	18) *Watching crowd departs*
		19) Women

* Denotes a Markan section omitted by Luke

The italicised incidents, being Luke's independent contributions, give clear indications of three of his editorial aims. Incidents 6 and 18 set the whole of the crucifixion on a public stage, watched by hosts of people who depart at the end beating their breasts (an expression of remorse peculiar to Luke—see Lk 18:13). Incidents 4 and 10 bind into the passion the theme of reconciliation and the salvation of humanity, thus letting shafts of sunlight pierce the gloom of the Markan narrative. 'They know not what they do' is a theme to be resumed in Peter's speech in Solomon's Portico at Acts 13:17; 'I know that you acted in ignorance, as did also your rulers.' Incident 14 again lightens the terrors of Mark's narrative, this time with a note of the serenity which will receive more majestic and theological treatment from John. It is also, characteristically a quotation of Psalm 31:6 with 'Father' prefixed, ancient scripture giving the resonance of fulfilment to Jesus's last words.

A more knotty problem is set by the overall pattern of Luke's editing of the entire narrative. There are the five additions just noticed and also three or four excisions (at the three asterisks in the central column and the small omission of 'Come down' etc. in Luke Incident 7.). Otherwise everything—and that means the bulk of the narrative—comes from Mark. But the central column shows much re-ordering of the incidents in Mark with only two short runs in the same order (7 and 8, 10, 11 and 12, 15, 16, 18) and these interrupted by omissions. The effect of all this is to give Luke's version so distinctive a character that scholars have resorted to theories of Luke having a source independent of Mark. Such hypotheses are made questionable by the opposite pull of the problem, the large amount of Markan material used, though in terms of the presuppositions of conservative source criticism they may be inevitable. As a 'scissors and paste' rearrangement by an unimaginative evangelist approaching Mark with no strong aims, the patterns in the diagram are incredible. To handle Mark so freely (and the evidence that it *is* Mark is heavy), Luke worked not with his nose close to the page but rather with Mark's passion memorised in his head and heart where it was changed by the influence of his own concerns in a way which is simple in execution but complicated in result. Material in the head and the heart is more malleable, and particularly more easily re-ordered, than material on the page. An instance is given by the three appearances of the figure (8) in the central column: three incidents in Mark, spread through the narrative at his incidents 2, 9 and 13 are brought together by Luke who conflates Mark's two givings of drink into one which he attaches to the 'save thyself'[20] which he has derived from Mark 15:30 and gives to the soldiers who offer the vinegar. Two things are happening here. The first is simple: the abolition of a doublet by conflation. The second is the development of the 'save thyself' theme. In Mark it occurs first at 15:29f., appended to the jest about detroying the temple which Luke, consistently and with regard to historical distinction, omits as he did in the examination before the council. Mark reiterates 'save thyself' in the taunt of the scribes ('rulers' in Luke) and Luke follows him. It is then repeated twice more in Luke, by the soldiers who offer vinegar (Lk 23:36) and by the obdurate malefactor (Lk 23:39). The paradoxical pathos of the unsaved saviour who submits to the will of God and the nation's leaders is thus a free amplification of a germinal theme in the source into a dominant motif: a signal that Luke is using Mark with a freedom born of a thorough and imaginative acquaintance which does not have to work exactly on the text.

The editing at the beginning of the narrative is in the interests of clarity. For his first three incidents Luke chooses from Mark those sections (Mark Incidents 1, 3 and 7) which set the scene in the way he prefers when managing a large tableau. A precise and momentous frame is thus provided for Jesus's 'Father, forgive them'. The casting of lots follows in loyalty to Markan order, then the characteristic widening of scope by the addition of people standing and watching. After this the reactions of rulers and soldiers are given consecutively although they are far apart in Mark, and the title over the cross made the centre and turning point of the whole passage. It shares this position with the contrast between the two criminals which is one of the most memorable achievements of Luke's *midrash*. Mark had told him that they were crucified on either side of Jesus, but with a powerfully laconic brevity which adds to the degradation of Jesus's death—particularly when they too join in the reproach of the chief priests. Luke's lively curiosity about human nature, combined with his sympathy for the lost and the least, is not content with this. Two other concerns of his are also brought to bear: his continual preoccupation with repentance and his insistence that Jesus's saving work should go in the teeth of destruction (see the healing of the servant's ear and the reconciliation of Pilate with Herod). The good criminal's rebuke to his fellow is God-fearing and a further announcement of Jesus's innocence. His words to Jesus find a curious parallel in a tale told by Diodorus (34:2, 5–8) of a slave deluded by ideas of royalty who is mocked with, 'Remember me when you come into your kingdom'. These two malefactors with their contrasted attitude to Jesus may be seen as male counterparts of Martha and Mary (Lk 10:38–42). The incident closes with two typically Lukan notes: the marking of the time as another 'today of salvation' and the belief that at death men pass immediately into hell or paradise (see the rich man and Lazarus Lk 16:19–31).

Hereafter the narrative is edited in a way which dissipates the Markan impact and horror. Mark 15:37–39 is dismembered and rearranged, and so deprived of its cumulative force. Instead of the cataclysm of loud cry—death—rending of temple veil—'truly this man was the son of God', we have the rending of the veil put with the other omen of the eclipse[21] and so made less eminent, the loud cry articulated in serene committal, the death followed by the centurion glorifying God with a further declaration of the laboured theme of Jesus's innocence instead of Mark's inexplicable and divine revelation of Jesus's identity. The return of the crowds at the close gives a sense of mourning and foreboding.

The burial is ἐν μνήματι λαξευτῷ, in a tomb of carved stone. Luke envisages a mausoleum in the Greek style rather than the cave of Mark and (more clearly) Matthew, adding that, like the donkey which Jesus rode, it has not been used before—a modest and derivative indication of new beginnings. Joseph of Arimathea is more fully described than in Mark. He is 'a good and righteous man who had not consented to their counsel and deed', thus to be paired with his fellow-councillor Gamaliel in Acts 5 as a member of that little remnant of sympathetic Jews who form a link between nation and Church in contrast with the larger national apostasy. With 23:54f. Luke adds careful notes of time which show the obedience of Jesus's followers to the law. They rest 'according to the commandment'.

The accounts of the finding of the empty tomb are notoriously different in each gospel. In Mark the women met a young man, possibly connected with the one who ran away naked from Gethsemane, in Matthew an angel (which connects with the angel who appeared to Joseph in his nativity stories and the legions of them referred to by him at Matthew 26:53), in Luke two men[22] in dazzling apparel. 'Dazzling apparel' recalls Jesus at the Transfiguration. Two men figured there too, Moses and Elijah who 'appeared in glory' (Luke's addition). There will be 'two men in white robes' at the Ascension (Acts 1:10). It is difficult not to make the association suggested by the clothing and believe that these two men are the same in each instance—and so are Moses and Elijah. If so, a characteristic link with the old scriptures is fastened. The message which they give is different from Mark's version. Instead of the puzzling and unresolved 'He goeth before you into Galilee', which Matthew retailed but resolved in his last scene on the mountain in Galilee, Luke has ' "remember how he spake to you when he was yet in Galilee saying that the Son of Man must be delivered into the hands of sinful men and be crucified and the third day rise again." And they remembered his words.' It is all changed, as we might expect, into an instance of historical reminiscence and prophecy fulfilled. The next step after tying this connection with the past is to tie one with the future. Instead of Mark's terrified flight from the tomb the women go in good order to tell the apostles who form the essential link of witness between the past of Jesus's life and the present of the Church. Even if they regard it as idle talk, they

117

have been told—and will come round to it later. A scene of historical recapitulation rather than holy dread thus marks another milestone on the road of the gospel's divinely ordained progress. Luke's last treatment of Mark is consistent with the way he has dealt with him throughout.

[1] Q. Quesnell *The Mind of Mark* Pontifical Biblical Institute, 1969, is a recent and valiant attempt, but see D. E. Nineham's review in *Biblica* 55, 1974, pp. 127–31

[2] According to Austin Farrer, *A Study in Mark*, London 1951, a very sophisticated one—but there is little evidence that *Luke* discerned or approved it all.

[3] These sections are dealt with in the next block, but are put here because Jesus's withdrawal marks a pause in the activity which begins with this block.

[4] The use of *wisdom*, by which God is known in the human world, is a telling example of development: once in Mark, thrice in Matthew, six times in Luke.

[5] Though not its *raison d'être*—the Matthean version will be used at Lk 11:14–26

[6] See pp. 375–8 of my article in *Journal of Theological Studies*, October 1973

[7] See John 1:6–8, 19–36; 3:22–30

[8] See John M. Hull, *Hellenistic Magic in the Synoptic Tradition*, S.C.M. Studies in Biblical Theology, Series 2, No. 28, 1974, pp. 105–15

[9] Creed, *The Gospel According to St Luke*, London 1930, p. ix

[10] Nineham, *Saint Mark*, Harmonsworth 1963, p. 197

[11] Nineham, p. 202

[12] See Haenchen *The Acts of the Apostles*, pp. 468 ff

[13] I cannot agree with J. L. Houlden in his excellent *Ethics and the New Testament*, Harmondsworth 1973, p. 63, that Lk 16:17 ('It is easier for heaven and earth to pass away, than for one tittle of the law to fail') 'must surely be ironical'. Admittedly it is at variance with Lk 16:16 but such minor muddles are common enough in Luke and evidence of his regard for the Law is massive—see Lk 1 and 2 particularly.

[14] M. D. Goulder, *Midrash and Lection in Matthew*, S.P.C.K., London 1974, p. 17.

[15] Ibid., p. lxi

[16] There are problems of textual criticism here. See Creed, pp. 263 ff. Theological considerations make Lk 22:19–20 acceptable, however.

[17] But does it succeed? Usually the first effect of grief is sleeplessness.

[18] Luke seems to be recollecting 2 Kings 8:11: 'And he [Hazael] settled his countenance steadfastly upon him [Elisha], until he was ashamed: and the man of God wept.' The tears are for the destruction to come upon Israel. The resemblance is of content rather than vocabulary in this instance.

[19] For the textual difficulties here see Creed *ad loc*.

[20] All that remains of the raillery of Mark's passers-by 'Ha! Thou that destroyest the temple and buildest it in three days, save thyself' (Mark 15:29f.). Luke insists that the destruction of the temple is a matter of prophecy for Jesus and not (even proleptic) achievement.

[21] See J. F. A. Sawyer, 'Why is a Solar Eclipse mentioned in the Passion Narrative (Luke 23:44–5)?', *Journal of Theological Studies*, April 1972

[22] But the disciples on the road to Emmaus retail the women's story as a 'vision of angels', as if Matthew 28:2 were in mind.

6

Using Matthew

THE RELATION of Luke's Gospel to Matthew's is usually explained
by resort to the hypothetical and vanished source Q which, combined with the priority of Mark, has the happy result of attributing
a high degree of historicity to all three synoptic gospels alike. But
it is a theory which has benefited too much from a one-sided
distribution of scholarly labour, neglecting the 'simpler, competing
possibility'[1] that Luke used Matthew. This possibility was explored
by Jameson[2] and Lummis[3] at the time when the two-document
theory (or four-document, if M and L are included) was receiving its
classical expression in the work of Streeter, but their voices were
drowned in the widespread celebration of 'assured results'. In more
recent times it has been aired by Austin Farrer[4] and B. C. Butler[5]
but has remained a minority view and even an eccentricity.
M. D. Goulder[6] has, however, now achieved something previously
thought impossible: a thorough and learned explanation of
Matthew's gospel without resort to Q, its exegetical function being
taken over by the application to Mark's gospel of the techniques of
midrash and the demands of the liturgical year. I have myself found
no intolerable strain in writing a commentary on Luke's gospel[7]
supposing that Matthew's was its second Christian source, though
it was necessary to state with unusual emphasis that the Old
Testament scriptures formed a source at least equal in importance
to Luke to his two Christian documents. The practical test is the
most convincing, but it requires more explanation than I was able
to give then of why it worked. This chapter is an attempt to give it
substance.

There is a difference between the way Luke handles his two

Christian sources. With Mark he is more inclined to keep the order of his original than with Matthew. It must not be put more strongly than that. The impression that Luke almost never deviates from Mark's order, and almost never keeps to Matthew's, is common in the classroom but denied by the facts. We have seen that Luke frequently re-orders Mark and shall see that more often than not he uses Matthean material in its original sequence. But the difference is observable and remains. It is also quite understandable. To the most superficial reader, Mark is memorable for his narrative, Matthew for the teaching which is his great legacy to the ordinary Christian. Mark is Luke's leading source for story, Matthew for instruction. He applies his historical mind to them both, but obviously teaching is easier to shift about and re-arrange than narrative—particularly when it comes in the pithy little apophthegms, so easily absorbed and recalled *ad hoc*, of which Matthew is a master.

A question interposes itself at this point. If Luke had Matthew why did he use Mark at all, since Matthew retails nearly all of his work in abbreviated form? Part of the answer is in the question. Matthew's version of his Markan material is so abbreviated as often to lose the impact of the original along with the details which give it a note of authenticity. The other part of the answer is in the well-worn testimony of Papias.[8] This Bishop of Hierapolis, who died in the first half of the second century, knew an elder who used to say that Mark was 'the interpreter of Peter' and 'wrote accurately (ἀκριβῶς) as far as he remembered them the things said and done by the Lord, but not, however, in order (οὐ μέντοι τάξει), for he had neither heard the Lord nor been his personal follower but at a later stage, as I said, he had followed Peter. . . .' The elder, in other words, was not uncritical of Mark ('not in order'), but accepted his accuracy on the strength of his Petrine authority. Luke's use of Mark, together with his revisions of his order, suggest strongly that he shared this view and possibly this tradition. He was writing around the same time as Papias was conversing with his elder or writing his testimony. He, too, seems to have believed Mark's book to have authority and to have found it less than entirely adequate, in particular from the point of view of historical order. In any case, we know that Luke had Mark's book. He would have needed strong reasons not to use it.

Having said that, the main point remains. An editor using both Mark and Matthew will not get far unless he prefers Mark for narrative and Matthew for teaching. It follows that he will use each differently. Teaching, especially when it is in the form of nutshells of wisdom, can be used *ad hoc* and *ad rem*. It is easily stored in the mind and easily shifted from place to place. Its position in the Matthean anthologies (particularly the famous five discourses) need not be final and, as in an ordered library, makes it all the easier to remove units at will. With narrative the reverse applies. Much of it is simply immovable because its *raison d'être* is tied up with its position in the unified story: for example, the beginning of the ministry or the central turning point or the last days. Teaching material out of order is of its nature more likely than narrative out of order. Luke will not deal with Matthew and Mark in the same fashion.

Against the view that Luke used Matthew at all, it has been objected by G. M. Styler[9] that there seems to be no explanation of why he 'has consistently ignored Matthew in any passage where he follows Mark', and 'has made no use of Matthew's narrative where Mark has no parallel account—e.g. of the nativity stories and the resurrection appearances.' The first point is acutely dubious. In a footnote, Styler adds 'or almost entirely ignored' and refers to a previous footnote—but without revoking his 'consistently'. There are numerous agreements of Matthew and Luke together against Mark in passages where they are both using him. These have to be dismissed as coincidental stylistic improvements, or coincidental textual corruptions made at a later time, or evidence of two editions of Mark if Styler's point is to stand. His second observation is perplexing. Mark has no account of the healing of the centurion's boy. Matthew and Luke do. However, Matthew's story of Jesus's birth and resurrection appearances are the chief battleground. If it can be shown that there is plenty in common between them and Luke's accounts, that Luke's versions could well depend upon Matthew's while using much other material, then the first game in the match against Q is won.

1. *Infancy and Resurrection Stories*

The material common to Matthew and Luke in the birth narratives can be listed.

1) *The name of Jesus's father* (or more accurately, step-father). In Mark the Lord is described as 'the carpenter, the Son of Mary and brother of James and Joses and Judas and Simon' (Mk 6:3). Matthew and Luke change this, in one of their many agreements against

Mark, to 'the carpenter's son' and 'Joseph's son' respectively, Luke omitting the names of the brothers (Mt 13:55; Lk 4:22). Matthew was the first evangelist to give a name to Jesus's father, the name of the great dreamer of the old dispensation for the dreamer of the new (Mt 1:20; 2:13; 2:19), with a midrashic aptness which casts some doubts on its historicity. Luke takes Matthew's Joseph for granted in more senses than one: he is present but far from prominent. He also repeats Matthew's ornate irrelevance of a genealogy (with differences and similarities) which traces Jesus's descent through a man who was not, on his own evidence, his father. Luke's addition of 'as was supposed' (Lk 3:23) does not dispel the discrepancy, but betrays the editor.

2) *The Spirit*. Matthew, again by *midrash*,[10] makes the Holy Spirit Jesus's begetter: 'That which is conceived in her is of the Holy Ghost. And she shall bring forth a son' (Mt 1:20f.). Luke repeats this doctrine, putting it into a conversation between Mary and the angel—a greater sophistication possible in a second version: 'You will conceive in your womb and bear a son' (Lk 1:31) and 'the Holy Spirit will come upon you' (Lk 1:35). Luke is building on Matthew's foundation. As far as we know, the idea of Jesus being born of a virgin entered Christian tradition with Matthew, whose source for it was the Septuagint version of Isaiah 7:14. It was thus a midrashic development, like the other instances in his infancy narrative with their outright quotations of the ancient texts concerned, and characteristic of his artless bid for Christian possession of the scriptures. Luke has a lower and more subordinate christology than Matthew. The idea of the virgin birth is thus not essentially necessary to his christology[11] and indeed pushes it to a higher pitch than it reaches elsewhere in his work and particularly in Acts. For him, the Christ's heavenly aspect is bound into his ascension and not his birth. In traditional terms, his christology is a matter of manhood taken up into God rather than of Godhead coming down into man: in contemporary terms, of 'take-off' rather than 'landing'. The virgin birth is thus an idea not integral to his thinking: so it is reasonable to look for another source—and for that we need go no further than to Matthew. That he should have included it at all betrays his debt to his predecessor.

3) *The Angel*. As in Matthew, so in Luke, the announcement of Jesus's birth is made by an angel. Luke takes things further by giving the angel a name, got from the book of Daniel: as with 'Joseph' in Matthew, a characteristic feature of secondary development.

4) *The name.* The angel gives Jesus his name (Mt 1:21; Lk 1:31) in exactly the same words in both versions: 'and thou shalt call his name Jesus'.

5) *The time.* Matthew times Jesus's birth by noting that it was 'in the days of Herod the King' (Mt 2:1), and giving Herod a major role in his tale. Luke gives Herod nothing to do but starts his narrative 'in the days of Herod, King of Judea'. Matthew foreshadowed Luke's interest in historical dating which, more under the influence of Old Testament narrative, Luke uses more fully than his predecessor (2:1-3; 3:1-2).

6) *The journey.* The journey of the holy family was the dominant feature of the last part of Matthew's story. Luke uses this motif and exploits it by having three journeys—which is not surprising in a writer so enthusiastic about travel as a means of salvation history. He has the journey to Bethlehem, the first journey to Jerusalem for purification and the second for Passover. The reasons for the completely different routes of Luke's three journeys from Matthew's one will be given below. That they occur at all seems to be due to Matthew, who was no doubt himself indebted to Mark's picture of Jesus's continual travelling.

7) *Places.* According to Mark, Nazareth was the place of Jesus's origin (Mk 1:9 and four instances of 'Jesus of Nazareth'). In spite of this, Matthew has him born in Bethlehem—because his Bible tells him so. The prophecy of Micah 5:2 must be fulfilled: a motive which is overtly betrayed at Matthew 2:6. The journey down to Egypt allows Matthew to accommodate Mark's strong tradition about Nazareth by having the family settle at Nazareth instead of Bethlehem, where they began, on their return. Luke abandons Matthew's Egyptian journey for reasons to be given later (p. 127), so that particular solution is not open to him. But he achieves a scheme of his own which does more solid justice to the tradition of 'Jesus of Nazareth'. His tale of Jesus's birth begins there (2:4) as well as ending there (2:51), so that Nazareth becomes the base—though not the birth place. It follows that Bethlehem instead of Nazareth must be reached at the end of some special journey—caused this time by the famous census. Luke thus joins with Matthew in making, with differences, a particularly intricate geographical manoeuvre for the same theological reason. Bethlehem is Jesus's birthplace, although Nazareth was his home because he is David's son, as Mark had also told (Mk 10:47) and because God's word through Micah cannot return to him empty. It is very difficult not to

believe that one evangelist is indebted to the other when they share a complication. Matthew is not the best of stage directors and with him the shifts of location stand out with the crudity of historical improbability (why go all the way to Egypt to get out of Herod's range?) which has long led critics to acknowledge that his hand is behind it all. Luke, however, has woven the movement into his tale with a sophistication which never jolts the reader or takes him out of Palestine. Goulder's judgement is vindicated: 'What Matthew has done with brilliance, he has done with genius.'[12]

8) *Visitors*. In both gospels visitors come to see the child. In Matthew they were the Magi following the star, in Luke the shepherds following the directions of the angels—a celestial sign in both instances. The different visitors fit the programmes of each evangelist. Matthew's birth stories are memorable for the parts played by the high and mighty—Herod and the Magi; Luke's for their setting amongst the humble and poor—Zechariah the country clergyman, women, shepherds, Simeon (just 'a man' who comes into the temple, despite his being made a priest in later iconography) and Anna the widow. Luke's reasons for dropping Matthew's Magi will be seen later (p. 126).

9) *Family trees*. Both gospels have genealogies with common features[13] which suggests a literary debt. That Luke is the debtor is evident from his further backward projection, which marks him as the later: he goes back to Adam instead of Matthew's Abraham. He wisely postpones giving his genealogy until his story is fully under way. His preface shows his interest in capturing the reader's sympathy; an object much better achieved by first telling him the story than by confronting him straight away with the less engaging genre of a list of ancestors. That he had a genealogy at all shows his loyalty to Matthew and to the old Jewish historians.

None of these resemblances is negligible. The first, fifth and ninth are not as important to Luke's tale as to Matthew's, but then their very survival in Luke's version is the more striking as an acknowledgement of debt. The rest are integral to Luke's tale and more cleverly integrated into it than in the original. Without the virgin birth, the angelic visitation and naming, travel, Bethlehem and the heaven-bidden visitors, what would be left of Luke's marvellous story?

Yet Luke's version impresses the reader more by its contrasts to Matthew's than by its resemblances. They are in different worlds.

In the first place this is attributable to the skill with which Luke has woven the Matthean threads into his own fabric: a tapestry made of Old Testament skeins, handled, along with the Matthean threads, with the high craftsmanship which weaves them into the story instead of letting them jut out from it like Matthew's quotations. At the beginning of his work, a writer's pent-up energies and skills work at full pitch. In terms of *midrash* this will mean a more daring, allusive and creative use of material than the copying which sometimes sets in later with fatigue. It was the same with Matthew whose birth stories at the beginning of his book are his most original narrative achievements and with Mark whose prologue (1:1–15) is so packed with allusion and promise.

Secondly, the difference between the two versions has come about by the large amount of Matthew's works which Luke has refused to use. Why?

1) *The Magi*. If Luke's is the gentile gospel their omission is inexplicable. But we have seen from his editing of Mark that such a designation is seriously misleading. Luke omitted Jesus's encounter with the Syro-Phoenician woman, together with the entire journey into gentile territory in which it is set. Acts, on the other hand, is full of such expeditions. Luke will keep Matthew's gentile centurion off-stage at the cost of much artificial coming and going by delegations. But in Acts Cornelius, also a friend to the Jews, though he is the centurion's *alter ego* and at first sends a deputation to Peter, is allowed to meet Peter and become a full member of the Church. In Luke's temporal scheme the gentiles are the Church's business and its founder's only in prophecy which awaits fulfilment. This clear and major decision excludes the Magi from the beginning of the gospel.[14]

2) *The massacre*. Matthew works in black and white. In Mark Herod (the Tetrarch, though not so designated), is a weak, bad man. Matthew's Herod the King is given his son's wickedness but not his weakness. He is a monster of iniquity. Luke works in colours, giving touches of goodness to the bad characters and touches of badness to the virtuous. In particular he loves to portray rulers and governors as ambiguous persons rather than decided enemies of Christianity. He treats Herod the Tetrarch and the officials in Acts so. He virtually omitted Mark's account of the death of the baptist—probably for these reasons amongst others. Matthew's account of Herod's attempt to kill Jesus with a wholesale massacre of children is unacceptable to him *a fortiori*. Above all his first two chapters are

designed to make a smooth and snug joint with the Jewish world, which this tale of raging opposition from the Jewish king could destroy utterly.

3) *The journey.* In Matthew the journey down to Egypt and back has as its overt point the exodus fulfilled in Jesus. But Luke's exodus is later. ('His exodus which he was to accomplish at Jerusalem' 9:31.) The hinge between the two volumes of his great work is to be the exodus passover feast which will signal the birth of the new people of God. Once again we notice the effect of Luke's strict historical scheme. Further, the author who omits Mark's gentile journey by Jesus will not be inclined to include Matthew's.

4) *Joseph.* Luke reverses Matthew's priorities by pushing him into the background and raising up Mary in his stead. This is typical of a writer who, following ancient precedent, gives women prominent roles in salvation history, thus accentuating the wonder of God's deeds. Luke's tendency to magnify her re-emerges at Acts 1:14 where she is one of the company of the first believers providing an essential link between the Church and its origins. The tendency will be taken further again in John's gospel with the marriage at Cana and the mother's presence by her son's cross.

Does Luke show any knowledge of Matthew's resurrection appearances? The first, at Matthew 28:9f. is so slight as to furnish little evidence one way or the other. The two women departing from the tomb are met by Jesus with 'Hail!', take hold of his feet and worship him. He then tells them not to be afraid but go and tell the brethren to go to Galilee where they will meet him. Luke's omission of the direction to Galilee is consistent with his strategy. Whatever Mark or Matthew may say, he is convinced that the resurrection appearances took place where the Church began—in and around Jerusalem. The main feature of this tale of Matthew is an encounter of Jesus with two women in the way after the discovery of the empty tomb. Once that is stated, the possibility emerges that this could be a seed of Luke's Emmaus story where men take the women's place and the whole is told with a sensitive detail which has put Matthew's little incident, amounting to no more than a link between the empty tomb and the final appearance, into the shade. Matthew's second resurrection appearance is at 28:16–20. Luke naturally has no use for its Galilean setting, but Matthew's note that 'some doubted' gets dramatic and more historicised treatment from him when he has the apostles suppose the women's report to be an idle tale. He takes Matthew's 'doubt' to refer to the resurrection, though in Matthew it bears a more moral and less intellectual meaning (see Mt 14:31). The two on the road to Emmaus have lost their faith and Jesus, when eventually he appears to the eleven, immediately demands 'Why are you troubled and why do questionings arise in your hearts?' The physical emphasis on feet in Matthew's first tale re-appears here, amplified, to his 'See my hands and my feet'. Both motifs, doubt and the physicality of Jesus's risen body, will receive their definitive treatment with Thomas in John's gospel. The rest of the incident is the command to mission among the nations, making disciples, baptising and instructing. This is echoed at Luke 24:47 ('unto all the nations'), but much more than that, it could well be the germ and incentive for the writing of Acts. He could scarcely owe Matthew a greater debt. The promise, 'Lo, I am with you always . . .' disappears. Like John, Luke believes that the Spirit is the divine presence in the Church after the ascension. Jesus is elsewhere, above the sky at God's right hand (Ac 7:56). The epochs of history are thus distinct. The stories about the risen Jesus at the end of the gospel present the gradual awakening of the disciples to God's great deed and so form the essential narrative link to the Church of Acts and its preaching.

2. In Order (Luke 3:7—4:13; Matthew 3:7—4:11)

Widespread acceptance of Q, with its basic conviction that Matthew and Luke worked independently of one another, has blinded the eyes of many scholars against the resemblances between their two infancy narratives, and so excused them from attempting any detailed explanation of the differences. It is practically impossible to see what one does not expect to see. Attention has also been diverted from the fact that from the preaching of John (Mt 3:7; Lk 3:7) to the end of the temptations (Mt 4:11; Lk 4:13), Matthew and Luke present much common non-Markan material in the same order. Streeter's famous knock-down argument for Q acknowledges this only to ignore it. 'Subsequent to the temptation story there is not a single case in which Matthew and Luke agree in inserting the same saying at the same point in the Markan outline.'[15] That argument will be taken up again. For the moment we need only notice that Streeter's 'subsequent to the temptation story' shows him choosing his ground with more care than justice and tacitly allowing that there is no need of the Q theory up to the end of the temptation story. Here is a substantial stretch where Matthew and

Luke agree in inserting the same sayings at the same point in the Markan outline.

This is unusual, as Streeter noticed, and so requires explanation. It is rare for Luke to use his two Christian sources at once. His gospel is characterised by the use of one at a time and for a good stretch. He edits Mark with only the occasional reminiscence of Matthew creeping in and *vice versa*. Obviously this is much the easier course, particularly since he has a third source to refer to in his ancient scriptures. But every writer knows that at the outset of his work, with hopes and energy running high, he expects to achieve something more than, and different from, that which the exigencies of the task produce in the end. So at the beginning of his work Luke labours for a more equally blended synthesis of Mark and Matthew than he finds possible in the final outcome. He is helped by the historical character of Matthew's contribution here, the teaching being more pointedly related to the Markan story than in Matthew's longer discourses. Luke's first two chapters were also a highly articulated *tour de force* in the building of a septuagintal superstructure upon selected Matthean foundations. From Luke 3:7 to 4:13 he runs Matthew and Mark in harness. Here a reading which attempts to show that he is using Mark alone is as impossible as one which assumes that Matthew or Q is the sole source. It cannot even be shown that one or the other is the leader throughout. For instance, in 3:16 and 17, 'I indeed baptise you with water' is Matthew word for word, ignoring Mark's past tense 'baptised' 'There cometh' is from Mark ignoring Matthew's 'He that cometh'; 'unloosing' the shoes agrees with Mark against Matthew's 'bearing' the shoes; verse 17 is a thorough debt to Matthew.

The omissions and additions with which Luke edits Matthew's text are all explicable. Matthew starts with 'And in those days . . .' (Mt 3:1). The dating is vague but historically an advance upon Mark who gives no note of time at all. Luke's elaborate dating in 3:1f. goes further still and is in septuagintal style. In quoting from Isaiah 40 he agrees with Matthew by omitting Mark's added and unacknowledged citation of Malachi 3:1. But he then takes the quotation two verses further until it reaches a prophecy reminiscent of Simeon's: 'and all flesh shall see the salvation of God', salvation being one of his grand themes. Unlike Matthew he omits Mark's description of John's clothing because it presents him as Elijah-come-again, a role which he prefers to reserve for Jesus. John, he has already noted, will work 'in the spirit and power of Elijah'

(1:17). But that makes him more like the junior Elisha, spirit and power being the 'double share of your spirit' (2 K 2:9) which Elisha asked and got. Luke's amplification of John's preaching is clearly a secondary addition, muting Matthew's climactic ending 'hewn down and cast into the fire' (Mt 3:10), and adding typically practical moral advice to the mutitudes, the publicans and the soldiers. The first two are favourite classes with Luke. At the outset at 3:7 he changed Matthew's Pharisees and Sadducees as the target of the Baptist's preaching into 'the multitudes'. It is a sure sign that he is editing Matthew when at 3:10 he puts 'and the multitudes asked him . . .' He seems to have forgotten his editing work at verse 7, in spite of which he has retailed the teaching in verses 8 and 9 as if it were directed at Matthew's Pharisees and Sadducees. The crowds and the publicans are favourite classes with Luke. The soldiers may show his historical awareness of Palestine as an occupied country but could as well be the Jewish soldiers of Antipas. In any case all three categories show a widening of the scope of John's preparatory message into a secular world beyond the confines of Matthew's intra-Judaic religious quarrel with Pharisees and Sadducees. The editorial parenthesis of 3:15, raising the question (developed at John 1:19ff.) whether John is the Christ, is necessary in order to rejoin Matthew and Mark. The further parenthesis at 3:18–20 removes John, of whom Luke has already had far more to say than his predecessors, from the scene. The omission of the rather clumsy dialogue between John and Jesus at Matthew 3:14f. ensues. Unlike Matthew, Luke has already made their relation clear in his infancy narrative. He is glad to agree with Matthew in omitting Mark's 'he saw' (Mk 1:10; Lk 3:21) and so make the event more public.

Luke divides the baptism from the temptations by his genealogy. The beginning of Jesus's public work is a natural enough place for the presentation of such credentials—Luke has already emphasised the public nature of baptism at 3:21 ('when all the people were baptised'). Possibly also, as a Christian in more spacious circumstances than his predecessors, he does not like Matthew's suggestion that temptation follows immediately upon baptism, although Matthew had diluted Mark's insistent 'and straightway' to a more moderate 'then'. Goulder says, 'It was inevitable that Luke should prefer the full Matthean temptations to the brief Markan note: the puzzle to commentators has been the reversing of Matthew's second and third temptations'[16] and explains it by an historically ordered Moses typology. Moses at Exodus 2:20 was bidden by Jethro to eat bread, then he went to Horeb the mount of God and was told 'When you have brought the people out of Egypt you shall serve God upon this mountain' (Ex 3:12). Another further explanation is possible. If the question is put the other way about, 'Why is the Jerusalem temptation the last?' the answer could be, 'Because Jerusalem is the end and goal of Luke's gospel.' The temptations are thus made prophetic of Jesus's course. That such an historical frame is in his mind is suggested by Luke's final editorial strokes which look forward to the far end of his gospel: the ministering angels are postponed until the agony at 22:43 (where one is enough) and an ominously prophetic note of time is substituted: 'The devil . . . departed from him for a season' (4:13).

3. *The Sermon (Luke 6:20–49, Matthew 5:1—7:27)*

Luke does not have the sermon 'at the same point in the Markan outline' as Matthew. Streeter is obviously, if superficially, right. But two further points modify his judgement.

The first is that Luke puts it at a similar point. Matthew put the sermon after Mark 1:16–20 (which is the call of the first four disciples), followed by Mark 1:39 (which is a note of preaching and cures) amplified with words of his own and with reference to Mark 3:7 for geography. Luke has it after Mark 3:13–19 (which is the call of twelve disciples on the mountain), followed by Mark 3:7 (which becomes a note of general healing edited to include preaching as well). So both Matthew and Luke have the sermon soon after a reference to Mark 3:7, although they quote that verse at different points in the larger scheme. More striking is the fact that they both have it after a calling of disciples and a ministry to the crowd—a remarkable coincidence which demands explanation and is best explained by one of them knowing the other.

The second point is that for all this similarity, Luke has his reasons for putting the sermon at a point in the Markan outline different from that chosen by Matthew. Streeter's argument against Luke using Matthew was that it requires us to imagine Luke removing non-Markan material from Matthew where it is always in 'exceedingly appropriate' contexts, only to put it in different contexts of Mark 'having no special appropriateness'.[17] That pleading has no force here, for if a calling of four followed by a crowd scene was an exceedingly appropriate place for Matthew to put the sermon, then a calling of twelve followed by a crowd scene is just as good for Luke. Streeter's next sentence is a famous piece of sarcasm. 'A theory which would make an author capable of such a proceeding would only be tenable if, on other grounds, we had reason to believe he was a crank.' So far we have found no more reason to believe Luke to have been a crank than Matthew. Streeter's argument is left with no force at all if Luke is discovered to have sound and sane reasons for putting the sermon at the later point which he prefers. It could be that Matthew's placing of the sermon does not seem so apt to him as it does to Streeter. He and Matthew are, after all, different writers with different skills and preferences: Matthew the master of the great speeches and Luke the master of the great story. Matthew has the sermon very early, making it the first major event in Jesus's public ministry, preceded only by the call of the four and sketches of the Lord's preaching and healing. He exercises his special skill as soon as he can. So does Luke, for he edits Mark at the outset so as to achieve the narrative order which he promised. First Jesus's ministry is thoroughly established by his prophetic manifesto at Nazareth followed by two particular healing miracles and some general ones. Then the four are called in the grand context of the miraculous catch. This is followed by more healings, the call of Levi, and sharp arguments with the opposition culminating in the dispute over the cure of the withered hand. Then the twelve are called on the mountain—and the time for the sermon has come. This arrangement means that the manifesto at Nazareth has taken the sermon's place as the opening tableau to set the scene of the ministry. Luke's scheme tells a developing story beginning with Jesus on his own, then gathering his followers as he works; a process which culminates in the calling of the twelve which marks the completion of the first stage of the founding of Christianity. Only when he has constructed this well-articulated platform of historical narrative does Luke think it appropriate to have a sermon about godly living.

The relation of Luke's sermon to Matthew's is best set in a synoptic diagram (see opposite).

Two features concerning order emerge clearly from this tabulation. Both sermons begin with the same teaching and end with the same teaching, which is another remarkable coincidence if Matthew and Luke are arranging Q material in complete independence of one another. Between the beginning and the end, most of the sayings are in the same order. There is only one major transposition: of the 'do as you would be done by' saying from a late point in Matthew

Matthew 5:3—7:37	Luke 6:20-49
8 blessings	4 blessings, 4 woes
Salt and light	(14:34 11:33)
Law and prophets	(16:17)
Murder and anger	
Reconciliation before judgement	(12:58f)
Adultery	
Offending eye and hand	
Divorce	(16:18)
Oaths	
The other $\begin{cases} \text{cheek} \\ \text{garment} \\ \text{mile} \end{cases}$	Love your enemies The other $\begin{cases} \text{cheek} \\ \text{garment} \end{cases}$
Give!	Give!
	Do as you would be done by
Love your enemies	Unconditional love
Your Father's sun and rain	Love your enemies
Unconditional love	God kind to ungrateful and evil
Perfection like your Father's	Mercy like your Father's
Hidden righteousness	
Almsgiving	
Prayer	
Lord's prayer	(11:2–4)
Fasting	
Treasure	(12:33f.)
The eye	(11:34–36)
Two masters	(16:13)
Anxiety	(12:22–31)
Mutuality of $\begin{cases} \text{judgement} \\ \text{measuring} \end{cases}$	Mutuality of $\begin{cases} \text{judgement} \\ \text{measuring} \end{cases}$
	Blind guides (Mt 15:14)
	Disciple and master (Mt 10:24)
Mote and beam	Mote and beam
Pearls before swine	
Ask and receive	(11:9–13)
Do as you would be done by	
Narrow gate	(13:23f.)
False prophets	
Trees known by fruits	Trees known by fruits
	*Good man and bad man
	(Mt 12:34f.)
Lord! Lord!	Lord! Lord!
... I never knew you	(13:26f.)
Two houses	Two houses

* Matthew repeats the saying about trees at 12:33 and follows it with the good man and the bad man.

(7:12) to an earlier one in Luke (6:31); but of all the sayings in Matthew which the ordinary Christian has by heart and so can quote whenever occasion arises, this is chief. The other change is Luke's extra use of 'love your enemies . . .' at an earlier stage than Matthew, which emphasises the doctrine by making it the heading over the instances of love—giving the other cheek and the other garment—as well as being a deduction from them. With Luke, as with so many later Christians, it becomes the key note of the whole sermon. The diagram shows many omissions, which altogether make Luke's sermon a quarter the length of Matthew's. The brevity is deliberate. Matthew, by interesting the reader in ethical truths, diverts his attention from the narrative so long that he forgets it until chapter 8 suddenly lands him once more in the historical world. Luke's preference for history demands something shorter— he even interrupts his abbreviated version at 6:39 with 'he spake also a parable unto them', using a saying from later in Matthew. The wish for brevity accounts for many of the omissions. When Luke uses a Matthean passage later in his story (indicated in the table by brackets) it is clear that he neither disapproves of it nor is unattracted by it. He is simply cutting the cloth. There is some material which Luke omits here and never uses. It is mostly concerned with details of the practice of religion in a Jewish–Christian community: oaths, alms-giving, prayer, fasting, the recognition of false prophets, relations with the synagogue and its doctrine. These are local rules and probably out of date by Luke's time. Murder and anger, adultery and lust, though far from being locally limited, are not aspects of human behaviour on which Luke cares to dwell (beyond the summary of the law at Luke 18:20) as problems for the Christian. Further, the polemical contradictions of the old law do not suit his apologia for a law-abiding (i.e. torah-abiding) Church which practises true Judaism in an organic historical development. His sense of Christianity as a public religion, not done in a corner (Ac 26:26), goes against Matthew's doctrine of hidden righteousness which also disappears. The omission of 'ask and you will receive' is much more apparent than real. Luke gives it handsome treatment in his parables of the importunate widow and the friend at midnight.

It is now possible to follow Luke as he goes through Matthew's sermon to make his own. A noticeable lapse of coherence and clarity will occur about two-thirds of the way through. He begins with four blessings and four matching woes. This means that he agrees with Matthew in having eight sentences but amends him by making his eight out of four positives and four negatives. Similarly at 11:42–52 he will break Matthew's seven woes on the Pharisees into three on them and three on the lawyers,[18] omitting the specialised and, no doubt, out-dated woe upon swearing by the gold of the temple. The Matthean beatitudes which Luke keeps are all to do with deprivation (poverty, hunger, weeping, persecution). The four which he omits are all to do with positive qualities (meekness, mercy, purity of heart, peace-making). He has no quarrel with the latter category, but a major aspect of his theology requires his own arrangement. The balancing of blessings and woes is obviously appropriate to the author of the double-edged theology of the Magnificat. He has learnt it from the Old Testament and particularly from the Book of Deuteronomy (see Deuteronomy 11:26, 'I set before you this day blessing and curse' and 28). He insists throughout his work, and above all in his grand theme of the rejection of old Jewry and the triumph of Christianity, that blessing and woe are the simultaneous effects in history of God's visitation. They are worked out consistently in the fulfilment and exaltation of the deprived and needy, the emptying and abasement of the rich and mighty. His second and third blessing and woes on the hungry and the weeping, the full and the laughing, are marked by the insertion of 'now', a little word which occurs thrice in Mark, four times in Matthew and twelve times in Luke. It betrays the editing hand of the historian concerned with temporal distinction between present and future. The deprived and the satisfied exist simultaneously at present, and so they will in the end—but with their roles reversed. The story of the rich man and Lazarus (Lk 16:19–31) will make it clear again. The beginning of his sermon is thus a deliberate job of editing, clearly marked by the stamp of his theology and structure. The greater sophistication of its double scheme is balanced by his simplified and secularised versions of Matthew's blessings (no 'in spirit' for the poor, no 'after righteousness' for the hungry), and the greater immediacy of his 'you' instead of Matthew's 'they'—though this involves him in the slight awkwardness of 'blessed are the poor for yours, etc.' which betrays his secondariness.

A large omission follows as Luke skips a wealth of Matthean material, some of it to be used later. At Matthew 5:39 and Luke 6:29, he reaches a point where the themes which marked his blessings and woes find more material. The promises to the have-nots take effect on the human plane when men allow themselves to be insulted or deprived: 'Your reward shall be great and ye shall be sons of the Most High for he is kind towards the unthankful and evil.' The reversal is perfected by the practice of a love as generous as God's. As we have seen, Luke has two instances of Matthew's single 'love your enemies', and transfers to a climactic position at the end of the section the promise of sonship to those who imitate God's generosity (Mt 5:45). He makes it more striking by omitting the references to the good and the just, leaving the unthankful and evil alone as beneficiaries. His characteristic 'Most High' creeps in and reference to the sun and the rain go out. Of greater importance is the change to mercy instead of perfection as the divine attribute to be imitated, since this is in line with the whole theme of Luke's sermon, and also betrays his knowledge of Matthew's blessing on the merciful (Mt 5:7) which he omitted before.

As usual it takes close scrutiny to notice all these omissions and alterations. For the ordinary reader the change from the reversals of fortune promised at the outset to the reversal of natural ethics which follows is a natural and interesting development. The whole of the section is a practical commentary on the blessings, showing how those who are ready to give and to go without in the present are instruments of God's purpose and heirs of his promise.

The next section, Luke 6:37–45, does the same for the woes, but less adequately. Its theme is wickedness and judgement, matching the previous treatment of goodness and mercy. They are dealt with in terms of the mutuality and cause and effect which ran through the preceding teaching. To get to this point Luke has again omitted much Matthean material. Here too the details of discipleship, such as almsgiving, prayer and fasting, find no place in his book, with the exception of the Lord's Prayer which appears later, as does the teaching about singleness and trust. At Matthew 7:1 Luke at last finds matter to illustrate his second theme of condemnation. He takes Matthew's 'judge not and you shall not be judged' and hammers it home with his added 'condemn not and you shall not be condemned'. His obstinate optimism matches these two negative commands with a pair of positive ones with the same structure, 'release' and 'give', thus repeating his method with the opening blessings by balancing the light and the dark. As he puts his hand to the critique of wickedness, he glances over his shoulder at the happier concerns he is leaving. The parables (or proverbs) of the blind leading the blind and the teacher and his disciple, both come from elsewhere in Matthew (15:14 and 10:24f.) and are the kind of short apophthegm which is easily remembered without reference

136

to the text. The root of evil is the sense of moral superiority ('woe, when all men speak well of you!'). But Luke does not have Matthew's skill in organising short aphorisms into an articulated architecture. Only with the saying about the speck in the eye is the command not to judge given its graphic definition. The preceding two verses have prepared for it, if they have also interrupted it with that clumsiness of unnecessary editing which is one of Luke's most irritating faults. Unfortunately for Luke, Matthew's subsequent material is not about judgement and wickedness but returns to discipleship. When Matthew at last seems to oblige him it is with a warning against false prophets which he omits, probably because this was a local problem of Matthew's which did not bother him. But he uses its moral conclusion: the fig and the thistle, the good tree and the bad. Interestingly he recalls Matthew's other use of this image at Matthew 12:33–35 where it is overtly developed, as it is not here in Matthew, in application to the good and bad heart: it appeals to Luke's love of wisdom and interest in the human heart and gives him extra material for his present concern with judgement. Judgement sharpens Luke's version of Matthew 7:21. Matthew has, 'not every one . . .' Luke uses the more direct 'you' again, and has 'and why . . .?' Crisp rebuke compensates for the omission of Matthew's eschatological *dénouement* (used later at Luke 13:26f.). But Luke's happier temperament seems to have stopped him exploring evil and its punishment as thoroughly as goodness and its reward. The closing illustration of the two builders unites blessing and woe. Matthew is adapted in the interests of realism. The sensible man is a thorough urban builder, digging and going deep for his foundations: a touch which gives a better connection with the previous doctrine about the foundations of conduct in the heart. The catastrophe is not a grandiose conjunction of rain, wind and flood, but a river bursting its banks.

Luke's sermon has a consistent and simple architecture. At the outset blessing and woe are pronounced. The blessing of the good life is then described, briefly contrasted with bad living which, in its turn, is judged in the ground of the heart. The two are contrasted at the end with the moral: foundations tell. There are signs of writer's fatigue precisely where we would expect them: two-thirds of the way through at verses 39 and 40, after which energy returns in sight of the finishing post. At no point has invocation of the Q hypothesis proved necessary to the understanding of the sermon. This is scarcely surprising since silence or ignorance about Luke's techniques and motives has played a considerable role in its survival and support. It has also been possible to follow and explain Luke's use of Matthew without being forced to conclude on these, or any other grounds, that he was mentally deranged.

4. A Christian Deuteronomy (Luke 9:51—18:14; Matthew 8:18—24:41)

The large tract from Luke 9:51—18:14, is one of the great riddles of gospel study. The strong sense of narrative development which sustains Luke's work seems here to weaken into insignificance, leaving a huge job-lot of loosely connected incidents, parables, debates and discourses, without any strong strategic control. To call it 'the travel document' is forced. The resounding beginning at 9:51f. certainly makes the title look appropriate. In grand septuagintal language and imagery, Luke sets Jesus and his disciples on the way to Jerusalem. But thereafter this sense of direction is very slight. At 13:22 the reader is reminded that Jesus is 'on his way through cities and villages, teaching and journeying on into Jerusalem', and at 17:11 that 'on the way to Jerusalem he was passing through the midst of Samaria and Galilee'. Otherwise there is little more than a general sense of Jesus moving about, and even that is absent for long stretches when he is sitting at table. So 'the only safe name by which one can call it is "the central section"—a title which states a fact but begs no questions'.[19] Even that is not as safe as it sounds. The centre of Luke's Gospel, inherited from Mark, is the transfiguration and the events surrounding it which reveal the Christ. In Mark the transfiguration is flanked on either side by predictions of the Passion, in Luke by two missions as well: of twelve before it, and of seventy after it, which make its centrality stronger still.

So what is Luke up to from 9:51 to 18:14? The only certain answer has been that he is not editing Mark. The section is made of Matthean material mixed with his own. The two older methods of gospel criticism have their reasons for pushing the question no further. The form-critic is pleased to see a congeries of bits and pieces. His theory of the composition of the gospels is confirmed and brilliantly illustrated by it. The traditional source-critic, positing and defending Q, recognises that Matthew has ordered the Q material with magisterial control into five great speeches, which contrast strikingly with the apparent chaos of Luke's use of it. This disorder is seen as an argument for Q: for how could Luke have been such an editorial hooligan as to pull down Matthew's excellent and obvious structure in order to make—nothing in particular? Either Luke did not know Matthew, or if he did, he was a crank (which is intolerable and on other grounds improbable). Luke 9:51—18:14 is thus left as a mixture of Q and peculiarly Lukan matter, distinction between the two being vague in some cases, on no particular plan but very probably keeping more than Matthew of Q's original and random order together with more of Q's original wording. It is thus no more in the interests of Q than of form-criticism to discover here a monumental, well-articulated plan like Matthew's. Yet these well-worn explanations are unsatisfactory and suspect precisely because they depend upon a studied lack of curiosity about the purpose of so large a section. Conversely, in attacking Q, Austin Farrer's strategy had only to be the demonstration of some connected plan of distinctly Lukan character. He achieved it over certain limited stretches by showing incidents in sequence with thematic connection and development, but fell short of treating the entire thing (*Studies in the Gospels*, pp. 55–86).

The explanation of the entire thing has already been noticed in Chapter 4. Deuteronomy is Luke's model, the template which determines the position of pieces within the whole. It exercises the same power as Mark in other long sections: less overtly but just as continuously. Like Deuteronomy, this section of Luke begins with the sending out of forerunners and messengers. Thereafter many apparent jumps and dislocations in the scheme are explicable by parallelism to Deuteronomy. It is worth giving some examples straight away. The lawyer's question 'What shall I do to inherit eternal life?' and Jesus's answer 'Thou shalt love the Lord thy God . . . and thy neighbour as thyself', followed by the story of the Good Samaritan, come suddenly after Jesus's celebration of the return of the seventy. The incident in the house of Martha and Mary comes as suddenly after that. In Deuteronomy the events on the threshold of the promised land are followed by the Ten Commandments, summarised in the words used by Jesus in answering the lawyer. No mercy for the foreigner then contrasts with the Samaritan's mercy in Jesus's story. Deuteronomy's subsequent doctrine that man lives not by bread alone but by every word from God's mouth is illustrated by Martha and Mary. Debate about casting out demons by the finger of God (Lk 11:14–26) is a switch from teaching about prayer (Lk 11:1–13), explained by Deuteronomy's parallel argument with a nation obdurate in spite of its possession of the tables of stone written by God's finger. Cleanness before God is dealt with at Luke 11:37-44, as at Deuteronomy 12:1-16. Wealth and godliness are the themes of teaching at Luke 12:13ff. in parallel with Deuteronomy 12:17ff. Divided families are spoken of at Luke 12:51-53, and at Deuteronomy 13:6-11. At Luke 13:10-21 the release of the bent woman on the seventh day coincides with Deuteronomy 15:1-18 which enjoins releases from debt and slavery every seventh year. The excuses given by those invited to the supper at Luke 14:15-35 are very close to the grounds for exemption from military service in Deuteronomy 20. In chapter 15, Luke deals with lost and found, a father and his ill-behaved sons. So does Deuteronomy 21:15—22:4. The injunctions against oppression of the poor in Deuteronomy 24:6—25:3 are parallel to the story of Lazarus and the rich man in Luke 16. C. F. Evans's synoptic table[20] gives more instances. Anyone who reads Luke 9:51—18:14 with that table at his elbow will be struck by the way in which Luke's apparently wayward changes of subject are explained by it time and again.

The important consequence for the study of Luke's use of Matthew is that this section is not, in its architecture, an edition of Matthew but a Christian Deuteronomy—a handbook on the Christian life in the historical setting of a journey to Jerusalem, just as Deuteronomy is a guide for the devout Jew set in the historical perspective of the journey into the promised land with Jerusalem, the place where God will cause his name to dwell, as its centre. Like Deuteronomy it deals with discipleship within a settled secular *milieu* and is pervaded by the note of joy.[21] Such a guide-book would be bound to draw on Matthew's material if it were available—what would anybody's picture of Christian living be without Matthew? But handling of Matthean material is a secondary and dependent concern, and this takes much of the vexation out of the argument. If Luke were simply editing Matthew, then 9:51—18:14, for all its connected passages, would contain ruptures which make the editing look extremely odd. But he is not. The thread through the labyrinth is Deuteronomy. Matthew is secondary. To change the metaphor Deuteronomy is the string on to which Luke threads teaching material from Matthew and from his own resources. To the modern reader such a strategy looks odd to the point of absurdity. To the Christian writer of Luke's generation, cherishing and exploiting the Jewish scriptures as his bible and source for the story of the

Christ who fulfils them, hearing them read week by week in church, it was a triumph of theological logic. Besides, Luke was a writer combining the roles of historian and moralist, and nowhere are these two concerns more splendidly woven together than in Deuteronomy's amalgamation of promise and command with historical process.

For all that, Luke's building of a Christian Deuteronomy does not involve a complete or wanton destruction of Matthew's order and architecture. Substantial traces of both survive in his scheme.

The architecture of Matthew's presentation of Jesus's teaching is one of the famous wonders of the gospels. Five great discourses deliberately set, concluded and bound together by unity of theme, give it a monumental clarity. They are:

1. Matthew 5—7   Sermon on the Mount   (Pentecost)
2. Matthew 10   Mission Charge   (New Year)
3. Matthew 13:1–52 Parables of Gathering (Harvest)
4. Matthew 18   Church Discipline   (Rededication)
5. Matthew 23—25   Judgement   (Passover)

The last column notes the feasts in the Jewish liturgical year for which, according to Goulder, each discourse was designed. If, as seems likely, they were not observed by Luke's church, the necessity for preserving Matthew's scheme was removed. Nevertheless Luke 6:20–49 was demonstrably a potted edition of Matthew's Sermon on the Mount, and Luke 10:2–16 will emerge as an abridgement of Matthew's Mission Charge. Matthew's great fifth discourse survives in two reduced and separated blocks: the polemic at Luke 11:39–52 which is a version of Matthew 23, the eschatology at Luke 17:22–37 which is a version of Matthew 24. The third and the fourth of Matthew's discourses are reduced to scattered fragments. The reason is simple. Matthew's sermons are planted in Mark's outline, and at times Luke works on Mark with very slight attention to Matthew. Matthew's third and fourth discourses occur at points where Luke is busy with Mark and betrays his knowledge of Matthew only in little details. In Chapter 8 he uses Mark's parables of seed-time and harvest (keeping one of them for use at 13:18f.) rather than Matthew's expanded version of them in his third discourse. At 9:43–50 he uses Mark's account of disorder among the disciples instead of Matthew's fourth discourse. Yet the other three great Matthean speeches remain recognisable in Luke. Like the walls and arches of a ruined monastery, they are much reduced by being used as a quarry for the building of the manor house by the Tudor supplanter. A good deal has disappeared. But what remains is enough for reconstruction of its history. Very striking in this instance is the fact that the three Matthean discourses which Luke leaves standing (though diminished) are in their original order as if units, such as archways, from the monastery have been incorporated in the manor house.

$$\begin{aligned} &\text{Matthew } 5\text{—}7 = \text{Luke } 6:20\text{–}49\\ &\text{Matthew } 10 \quad = \text{Luke } 10:2\text{–}16\\ &\left\{\begin{array}{l}\text{Matthew } 23 \quad = \text{Luke } 11:39\text{–}52\\ \text{Matthew } 24 \quad = \text{Luke } 17:22\text{–}37\end{array}\right.\end{aligned}$$

Within this architecture there are coincidences of the order in which Matthew and Luke put the sayings which make up the speeches. These are strong and numerous in the first two chapters of Luke's Christian Deuteronomy, 10 and 11. They weaken and become much scarcer in Luke 12. In Luke 13:24–29 four Matthean sayings, making up two pairs (Mt 7:13 and 14, 22 and 23), occur in order. Then in Luke 14—16 Matthean order is disrupted and higgledy-piggledy. It re-asserts itself in Chapter 17, first with a short run (Lk 17:1–4; Mt 18:7, 6, 15, 21–22), then with the eschatological section at 17:22–37 in which material from Matthew 24 comes in the order of verses 23, 26, 27, 37, 38, 39, 17, 18, 40, 41, 28. A graph of Luke's attention to Matthew's order would show a line kept high at the outset, then declining with some undulation to a low level just before the half-way mark and only recovering in sight of the end. So in the first two chapters of his Christian Deuteronomy, Luke manages to use both Deuteronomy and Matthew in order. It is an editorial *tour de force* which (as before) he cannot sustain. In chapter 12 it disintegrates and instead Luke works on Deuteronomic order alone, richly embellished with his own material and a much smaller amount of stuff quarried here and there from Matthew. Only in the second half of Luke 17 are Deuteronomy and Matthew in something like harness again under the theme of judgement. Vincent Taylor thought that 'coupled with the other arguments in favour of Q, the manifest signs of a common order in Matthew and Luke raise the hypothesis to a remarkable degree of cogency, short only of demonstration.'[22] That is an exaggeration based on a logical jump, accompanied by the usual conviction that the hypothesis of Luke's dependence on Matthew has been 'long abandoned'. Q, being an hypothesis, cannot be destroyed but only abandoned as unnecessary because another hypothesis explains the case as well or better. It will not be difficult for the theory of Luke's dependence on Matthew to make better sense of Luke 9:51—18:18 than the Q hypothesis which, as we have seen, prefers to make little or none. It need only show that Luke's Christian Deuteronomy can be read as a re-ordering and editing of parts chosen by him from Matthew's gospel, according to the Deuteronomic scheme and to criteria integral to his theology and literary craftsmanship. The use of Deuteronomy as a framework so appropriate to Luke's debt to the Old Testament amalgamation of history, theology and ethics, which it exemplifies, has gone a long way towards this already. The matter must be taken further, not by prolonged polemic against Q, but by the happier and more rewarding path of understanding Luke. If we seek his doctrine in form and content, deliverance from Q will be added unto us.

The overall character of the section is easy to appreciate. It is a compendium of teaching, often interrupted by little narrative notes which are rarely more than one verse long but keep things on the move. This suits its position: not central but rather an interim or extended bridge between two centres. The transfiguration and the events surrounding it have crowned the narrative leading up to them by making clear Jesus's identity and mission. The Passion and the events surrounding it will again gather up all that has gone before and point the drama towards the future of Acts. Teaching finds its place between these two, like a beam supported by two great pillars[23]. In this it closely resembles Deuteronomy, its source, which also occupies an historical position between the past of the exodus and the future in the promised land, and consists of instruction which continually refers back and forth to these two definitive events.

Luke's basic strategy with Matthew fits this scheme. He cuts and redistributes the discourses to let the historical element flourish the more. We have already seen him abbreviating the Sermon on the Mount to a size which does less to distract attention from the narrative. So here Matthew's mission charge of 38 verses compares with Luke's of 15. And whereas Matthew leaves a major loose end in his story by telling us nothing of the success of the mission or even of the return of the missionaries, Luke does so in resounding style, greatly enhancing the historical particularity of the charge. Matthew's fifth discourse—a massive structure of three chapters— is divided into two main sections: the woes at Luke 11:42–52, and the eschatological prophecy at Luke 17:23–37. Other parts, such as the oracle against Jerusalem, are used elsewhere (Mt 23:37–39; Lk 13:34–35). The result of such breaking up is not a mess but a new creation: a single tract of teaching relieved by frequent and various narrative settings and enlivened by stories peculiar to Luke, such as the Good Samaritan, the Prodigal Son, the Unjust Steward, Martha and Mary, the Rich Man and Lazarus, the Pharisee and the Publican, which add so much vivacity, movement and body to the whole.

The tract Luke 9:51—18:14 also has its own thematic development. As we might expect of Luke, it is set in an historical order. First things are put first by a beginning with calls to discipleship. Last things are put last by a conclusion which teaches the coming of the kingdom and judgement. Hopes are thus raised that the intervening material is also in an historical order, and the hopes are fulfilled. The call of the disciples is followed by their successful mission, the basic things of the disciple's life are illustrated by the Good Samaritan loving his neighbour and Mary's love of God developing into teaching about prayer. Then, with its historical and spiritual basis established, the Beelzebub controversy brings the kingdom up against its enemies: a confrontation which is seen as an opposition of sound perception against the perverted and superficial vision of the Jewish leaders who are castigated in the woes which follow and prophesy the doom of the Jewish nation, rooted in its failure to see or react positively to the crisis. Luke shows the disciple's role in this world of dispute: trust, readiness, faithfulness and a clear head. From this fundamental contrast emerges the major theme of the historical problem of the Jewish nation, which comes into the open again at Luke 13:5ff. and gets covert dramatic treatment in the healings of the bent woman and the dropsical man, both polemically set on the sabbath day, and the parable of the Supper. The moral stories of the Prodigal Son and the Unjust Steward exemplify by contrast the positive reaction to crisis which the nation lacks. Judgement concludes the whole. The history of the beginning of Christianity thus underpins and shapes the whole section. The Church is called, sent, established, flung into controversy with the opposition, contrasted with the ancient people of God, and the whole story pointed towards judgement. Central to

144

it all is Luke's grand theme of the passing of religious initiative and authority from Israel to the Christian Church.

The imposition of a simple pattern of three on Matthean material is less important but a common feature of Luke's editing.

1) At Matthew 8:18–22 a scribe offers to follow Jesus and is warned of the rootless existence incurred. Then 'another of the disciples' is refused leave to bury his father before following. Luke adds a third who is refused leave to say goodbye to his household, thus contrasting with the source of this incident: 1 Kings 19:19–21, where Elijah allows his disciple Elisha to give a farewell feast.

2) Matthew 7:9f. is a pair of proverbs about asking: 'What man is there of you who, if his son shall ask him for a loaf, will give him a stone, or if he shall ask for a fish, will give him a serpent?' Luke adds a third 'Or if he shall ask for an egg, will he give him a scorpion?' (Lk 11:12). Mentions of scorpions are rare in scripture which makes it more striking that of the four in the Old Testament, one occurs at Deuteronomy 8:15: according to Evans, falling in the very section of Deuteronomy which is synoptically parallel to Luke 11:1–13 (though this particular parallelism escaped his notice).

3) The woes at Luke 11:42–52 are a major instance of Luke's editing of Matthew. First they are abbreviated from seven to six and then they are divided into two sections, against Pharisees and against lawyers: a procedure strongly remiscent of Luke's reduction of the blessings from seven to four, followed by a second section of four matching woes. Here the six are divided into three and three, but the same deliberate editorial hand is obviously at work.

4) At Matthew 5:25ff. the perils of litigation involve two officials—judge and officer. The parallel Luke 12:58f. has three: magistrate, judge and bailiff—unless 'magistrate' and 'judge' are synonyms.

5) Luke's edition of Matthew's Great Supper is memorable for the three invited guests with their three excuses for declining. In Matthew there are two who 'made light of it and went their ways, one to his farm, another to his merchandise', and a third category of 'the rest' who emulate Mark's tenants of the vineyard (Mk 12:3–5) by killing the Lord's servants. Luke's first two refusers follow Matthew's: the farm = the newly acquired field, the merchandise = the newly acquired oxen. Luke's third is the newly-wed, and he comes from the Old Testament. In Deuteronomy 20, according to Evans synoptically parallel to this parable in Luke, the newly betrothed man is excused military service. The use of direct speech in all these instances is also typical of Luke (Lk 14:15–24).

6) Luke 15 contains the grandest example of editing Matthew into a pattern of three. The chapter begins with the lost sheep, retold so as to make the central point a change of heart in the lost rather than the seeker's expedition. To this Luke can add with ease a second in the same mould, using his stock-in-trade of woman and money, and crown the whole with his version of Matthew's two sons (Mt 21:28–32) of whom one, in his version, is lost and found. Again two Matthean ingredients are spun into three, and again the third draws on the Old Testament.[24]

Six examples with a wide spread are enough to show a clear consistency of workmanship in Luke 9:51—18:14. Of the six, four of the third members which Luke adds to the material are borrowed from the Old Testament: one from the Elijah saga, one (the two brothers) from stories about brothers in Genesis together with legislation about them in Deuteronomy, and two from Deuteronomy. This points inexorably towards the consistency being Luke's, for these are among his favourite scriptures.

Still on the secondary scale, Luke's editing of Mark shows a particular fondness for the dinner table as a setting. He extended the debate over the supper which followed the call of Levi, and did the same with the incident of the woman with the ointment. He will amplify the tradition of the Last Supper by making it the occasion for a speech by Jesus on the nature and destiny of the Church. The writers of *Esther* and of the *Epistle of Aristeas* had also used banquets as scenery. Luke shows his affinity with these later Jewish story-tellers, and with the Jewish and gentile bourgeoisie of his own day for whom the meal was the occasion for high-minded religious and philosophical discussion, a setting which the Jewish Passover shared with Plato's symposium. In Luke 9:51—18:14 the table is an ideal vehicle for giving some historical actuality and particularity to didactic material in search of a setting· At Luke 11:37–52 it provides a background for teaching. Luke 14 opens with Jesus going 'into the house of one of the rulers of the Pharisees on a sabbath to eat bread'. The dropsical man is healed at table, etiquette for guests and hosts put forward as theological ethics (influenced by Matthew 23:6 in which the Pharisees are criticised for loving the chief place at feasts), and crowned by Matthew's banquet parable. At Luke 14:25 this setting seems to be abandoned, but it is referred to again at Luke 15:2 and plays a major role in the story of the rich man and Lazarus at Luke 16:19–31 and in the illustration of the servant as waiter at table at Luke 17:7–10. Only at Luke 17:11 is another scene of action clearly delineated: 'On the way to Jerusalem he was passing along between Samaria and Galilee.' There seems to be nothing to stop the reader imagining everything from 14:1 to 17:10 as table-talk having something of the character of a Christian symposium.

We have already seen that in the first two chapters of his Christian Deuteronomy, Luke uses much of Matthew's work and uses it in order. Further scrutiny will show that he deploys it according to deliberate purposes of his own which can be discovered elsewhere in his work. What follows now is therefore a commentary to show that the use of Matthew in this section is done according to the plan of Deuteronomy and with editing and connecting characteristic of Luke.

One of his purposes is to present Jesus as a prophet and the historical culmination of the old prophetic tradition. Evans considers this to be his main purpose, in particular Jesus's fulfilment of the destiny prophesied at Deuteronomy 18:18 that God would raise up a prophet like Moses from among Israel, and of Malachi 4:4–5 where in another great promise Elijah is linked with Moses and designated as the prophet who will come to convert the people before the great and terrible day of the Lord. Jesus is, for Luke, just such a new moral leader and just such a prophet of the end. He makes it concrete by giving him some of the characteristics of Moses and Elijah as his antetypes. This involved him in a contradiction of Mark when he edited his treatment of John the Baptist as Elijah-come-again. Of Mark's equation of the Baptist with Elijah there only remains Gabriel's prophecy that John will go before the Lord 'in the spirit and power of Elijah', making him more like the junior Elisha. When Jesus first appeared in public he made Elijah's tactics his own (Lk 4:25) and shared with Moses and Elijah the prophet's fate of rejection by his own people. The resurrection at Nain used Elijah typology in a bold and obvious fashion and ended with the unmistakable acclamation, 'a great prophet is arisen among us' (Lk 7:16). Nowhere is this Elijah typology, coupled with reference to Moses, stronger than at the outset of the Christian Deuteronomy—naturally enough since the transfiguration has just brought these two worthies onto the stage. At Luke 9:51 the days are near for Jesus to be received up like Elijah, and he sends messengers before his face like Moses (Ex 23:20). Incidents follow which compare Jesus with Elijah and mark differences. He refuses to emulate his antetype by calling down consuming fire (compare 2 K 1:10 and Si 48:1–14). The third of the would-be followers is treated less indulgently than Elisha by Elijah. Luke 9:51–62 is thus determined by Luke's historical typology, with Matthean material called in and expanded to fit it.

The mission of the seventy is driven by the sense of historical fulfilment and urgency generated in this previous section. Moses takes Elijah's place as the power behind the scenes: the leader of Israel who called in seventy elders to share his work (Nb 11:16ff. recalled at Dt 1:9ff.)[25] and sent forerunners ahead to blaze the trail for himself and the nation (compare Lk 10:1) who returned with fruits of harvest (Nb 13:23f. recalled at Dt 1:25). In spite of these good auguries, the Israelites were afraid to go forward because of the hostile men and cities in their path. However, after much wrangling they advanced with instructions to buy food and drink from the inhabitants of the land as they went. Sihon and Og resisted and their cities were detroyed. The Lord made his nation's cause his own ('The Lord your God who fights for you', Dt 3:22). Luke's selection of Matthean material is governed by this typology. Matthew 10 is the main source combined with the last two verses of Matthew 9 and the five verses (20–24) about doomed cities in Matthew 11. Having made the twelve spies of Deuteronomy 1:23 into the seventy delegates of Numbers 11:16ff., he first puts down a verse of his own to marry with the pioneering spies of Deuteronomy 1:23 and 24; 'He sent them two and two before his face into every city and place whither he himself was about to come' (Lk 10:1). Going on mission in pairs is to be the strategy in Acts. His first direct use of Matthew is in the next verse where he quotes Matthew 9:37–38 for its reference to harvest, which chimes with the fruit of the land brought back by the spies. Matthew 10:16 then provides a reference to hostility ('I send you forth as sheep among wolves') and Matthew 10:9–14 a guide to tactics to which Luke adds instruction about eating and drinking (compare Dt 2:28). The fate of hostile cities comes next in Matthew (Mt 10:15) with which Luke couples Matthew 11:21–23 which is on the same theme. Luke follows it, crowning the speech with a version of Matthew 10:40 ('He that receiveth you receiveth me . . .'), characteristically adding the negative of rejection in line with the theology first presented in the Magnificat, and also fitting with the resistance put up by Sihon and Og against God and Israel.

At this point in Luke the seventy go and come back and Jesus celebrates their victory. The narrative interjection splits Matthew

11:21–27 into two parts at the junction of verses 24 and 25. 'In that same hour' Jesus thanks the Father (Lk 10:21) which quotes both Matthew 11:25 and Deuteronomy 3:23 where Moses 'prayed to the Lord at that time'. The subsequent jump forward at Luke 10:23 to Matthew 13:16f. is explained by Deuteronomy 4:36, where Moses reminds the people that they have enjoyed the singular privilege of hearing God's voice and seeing his fire: Matthew's 'blessed are your eyes for they see and your ears for they hear' is appropriate and needs only an object for the seeing: 'blessed are the eyes which see the things that ye see'. So Luke's use of Matthew from 9:15—10:24 is done according to a well-articulated scheme as accessible to us as it was to him—the moralised history of Deuteronomy. The new people of God sets out to possess its destiny after the pattern of the old, and in doing so gets a foretaste of a greater future.

The long section devoted to the mission of the seventy is followed by the lawyer's question, answered by the summary of the law and the tale of the Good Samaritan. Emphasis switches from history to morals—but still morals in the form of story—with Luke making a great leap in his use of Matthew to Matthew 22:34–40 (with memories of Mark's version creeping in, e.g. 'strength' at Lk 10:27). Seen simply as editing of Matthew, this is arbitrary. Seen as editing of Matthew according to the scheme of Deuteronomy it makes perfect sense, for at Deuteronomy 5 Moses's historical recollections turn more strongly to ethics as he rehearses the Ten Commandments and gives a summary of them at 6:4. It is this summary which accounts for Luke's leap to Matthew 22:34–40 where it is quoted by Jesus in answer to a Lawyer's question, tilted by Luke from the rabbinic interest of 'what is the great commandment in the law?' to the more practical 'what shall I do to inherit eternal life?' which also reverts to Deuteronomy's insistence on the commandments as conditions of the inheritance of the land. The tale of the Good Samaritan then dramatises in characteristic Lukan fashion the love of neighbour;[26] and the story of Martha and Mary, the love of God. Martha is as busy with her serving as the Israelites were in gathering manna, and Deuteronomy 8 dwells on the perils of being so occupied with material things as to forget the primary lesson of attention to God's word (Dt 8:3, 14, 19). The Good Samaritan and Martha and Mary thus make a pair of stories interpreting Matthew's double commandment drawn from Deuteronomy to love God and neighbour. Mary's good part develops naturally into teaching about prayer for which the obvious Matthean materials are Matthew

6:9–13 (the 'Our Father'), and Matthew 7:7–11 (about asking, receiving and giving). God's providence is the object of prayer here as it is the subject of Deuteronomy 8. Luke needs little prompting to devote a section to prayer and embellish it with his story of the friend asking for bread at night, a *midrash* which gives dramatic body to the Matthean petition for bread, and makes a little story out of Matthew's 'ask and it shall be given to you' (Mt 7:7). Prayer is a favourite topic with him, as his editorial additions depicting Jesus at prayer testify (Lk 3:21; 5:16; 6:12; 9:18; 9:28; 11:1). It is the primary bond between God and his people (see Lk 1:10 where 'the whole multitude of the people' first appears at the outset of Luke's work 'praying'). His editing of Matthew's Lord's Prayer is consistent with his practice elsewhere. He omits 'Thy will be done' just as he omits reference to the will of God at Matthew 7:21/Luke 6:46; Matthew 12:50/Luke 8:21; Matthew 18:14/Luke 15:7; Matthew 21:31/Luke 15:11–32. He changes debts to sins, a word he uses eleven times against Matthew's seven and Mark's six, but leaves 'indebted' to betray his use of Matthew. He omits 'the evil one' here as elsewhere in his use of Matthew (Matthew 5:37 and 39 have no parallel in his work).

Next comes a controversy about casting out devils. It begins with a version of the cure of a dumb demoniac at Matthew 9:32–34 and Luke 11:14f. The reference in the last of these verses of Matthew to the Prince of the Devils naturally leads into the material from Matthew 12:24–30, and thence to verses 43:45 of the same chapter which depict the dangers of worse possession. The obvious question is why Luke should have jumped from the discussion of prayer to this aggressive controversy with obstinate opponents about the overthrow of evil forces. Yet again Deuteronomy gives the answer. From 9:1 to 10:11 it deals with the twin themes of the conquest of hostile forces (like the gigantic sons of Anak) and with controversy between God, Moses and the obdurate people. Some connection between Luke and Deuteronomy here has long been acknowledged, the singular phrase at Luke 11:20 'the finger of God' occurring elsewhere in scripture only at Deuteronomy 9:10; Exodus 31:18, and at Exodus 8:19. The link with Deuteronomy is made the stronger by the coincidence of themes. Luke first selects from Matthew 12:22–45 the material which deals directly with the conquest of demons: Matthew 12:24–30 and 43–45.[27] The saying about signs which comes between these two sections in Matthew (at Mt 12:38–42) will be used directly after the teaching about obedience which in Luke, as in Matthew, follows upon the comparison of the exorcised men with an empty house. The two versions of this doctrine of obedience are:

Matthew 12:46–50	Luke 11:27–28
'While he was yet speaking to the multitudes, behold his mother and his brethren stood without seeking to speak to him, and one said unto him "Behold thy mother and thy brethren stand without seeking to speak to thee," but he answered and said unto him that told him "who is my mother and who are my brethren?" And he stretched forth his hand towards his disciples and said, "Behold my mother and my brethren, for whosoever shall do the will of my father which is in heaven, he is my brother and sister and mother." '	'And it came to pass as he said these things a certain woman out of the multitude lifted up her voice and said unto him "Blessed is the womb that bare thee and the breasts which thou didst suck," but he said, "yea, rather blessed are they that hear the word of God and keep it." '

Both are about the primacy of obedience to God over ties of kinship and use a contrast between the ties of family and of religion. Characteristically Luke has made the speaker 'a certain woman of the multitude' who utters a blessing on Jesus's mother and her womb which echoes Elizabeth's 'blessed art thou among women and blessed is the fruit of thy womb' (Lk 1:42).

The postponed polemic about a sign (Mt 12:38–42) comes next. Here Luke's distinctive contribution is his different view of the significance of Jonah:

Matthew 12:40	Luke 11:30
'For as Jonah was three days and three nights in the belly of the whale, so shall the Son of man be three days and three nights in the heart of the earth.'	'For even as Jonah became a sign unto the Ninevites, so shall also the Son of man be to this generation.'

There is no reason to suppose that Luke has the earlier or Q version here; rather the contrary. Matthew's is characteristically allegorised and apologetic. Luke's is resoundingly harmonious with his major doctrine of Jesus as the unheeded prophet of repentance to the Jewish nation of his time. Signs are as constantly given to Israel as they are constantly ignored.

The verses about light which follow are from Matthew 5:15 *via* Luke 8:16 and Matthew 6:22. Doctrine in a nutshell travels fast and far. Luke's editing widens the radiance of the light from those in the house to those outside—the lamp is put on a stand so that people may see and enter. Luke 11:36 then describes the inner illumination of perfect sight. The wider world and the individual count for more than Matthew's ecclesiastical household. The passage goes well with Deuteronomy 10:2–11, which rehearses the signs which Israel saw when God delivered her from Egypt and insists upon inner obedience to his law which 'shall be for frontlets between your eyes' (Dt 11:18)—and so at the centre of vision. Deuteronomy goes on in Chapter 12 to command the cleansing of the land from the objects of false religion, the offering of tithes and sacrifices and regulations about blood. Luke's attention thus turns to Matthew's great diatribe against false religion, the attack on the Pharisees and Scribes in Matthew 23. He adds the saying about giving for alms 'the things which are within' (Lk 11:41), which goes well with his doctrine of the kingdom 'within' (Lk 17:21). The first extract from Matthew 23 which he uses (Mt 23:25–26) is about false cleansing and false piety. The next, Matthew 23:23, is about tithing. His characteristic re-ordering of the woes has already been noticed (p. 135). He singles out for emphasis the third against the lawyers which fixes on them the guilt for the blood of the prophets, adding the historical 'from the foundation of the world' and repeating Matthew's 'this generation'. Again Matthew's historical perspective is strengthened and refined.

To Luke's mind one of the greatest treasures of Matthew's gospel is its insistence on the inwardness of true religion, contrasted with misleading outward appearance. He exploits it in terms of his interest in what goes on in people's minds, and his conviction that at this central point the religiously suspect are nearer to God than the religiously respectable. The soliloquies of the Prodigal Son and the Unjust Steward, the penitence of the Sinful Woman and of Zacchaeus are classical instances of it. In his rearrangement of Matthean material, he has already followed the teaching about a sign for this generation (Mt 12:38–42/Lk 11:29–32) with the teaching about perception (Mt 6:22–23/Lk 11:33–36), thus earthing the large-scale problem in the human heart. So here the woes are followed by material in which the secret things of the mind interact with public events. Hidden hypocrisy (Mt 16:5–6/Lk 12:1) will out (Mt 10:26–27/Lk 12:2–3). Hidden faith and trust (Mt 10:28–31/

Lk 12:4–7) will also have its moments of disclosure, both at the last day (Mt 10:32–33/Lk 12:10, 8–9) and when Christians are brought to trial (Mt 10:17/Lk 12:11–12)—two crises of revelation which hinge upon obedience to the Holy Spirit (Mt 12:31–32/Lk 12:10). This ransacking of Matthew, some of it probably from memory and some from selective perusal of Matthew 10 and 12, is done to a logical scheme. This generation seeks a sign, but the only sign given is a call to repentance. It is a light which they cannot see because of their studied neglect of the inward side of things, which will, however, come to light in the course of history, when vengeance descends on the Jewish nation for its obduracy, and the Christian disciples make their true confession in confidence.

The switch to instruction about the uses of prosperity is explained (as we may expect by now) by the scheme of Deuteronomy which, in Chapter 12, looks forward to affluence in the inheritance of the land of promise and warns against the accompanying danger of slackness towards God. The minatory example of the rich fool opens Luke's discussion on the cue of a request to Jesus to adjudicate over an inheritance. The protagonist of the parable is typical in his wealth and his soliloquy, a thoroughly biblical fool in his forgetfulness of God (Ps 14:1; Pr *passim*). Matthew has had a hand in his midrashic portrayal. Unlike the trusting birds of Matthew 6:26, he reaps and gathers into barns. He flouts the teaching of Matthew 6:20 by laying up treasure on earth, not in heaven, and setting his heart upon it. Luke has made Matthew's moral instruction about worldliness and wealth into a story, just as he did with Matthew's teaching about asking. The story over, sections from Matthew 6 are quoted outright as the perfect commentary, to which Luke adds snippets from the eschatological Matthew 24 and 25 to point the fool's unreadiness for God's interruption of his careless ease. First comes his version of Matthew 6:25–34 and 19–21 at Luke 12:22–34. Then at 12:35–36 he recalls the wise and foolish virgins of Matthew 25:1–13 ('Let your loins be girded and your lamps burning'). The watchful servant has, as his reward for obeying the command of Matthew 24:42 ('watch therefore for ye know not on what day your Lord cometh'), the characteristically Lukan privilege of sitting down to table, waited upon by his Lord—an image which John 13:1–11 will exploit more memorably. The despoiled householder of Matthew 24:43–44 and Luke 12:39f. recalls the rich fool again. The same passage of Matthew, interrupted by a question from Peter, continues to descant upon the theme of preparedness

(Mt 24:45–51; Lk 12:41–48) which so occupies Luke with his sense of living in a long interim between two comings of Christ: a time of disciplines which Matthew had done so much to define. Matthew's ferocious temperament and black-and-white morality rejoiced to depict the exclusion of the reprobate. Luke, more aware of the greys of human existence, carefully reflects that there are reprobates and reprobates: some inexcusable because of their knowledge of the right, some less culpable because of their ignorance. He lives in a more pluralistic world than his predecessor, and adds his verses 47 and 48 accordingly and in line with the teaching of Amos 3 which promises particularly severe retribution for Israel precisely because God has known her and declared his will to her by prophets.

This strongly eschatological teaching needs, in Luke's view, balancing by reference to history. He is never against the eschatology or even the apocalyptic of his predecessors, but always concerned to earth it in history as a safeguard against fanatical explosions. 'You shall not listen to the words of that prophet or that dreamer of dreams, for the Lord your God is testing you', says Deuteronomy 13:3, and there is no doubt about the sort of prophet whom Luke distrusted, nor of what was for him the supreme trial. Verses 49 (recalling Elijah's fire-raising) and 50 are about the trials of Jesus's present. Verses 51 to 53 draw on Matthew 10:34–36 and are about the trials which beset the Christian reader of his time. The latter is characterised by divisions within families, echoing Deuteronomy 13:6–11, where members of a man's own family entice him from the worship of God.

Eschatology and repentance go together in Matthew from the preaching of the Baptist to Jesus's last discourse. The exhortation to repentance which now follows in Luke from 12:54 to 13:9 is thus a natural development for a mind permeated by Matthew's teaching. Luke gives his own twist to Matthew's doctrine of repentance, grounding it in historical perception—that ability to notice that the hour of destiny has struck which the rich fool so conspicuously lacked, which the faithful servant possessed and which the prodigal son and the unjust steward will exhibit splendidly. He uses two scraps of Matthew for this purpose: the weather lore of Matthew 16:2–3 changed by a more urban outlook and particularised from 'the times' to 'this time', and the injunction to be reconciled with one's adversary before the judgement falls (Mt 5:25–26; Lk 12:58f.). This latter is changed in its bearing by its change of context. Instead of referring directly to private behaviour, it is put on the public stage of history as a parable. It is likely that in Luke's mind, haunted by A.D. 70, the parties are the Jewish nation and Rome.

Deuteronomy 13:12–18 orders the destruction of any city which has gone after other gods, thus providing a connection between misfortune and sin which is the background for the discussion at Luke 13:1–5 of two disasters: the massacre of Galileans and the fall of the tower at Siloam. The phrase 'all the inhabitants' (πάντας τοὺς κατοικοῦντας) occurs at Deuteronomy 13:15 and at Luke 13:4. Luke's interpretation of Deuteronomy's commandment to destroy is both more tolerant and more universal in scope. It is not that those who perish are alone guilty; repentance is required of the fortunate too. The subsequent parable of the fig tree is another instance of interpretation more sophisticated than the material on which it works. In Mark and Matthew the fig tree is an acted miracle and a prophetic sign, signifying the doom of a fruitless nation. But turning it into a parable, Luke exonerates Jesus from apparently arbitrary and violent behaviour—and adds the year's grace. The fruit which the tree may yet bear is the fruit of repentance from Matthew 3:8. History and patience make a typically Lukan difference.

The light follows upon the dark, the release of the bent women (as 'daughter of Abraham' standing for the nation) upon the warnings of doom. The theme of release coincides with Deuteronomy 15:1–18 which deals with releases from debt and slavery. Set controversially (and in line with synoptic tradition) on a sabbath day and in a synagogue, it calls to mind Jesus's reply to those who had objected to his healing the man with a withered hand on the sabbath at Matthew 12:9–13—they would not hesitate to release animals on the sabbath. Matthew's sheep in a pit becomes an ox and an ass in a stall. The miracle is followed by the little parables of the mustard seed and the leaven from Matthew 13:31–33, which serve to make clear that the judgement and release acted out in the healing have more than a limited reference. They are prophetic, the germ and the yeast of more to come. As ever, Luke uses a story as a tableau to dramatise the teaching and point to the future. He has made this story out of the Christian and Jewish literature available to him. The tradition of healings on the sabbath and in synagogue in Mark and Matthew is filled out with the Old Testament materials we have noticed, to which may be added Isaiah's promise that the crooked would be made straight (Is 40:4), and the doctrine of the Psalms that 'the Lord raises up all who are bowed down'

(Ps 145:14 and 146:8: ἀνορθός in both cases and ἀνορθόω here at verse 13).

The pattern of few and many (the daughter of Abraham and the destiny of all his descendants, the seed and the tree, the yeast and the loaf) continues into the next section with the question, 'Lord are they few that be saved?' The answer is a collection of texts from Matthew 7—8 about the conditions of inclusion in the kingdom and exclusion from it—all subtly changed by Luke's subsuming them under his great theme of salvation in the course of history which takes over from Matthew's theme of the kingdom at the end of time. The coming of people from afar to sit down in the kingdom must, to him, be a prophecy of Acts rather than of the last judgement. The teaching is framed by reference to Jerusalem. At the outset it is noticed that Jesus is 'journeying on unto Jerusalem', and at the end comes the prophecy against the city from Matthew 23:37-39 at Luke 13:34. Deuteronomy gives the reason. In chapter 16 it commands attendance at the three great pilgrim feasts of Jerusalem, 'the place which the Lord your God will choose to make his name dwell there'. In chapter 17:2-7 it commands the death by stoning of the evil doer: a strongly ironical background to the stoning of God's emissaries in Matthew 23:37 and Luke 13:34. Deuteronomy goes on to describe the functions of authority, judges and ruler (ἄρχων). The people have a duty to abide by their decisions and they have a duty to obey God and not be lifted up above the brethren. Again Deuteronomy gives a setting to Luke's narrative where we now see Jesus at table in the house of a ruler (τῶν ἀρχόντων) of the Pharisees, battling with biased judicial authority over his right to heal a dropsical man on the sabbath. The miracle story itself is extremely slight, the man's complaint and cure being dealt with in a verse and half a verse. It is the controversy about the use and abuse of authority that counts, and carries over into the parables of seats at table which is aimed at those who seek to be lifted up above the rest. The connection of Pharisees with chief seats at feasts is given by Matthew 23:6. Again Matthew's sheep in a pit is altered, this time to an ox in a well which makes a connection with the ox and the ass which were referred to in the healing of the bent woman. These two sabbath miracles thus include the same Matthean saying in their construction. The table setting of the miracle is exploited in the sayings which follow: Luke's theology of reversal coming in the secular, not to say bourgeois, vehicle of etiquette. The provision of food for the Levites as described in

Deuteronomy 18:1–5 has roused Luke to this congenial theme, and Proverbs 25:6 is the source:

> 'Do not put yourself forward in the king's presence,
>   or stand in the place of the great.
> For it is better to be told "come up here"
>   than to be put lower in the presence of the prince.'[28]

The advice to hosts, with its orientation towards the resurrection of the just, is a trailer for the story of the rich man and Lazarus. It is virtually inevitable that Matthew's parable of the great feast (Mt 22:1–14), suitably edited with the reference to Deuteronomy 20,[29] should follow. Matthew's ferociously discordant ending is reduced to 'none of these men which were bidden shall taste of my supper', substituting a prophecy of the exclusion of Israel for Matthew's draconian parable of Church discipline, the expulsion of the improperly dressed guest. As so often the sense of history determines Luke's editing. It is also clear that, unlike Matthew and like ben Sirach, Luke moves in a world where dinner parties are a recognised form of hospitality given by ordinary people, and not the fabulous and dangerous banquets of despots.

With the change of setting from the table to the road the teaching turns to emphasise the strictness of discipleship—'the Way' of Acts 19:23 and 22:4. A man must hate this kindred and take up his cross. The directions about recruitment for battle in Deuteronomy 20 give the cue, particularly Deuteronomy 20:8: 'and the officers shall speak further to the people and say "what man is there that is fearful and faint-hearted? Let him go back to his house, lest the heart of his fellows melt as his heart." ' To a mind soaked in Matthew, such a text could bring to mind the stern summons of Matthew 10:37f., 'He that loveth father or mother more than me is not worthy of me, and he that loveth son or daughter more than me is not worthy of me.' In the illustration of the tower builder, Luke gives Matthew a characteristically graphic and down-to-earth interpretation. The strictness is not arbitrary or exaggerated. There is a price to pay for discipleship as for any momentous enterprise. The tower of Babel, that archetypal biblical erection, is in mind. The Deuteronomic setting of war emerges in the next illustration—the making of a treaty. 'When you draw near to a city to fight against it, offer terms of peace to it' (Deuteronomy 20:10) is reflected in Luke's 'He sendeth an ambassage and asketh conditions of peace.' Matthew's 'make friends with your adversary' could well be at work again, but we are now decidedly in a part of Luke's gospel where Matthew is an influence behind the scenes, rather than a text to be copied and edited. His influence is pervasive certainly, but less than direct.

Chapter 15 continues the theme of repentance which has been running for a long time now, and brings it to a definitive, secularised clarity. It is one of the chief glories of Luke's gospel and here the tale of the two sons shows his narrative skills at their very best. But it is no more a creation out of nothing than any of his work. Deuteronomy 21:15—22:4 shows itself plainly as a source. It is concerned with the division of inheritance between two sons, emphasising the right of the first born, even when he is the son of a less-beloved wife, commanding the stoning of any son who is disobedient, riotous and drunken, and giving rules for the reclaiming of lost property—ox, sheep, ass or garment. Deuteronomy's lost sheep cannot but recall Matthew's (Mt 18:12–13), which is edited to suit Luke's continual preoccupation with repentance. Matthew's interest was more in the shepherd; Luke's is more in the sheep. So he adds his verse 7: 'I say unto you that even so there shall be joy in heaven over one sinner that repenteth more than over ninety and nine righteous persons which need no repentance' a considerable and very characteristic amplification of Matthew's 'He rejoiceth more than over the ninety and nine which have not gone astray'. It is easy to add a second instance; indeed the reader can probably make up two or three more of his own using the same simple pattern. Luke's is marked by two of his commonest interests: a woman to pair with the man (as with Zechariah and Mary, Simeon and Anna, the bent woman and the dropsical man, etc.) and money. Matthew's lost sheep is the source for Luke's lost coin. But the second parable increases a difficulty. Do sheep repent? Does, still more absurdly, a coin? Repentance is something done by people, and the people presented by Deuteronomy at this point are sons: the son of the beloved wife and the son of the hated wife, the son who riots and drinks. Again, inevitably and immediately, a parable by Matthew, the two sons of Matthew 21:28–31 springs to mind. It opens the fascinating possibility that things may not be as black and white as the Deuteronomist thinks. The apparently disobedient son in Matthew turns out obedient, and *vice versa*. Matthew put it baldly. Luke wonders, as ever, what internal communings and reversal would have made it so, and finds the answer in the forefront of his mind—repentance. The problem set by the sheep and the coin is thus triumphantly solved by the two sons; one obdurate for all his virtue—the other penitent for all his vices. A tale emerges which is spun out of Deuteronomic and Matthean yarns with enrichments from ancient scripture (see pp. 75–77).

The happiness of a writer in his stride shines through Luke 15, and carries into the next chapter. The tale of the cunning steward takes to outrageous lengths the evangelist's conviction, so graphically presented by the contrast of the two sons, that the wicked may well have more to be said for them than the virtuous because God is 'kind towards the unthankful and evil'—and particularly the intelligently penitent. 'The sons of this world are, for their own generation, wiser than the sons of light' because they can recognise a crisis when they see it and take effective evasive action. They can repent. Deuteronomy speaks at 23:15–16 of the slave who has left his master and his right to be received 'into other houses'. At 23:19–20 it condemns usury. Luke tells of a servant caught out in his negligence, like the servant of Matthew 24:48–51, who, with the greater resourcefulness common amongst Luke's bad characters, debates with himself what to do so that 'when I am put out of the stewardship they receive me into their houses'. He decides to ingratiate himself with his master's debtors by cutting drastically the returns that the master expected from his transactions (according to Derrett,[30] usurious). So the rich man suffers in his pocket, the poor are relieved—and all because a resilient rogue makes a sharp change of mind and plan in the face of a crisis. There could hardly be a happier combination of Luke's favourite concerns. Matthew's contribution is from 24:45f.: 'Who then is the faithful and wise servant whom his Lord hath set over his household to give them their food in due season? Blessed is that servant whom the Lord, when he cometh, shall find so doing', coupled with the bad and negligent servant of the following verses (see above). To this Luke owes his characters: the lord, major domo, and those under him to whom he gives provisions—but with what a Lukan difference! He has already used this piece of Matthew at Luke 12:42. Only there, and here at 16:8, does he use the adjective φρόνιμος (wise). Matthew uses it seven times. It never occurs in Mark. The discovery of this Matthean source solves the minor problem of the identity of the lord who commends the steward. It is the same lord as Luke refers to in verses 3 and 5; as in Matthew, the lord of the estate, not Jesus, the Lord of the Church.

A salvo of maxims follows the tale which could as well be a sign of high spirits as of the embarrassment which has sometimes been posited as its motive. Such collections of short injunctions are a feature of Deuteronomy (e.g. 23:15–25; 24:5–9) and of Luke (e.g. 6:37–45; 12:1–12). Here the first two are apt comments on the tale. The others are about faithfulness which is the prime virtue of a steward in 1 Corinthians 4:2 (an additional source?), but connects only very loosely with what has gone before in Luke, more exactly with the parallel instruction at Deuteronomy 23:21–23 about being faithful to promises. Matthew is the source of Luke 16:13 (two masters), and of the sayings against the Pharisees at Luke 16:14–18. But the order is so random (Mt 6:24; 11:12; 5:18; 5:32) that Luke must be quoting Matthew's portable apophthegms from memory. The charge that the Pharisees justify themselves in the sight of men is the essence of Matthew's tirades against them. Verse 16 is famous as a foundation-stone of Conzelmann's theory of Luke's historical distinctions. It certainly clarifies the obscurity of Matthew 11:12 and 13 into a sharper historical diagram. The difference is in context. In Matthew the saying is set in a discussion of the Baptist's status. Here it defends, against Pharisaic attack, the rough and ready entrance into the kingdom which the tale of the steward has presented. Even if we allow some weight to the idea that Luke is somewhat embarrassed as well as exhilarated by his own daring in telling the tale of the Unjust Steward, it does not follow that the story is not his own. Every writer has had the experience of an enthusiasm taking him beyond the bounds of prudence and subsequently taking steps to ward off misunderstanding. So Luke 16:17 adds a *caveat*: the story is not a licence for antinomianism. The law has eternal authority. The apparently contradictory views found in the parable and in the teaching appended to it are both integral to the writer of Luke–Acts who tells the expansion of Christianity in terms of the free admission of all sorts and conditions of men, but without the uncompromising dispensation from the law insisted upon in Galatians. This is facilitated by the vaguer concept of the law which distinguishes Luke from Matthew and Paul.

The rule about divorce is put here because it comes here in Deuteronomy (24:1–4). It is an amalgam of Mark and Matthew, without Matthew's exception clause or Mark's reference to divorce by the wife, and shorter than either. Sexuality is far from being one of Luke's favourite themes (compare his omission of Matthew 5:27 and 19:12) and it is probably thanks to Deuteronomy that Luke retails this regulation at all.

After marriage and divorce Deuteronomy turns, at 24:6, to the rights of the poor and the duties of the rich towards them. So does Luke, with his tale of a rich man and a beggar (Lk 16:19–31). The leading source is a folk story about the reversal of the fortunes of rich and poor beyond the grave—preserved here and on an Egyptian papyrus of the first century.[31] It is so thoroughly congenial to Luke's biblical theology that it is not surprising that it should enter Christian tradition in his gospel, edited and decorated with Matthean features and touches of his own. Matthew 25:31–46 looms over it all: the last assize which condemns carelessness of the hungry, thirsty, naked, sick and imprisoned. But, as always in Luke's hands, the present bearing of eschatology is more strongly and graphically emphasised. In his view a man comes to judgement with his own individual death (see Lk 12:20 and 23:43). The dogs and the crumbs from the table are from the pleading of the Canaanite woman: 'even the dogs eat of the crumbs which fall from the master's table' (Mt 15:27, not Mk 7:28 where they are 'the children's crumbs'). Matthew's hell as a torture chamber here makes its only appearance in Luke. Unmistakable signs of his own hand, besides the grand theological message, are the opulent dinner-table setting, the central presence of his favourite Abraham in paradise (in Matthew's assize it is the Son of Man), angels, septuagintal turns of phrase such as 'lifted up his eyes' and 'and beside all this', references to Greek literature (see Creed p. 213) and to 'Moses and the prophets' as at Luke 24:27, the refusal to be convinced by resurrection which Paul will struggle with in Acts (23:6; 24:21; 26:8), the emphasis on repentance, the number five and the rich man's prayer.

Matthew 18, about care of the brethren, provides a quarry of morals to append to the tale. The new context changes their function from Matthew's concern for the Church to Luke's wider humanism. He chooses those which fit the occasion by condemning those who do not care for the 'little ones' and commanding repentance. He intrudes his favourite 'take heed to yourselves' (see Lk 12:1 and 21:34) and, as usual, reduces Matthew's numbers—from 'seventy times seven' to the more practically manageable 'seven times a day' (he uses 'day' twice as often as Matthew). As with the morals attached to the Unjust Steward, relevance diminishes with distance. Matthew's doctrine of continual forgiveness does not entirely fit the single change of heart required of the rich man's brothers. The subsequent teaching about faith depends on an artificial connection

—the apostles ask for an increase of it to cope with the stringent demands put before them. Luke does not have a developed notion of faith. As a ground for miracle he inherits it from Mark and Matthew. To these instances he adds the prayer of Jesus at Luke 22:32 that Simon's 'faith fail not', which seems to subsume it under his more cherished virtues of patience and perseverance. Here, his editing of Matthew's saying about faith (Mt 21:21; Lk 17:6) is curious in the extreme. He seems to have jumbled together in his mind (he can scarcely be working from the text) two Matthean instances: the faith as small as a mustard seed which could yet move a mountain (Mt 17:20), and the faith which would not only do what the master had done to the fig tree (συκῆ) but also uproot a mountain and throw it into the sea (Mt 21:21). Recollecting the συκῆ Luke substitutes a συκάμινος tree for the mountain and ends up with it planted in the sea—which must count as one of the most absurd casualties of *midrash*. To confirm that Luke is flagging after his major efforts at 15:1—16:31 we notice that the illustration of the servant waiting on his master has no discernible connection with what has gone before. Deuteronomy may be responsible, with its teaching at 24:14f. about the hired labourer's right to his wages before sundown. The well-to-do table setting and appeal to social degree show Luke at his most complacently bourgeois. The teaching is the sort that would come from the top of his head and the sober moral is a counterpoise to the extravagant teaching about faith: 'we have done that which it was our duty to do'. 'Unprofitable servants' is a memory of Matthew 25:30 (the end of the parable of the talents).

Looseness of connection continues to perplex the reader as he moves to the incident of the ten lepers. Editorially, this is the dark before the dawn, the flagging of energy before the last stretch such as we noticed in the Sermon on the Plain. After it eschatology and prayer will combine to make a tighter scheme. The miracle is an extra dramatisation of the words of Jesus about the centurion at Matthew 8:10 and Luke 7:9: 'I have not found so great faith, no, not in Israel.' Matthew is again the power behind the scene. Deuteronomy is here (Dt 24:17–22) concerned with the welfare of the stranger. Like the other miracles in Luke's Christian Deuteronomy, it is an allusive *midrash*. The single leper of Mark 1:40–45, Matthew 8:1–4 and Luke 5:12–16 is the obvious source, altered so that the ten are cleansed *en route* to obey the requirements of Leviticus 13:49f.: a symptom of Luke's regard for the law (see

Lk 16:17 and Ac *passim*). The petition 'have mercy on us' is drawn from the two blind men of Matthew 20:30 ('have mercy' occurs once in Mark, four times in Matthew, and three times in Luke, and so can be called a Matthean phrase). 'Thy faith hath saved thee' is a verdict on suppliants in Mark: the bleeding woman at Mark 5:34 and blind Bartimaeus at Mark 10:52. Luke uses it of the sinful woman (Lk 7:50), of the bleeding woman (Lk 8:48), of the blind man (Lk 18:42) and here—thus adding two uses to Mark's. Matthew has it only once (9:22). The Septuagint contributes reminiscence of the healing of Naaman the alien leper (2 K 5), though in accordance with his grand strategy Luke in his gospel prefers a Samaritan on the fringe of Judaism to a rank outsider. The most striking Lukanisms are the Samaritan and his glorifying and thanking God. It is, as Creed (*ad loc.*) says, 'an ideal scene'.

The Christian Deuteronomy ends with eschatology and judgement. This is just what one would expect of a writer nurtured on Mark with the apocalyptic Chapter 13 as Jesus's last discourse, and on Matthew with his expanded version of it. Deuteronomy itself points in its later chapters more strongly than ever towards the future, with many curses upon disobedience and blessings on obedience. A selection from Matthew 24 is introduced by the Pharisees' question 'when the kingdom of God will come'. Jesus answers that it will not come by observation to be pin-pointed here or there; it is 'within you' or 'among you'. This striking and singular phrase may be a version of Matthew's 'wherever two or three are gathered together in my name, there am I in the midst of them' (Mt 18:20), and so a definition of Luke's belief in the immanence of God's work within the commerce of history and everyday life—and even within the ordinary workings of the minds of 'the men of this world'. The saying goes well with another peculiar to Luke—about giving as alms 'the things which are within' (Lk 11:41). But if he is the initiator (and John the perfector) of the realised eschatology which Dodd tried to read back into his predecessors, he is still, unlike John, a convinced futurist: the N.E.B. margin allows the translation 'suddenly the kingdom of God will be among you'. The selection from Matthew 24 which follows witnesses to Luke's continued faith in futuristic eschatology. He picks extracts which dampen the fires of expectation without denying the doctrine of the last day by telling of that unpredictable suddenness which debars speculation. The first saying is his own and sets the tone: 'Ye shall desire to see one of the days of the Son of Man, and ye shall not see it.' Impatience will arise, but will achieve nothing. To Matthew's Old Testament historical reference to Noah, he adds Lot, repeating 'they ate, they drank' and appending Lot's wife as a warning against turning back. Deuteronomy 24:19–21 forbids turning back to pick up the gleanings of harvest which must be left for the poor.

Next, Deuteronomy insists upon the judge's duty to condemn the guilty and to acquit the innocent, setting Luke to his more sophisticated parable about the godless judge who did justice out of self-interest. We have seen him mixing the blacks and whites of Deuteronomy into grey before. The parable is an obvious pair with the friend at midnight (Lk 11:5–13), having the same construction—the grudging giving of men as a shadow of God's generosity. Verses 6–8 turn it to eschatological reference. The widow's pleadings are like the prayers of the elect for vindication. They will be heard— but will the elect hold out? The parable is thus not primarily about prayer but about waiting for the end. Prayer is all that the elect can do in the meanwhile, and the next parable shows how it should be done. Deuteronomy 26:12–16 has the dutiful Jew rehearsing the details of his obedience before God: 'I have given the tithe. . . . I have not transgressed any of thy commandments.' So does the Pharisee, adding with pride that this distinguishes him from the ruck of humanity. Matthew's critique of ostentatious Pharisaic piety included a contrast of its love of publicity with the privacy of the true disciple's prayer to the father in secret (Mt 6:6). Luke's parable makes a more graphic contrast between Pharisaic self-congratulation and true penitence. The prodigal son and his brother are called to mind. Matthew, to whom Luke owes so much of his doctrine of repentance and reversal, is given the last word—his doctrine again characteristically turned into a little story.

5. *Historical Development in Matthew*

Historicising has emerged as Luke's main editorial activity in dealing with material from Matthew—as it was with his treatment of Mark. He reduces or breaks up the five big discourses which hold up Matthew's action. He intersperses stories and incidents which have grown midrashically out of his material. And in his Christian Deuteronomy he sets the bulk of Matthew's teaching in the historical frame of the journey towards Jerusalem. But it would be a caricature to present Luke as the first Christian writer to bring temporal order to a chaotic tradition. We have seen that consciousness of history was part of Christianity from the first and that it developed through Paul, Mark and Matthew, to reach with Luke a definitive clarity which depends on the labours of his predecessors as much as on his own skill and vision. Time and again we have glimpsed Matthew's importance in this process as a mediator between Luke and Mark.[32] It is now time to give him his due in the story by an appreciation of the historiographical editing which he brings to bear upon Mark, so preparing the way for Luke and particularly in his greater use of scripture to this end.

The genealogy with which Matthew begins his work makes Jesus the climax of a past which goes back to Abraham. At 2:1 and 2:22 he fixes his life more precisely in history than Mark had done. 'Jesus was born in Bethlehem of Judea in the days of Herod the king' and came back from hiding in Egypt when Joseph was told in a dream 'that Archelaus was reigning over Judea in the room of his father Herod'. The infancy stories answer an inevitable historical curiosity about Jesus's origins, and do so by drawing on the riches of past prophecy. Just as Matthew goes beyond Mark's sudden beginning, so he adds to his equally sudden ending. The credibility of the resurrection is defended by stories at 27:62–66 and 28:11–15, designed to give an historical answer to Jewish scepticism. The appearance to the eleven on the mountain in Galilee ties up a loose end in Mark's story ('he goeth before you into Galilee; there shall ye see him', Mark 16:7), and links the Lord to the life and work of the Christian community. The stage is set for Luke's *Acts of the Apostles*. Between these two points he adds scriptural quotations to Mark's picture of Jesus to enhance his historical importance as the fulfilment of prophecy. The beginning of the ministry in 'Galilee of the Gentiles' is presented at 4:14–16 as fulfilment of Isaiah 9:1–2, the miracles of healing at 8:17 as fulfilment of Isaiah 53:4. At 12:17 Jesus is given a particular manner and character— that of God's servant in Isaiah 42:1–4. Mark's theory that Jesus was deliberately obscure in his use of parables has always vexed his readers. Matthew 13:35 invokes Psalm 78:2, 'I will open my mouth in parables: I will utter things hidden from the foundation of the world', thus increasing the aspect of revelation and giving an historical reason (the necessity that prophecy be fulfilled) for the whole puzzling exercise.

What happened to Judas? Mark 14:21 hinted at the worst: 'good were it for that man if he had never been born'. Matthew 27:3–10 settles the matter with added history worked out of scriptural prophecies:[33] the remorse, the return of the money, the suicide and the purchase of the Field of Blood.

John the Baptist is, next to Jesus, the most important figure in the development of Christian historiography. His close relation to the Lord required historical resolution and got it from each evangelist in turn with increasing sophistication and more intricate combination of building up and cutting back. Matthew 3:7–10 gives him his own moral message to Israel, set firmly in the historic lull for repentance before the storm of judgement. But when it comes to Jesus's baptism John must be kept at bay. Matthew 3:14f. gives him an expression of diffidence, over-ruled by Jesus's 'Suffer it now: for thus it becometh us to fulfil all righteousness'. The 'now' (ἄρτι) bears the emphatically historical meaning of 'at the present time'. God's will ('all righteousness') requires that it should be done at this point. Matthew's further treatment of John occurs in three sizeable sections:

1) Matthew 11:2–19 has John in prison hearing of 'the works of Christ' and sending his disciples to ask 'art thou he that should come or look we for another?' His doubt serves both to set him at a distance from Jesus and to provide the cue for definition of their relative places in history. Jesus answers the question by appeals to his work which show him to be 'him that should come'. He then expounds John's paramount significance, using the text of Malachi 3:1 which he had omitted at 3:3 (=Mk 1:2). But although John is the greatest man to date, 'he that is but little in the kingdom of heaven is greater than he'. Matthew 11:12 then links John and Jesus: both have proclaimed the kingdom of heaven (see Mt 3:1f.) and both have suffered from Herod's violence 'until now'. But the next verse separates them. John belongs with the prophets and the law as the end and climax of the long time before Christ. Who then is he? The exaltation and diminution which he has suffered so far are characteristic enough of Matthew (his view of the law is a more monumental example), but have scarcely succeeded in leaving a clear answer. He is (as Mark 6:15 had suggested) Malachi's Elijah who comes before the day of the Lord. Verses 16–19 bring the matter back to the historical present of 'this generation' which finds fault with both manifestations of divine wisdom—John's asceticism and Jesus's sociable indulgence. So a discussion which has ranged back in time into scripture and forward into the Church is brought back to its place in the gospel story.

2) Matthew 17:10–13 develops the resolution of 11:14: 'this is

Elijah'. Again John, as the Elijah who must come first, is kept at a distance from Jesus and again he is joined to him in suffering at the hands of men. The course of history imposes both the discrimination and the resemblance. Mark 9:9–13 is the source.

3) Matthew 21:23–32 follows Mark 11:27–33 and deals with the question of the chief priests and elders. 'By what authority doest thou these things?' Jesus's answer is an appeal to the recent past. 'The baptism of John whence was it? From heaven or from men?' Again 'this generation' refuses, quite literally, to respond, and so the discussion centres upon the historical crux of the self-disinheriting of unrepentant Israel. Again it is worked out in terms of the connection and the difference between John and Jesus. If they have ignored the forerunner they inevitably ignore the fulfilment, and the future passes to 'publicans and harlots'—a trailer for Luke's grand and more developed schemes.

Luke uses the first of these three numbered sections at Luke 7:18–35, putting aside verses 12f. for later use and omitting verse 14 altogether, because it makes John into Elijah—a role which he reserves for Jesus. This also accounts for his omission of the second section which develops the Elijah theme. When it comes to the third section Luke is working upon Mark, not Matthew, and so retails the older version, but his knowledge of Matthew 21:23–32 is possibly betrayed by 'answered and . . .' at Luke 20:3 and Matthew 21:24, and certainly by his use of the parable of the two sons in his story of the Prodigal Son. He leaves out the clumsy dialogue between John and Jesus at his baptism but takes Matthew's point by paring down John's part to a minimum. It begins to look as if Luke is not developing Matthew's development of John the Baptist but cutting it. The beginning of his book contradicts such an impression. At Luke 3:10–14 he gave John even more moral teaching and in his first two chapters he achieved all that Matthew did by didactic dialogue in his own favourite form of narrative, thus handling the connection and difference between John and Jesus in entirely historical terms. John's place in the temporal scheme is thus settled at the outset, an improvement which relieves Luke of the necessity of using all the subsequent material in Matthew (some of which is in any case unwelcome because of the Elijah connection), and the reader of any perplexity about John's standing. So Luke's treatment is a further development of Matthew's amplification of Mark, transformed by the greater narrative skill which we should expect of him.

The tragic history of the Jewish nation is one of Luke's continual and major preoccupations. The only direct references to it in Mark are at 12:1–12 (parable of the wicked husbandmen) and 13:14–19 (apocalyptic discourse). There is much more in Matthew, sometimes developed from hints in the early gospel. Mark gave a national setting to John's ministry by saying that 'Jerusalem and all Judea and all the region about Jordan' went out to meet him (Mk 1:5). Matthew develops this by giving John a message to the leaders of the nation, Pharisees and Sadducees as 'children of Abraham', which prophesies an historical doom: 'even now is the axe laid to the root of the trees: every tree therefore that bringeth not forth good fruit is hewn down and cast into the fire' (Mt 3:10). Luke, as we have seen, expands this again (Lk 3:10–14). The encounter with the centurion, who has a faith unequalled in Israel, is the occasion for Jesus to prophesy Israel's exclusion from God's kingdom. 'Many shall come from the east and west, and shall sit down with Abraham and Isaac and Jacob in the kingdom of heaven, but the sons of the kingdom shall be cast forth into outer darkness' (Mt 8:11). Matthew 11:20–24 is a prophecy against the Jewish cities of Chorazin and Bethsaida, unfavourably compared with gentile Tyre and Sidon. Historical references to Sodom in the past and to the day of judgement in the future seal their fate. Luke 10:12–15 retails it. The same attack on both flanks of past and future is thrown against this evil generation which 'seeketh after a sign' at Matthew 12:38–45. The judgement remains the goal. The men of Nineveh who repented at the preaching of Jonah and the Queen of Sheba who 'came from the ends of the earth to hear the wisdom of Solomon' give the verdict of past history. Prophecy against Israel naturally gathers momentum as Jesus reaches Jerusalem. Matthew makes two emphatic additions to Mark's allegory of the wicked husbandmen which tells salvation history from the nation's beginning to doomsday.

He first adds 'therefore I say unto you, the kingdom of heaven shall be taken away from you and shall be given to a nation bringing forth the fruits thereof' (Mt 21:43) and then a ferocious *midrash* of the stone of stumbling from Isaiah 8:14–15, 'on whomsoever it shall fall it will scatter him as dust', which is clearly turned towards A.D. 70, and the subsequent scattering of Israel. Mark's historical thrust is made inescapable, and in case there should be any lingering doubts or excuses, Matthew adds his own parable of the marriage feast which 'is nothing but a second version of the wicked husbandmen ... with Titus's armies and the burning of Jerusalem making their presence felt through the threadbare story.'[34] The two parables make up a concentrated historical and prophetic barrage against Israel.

As Christ's passion looms nearer, condemnation of the nation finds a foothold in present events—a step which will be essential to Luke's passion narrative. It is guilty of the blood of the Christ, as of the blood of God's emissaries in the past, and judgement for it all is impending. The last woe on the Pharisees (Mt 23:29–36) brings it home. They delude themselves about history, believing that they would not have killed the prophets as their ancestors had done. But this is precisely what they do, killing, crucifying, scourging in synagogues and persecuting from city to city. 'This generation' catches God's judgement through the Roman armies. The whole utterance is in the historical frame 'from the blood of Abel the righteous unto the blood of Zechariah son of Barachiah' (2 Ch 24:22) and beyond to the blood of Jesus and of the Christian martyrs. A prophetic lament over Jerusalem follows (23:37–39), bewailing her past crimes, present obduracy and future destruction. Only at the end of time will she hail the Christ. All that now remains for Matthew is to fulfil prophecy by giving an historical account of Israel incurring its own blood-guiltiness. This is done by the insertion, into Mark's account of the trial before Pilate, of Matthew 27:24f. Pilate washes his hands to show his innocence 'of the blood of this righteous man. And all the people answered and said, His blood be on us and on our children.' This is the terrible moment at which Israel seals its own fate.

Wrangling with his colleagues of the synagogue sharpened Matthew's interest in the historical roots of their quarrel. In the course of it he formed the theory of Christ's ministry and death as an irrevocable turning point in Israel's destiny which is integral to Luke's scheme. He also prepared the ground for Luke by the oracles which bring past and future to bear on 'this generation'. Luke has only to exploit and distribute such material more evenly throughout the story than he had done, so that it is never far from the reader's consciousness. The Lord 'was not sent but unto the lost sheep of the house of Israel' (Mt 15:24)—a more precise historical definition than Mark had achieved. But they paid him no attention. In his warm indignation Matthew comes near to saying that the only good orthodox Jews are dead ones: the prophets and saints of scripture who rise up from their tombs at the moment of Christ's death (Mt 27:52f.). From John's meditations on the work of his predecessors the definitive sentence will emerge: 'he came unto his own and they that were his own received him not' (Jn 1:11). For Matthew the *dénouement* of history, the answer to all its problems and tangles, is the day of judgement. Luke does not contradict this, but quietly goes about shifting the emphasis from time's end to its unfolding course, the judgement of history rather than the judgement beyond it. Again John will cap the historicising process, screwing it up so tightly that it bursts into eternity and the eternal now: 'now is the judgement of this world' (Jn 12:31).

The origin of the Christian Church is a theme which Luke explores in connection with the nation's downfall. Here too he stands on Matthew's shoulders and owes to him a wealth of ecclesiastical material. Matthew's preoccupation with law and order goes with a less exact and sophisticated historiographical technique. He does not hesitate to be anachronistic, having Jesus pronounce upon such concerns of his community as false prophets (7:15ff.) and the settlement of inter-Christian quarrels (18:15ff.). Jesus proclaims himself as the divine presence among the two or three gathered together in his name (18:20). He is occupied with the relation of Church to synagogue. Mark's brief mission charge (Mk 6:7-11) is much expanded in historical terms at Matthew 10:5-42. The twelve, like himself, are to seek out the lost sheep of Israel and not stray into gentile or Samaritan territory—that may come later (28:19). Luke owes much to this rudimentary but very important distinction, which Matthew himself is not precise about (see 8:5-13; 15:21-28 and here, 10:18). The mission is set between the prophetic past of Sodom and Gomorrah (10:15), and the future of the Church (10:21-33) which blurs into the present of the Lord's ministry, both being described as times of calumny, division and deprivation. So the work of the Church is seen, despite the haze, in a frame of temporal succession. Luke will dispel that lingering mist. In line with his historical concern, Matthew takes pains to have Jesus set the Church on firm and authoritative foundations during his own ministry. The verses which he adds to Peter's confession (Mt 16:17-19) achieve this in monumental style. Peter is congratulated on receiving a direct revelation from God. He is the rock on which Christ will build his Church, the wielder of the keys of eternal destiny. As a result the subsequent Markan rebuke loses much of its sting. Luke in his turn will make a sharper historical distinction. The Peter who establishes the brethren will be a matter for prophecy at the Last Supper, and realisation in Acts.

In the main however, Matthew's concern for the Church is more moral than historical. History serves ethics. His Christian community is a mixed bag. The vigilant rub shoulders with the careless, the sincere with the frauds, the men of long service with new converts, the worthy with the unworthy. The parable of the tares (13:26–29 and 36–43), a midrashic expansion of Mark's seed growing secretly, confronts this tangle and gives a temporal solution. It is not the task of men to sort it out, nor is the present the time to do it. It is God's business for him to accomplish at 'the end of the world'. Similarly the guest without a wedding garment of Matthew 22:11–14 is summarily dealt with by the king in judgement.[36] The parable of the labourers in the vineyard at Matthew 20:1–16 deals with the resentment of long-standing members of the Church against late-comers. Will there be no recognition of their greater labours? Again the decision is with God. History, the basis of their envious plea, is subject in final judgement to history's Lord who does what he likes with his own. Here too a development can be traced. In Mark a relatively crude, if forceful, view of history goes with a similar view of human nature—nobody apart from John and Jesus has much to commend him. Matthew's mixed disciples and mixed Church need more delicate historical treatment. Luke has both the finest appreciation of mixed motives in the individual and the most discriminating historical technique.

For all his scribal concern with ethics and his continual reference to the day of doom, Matthew's work is a decisive historiographical improvement upon Mark's. His more settled community allowed for curiosity about such historical questions as the status of the Baptist and the fate of Judas. A number of small touches here and there also show a more critical historical eye working on Mark. Above all Matthew's Church needed to see the story of Jesus in a more precise and integral relation to the time before it and the time after it. The scriptures were applied more—and more systematically. The subsequent destinies of Christianity and of Judaism were given a more pervasive bearing on the telling of the tale of Jesus. Luke improves on all this, but in the development of the Christian view of history Matthew's contribution is large and indispensable.

[1] Ropes, *The Synoptic Gospels*, Oxford 1960, p. 67

[2] *The Origin of the Synoptic Gospels*, Oxford 1922, p. 7

[3] E. W. Lummis, *How Luke Was Written*, Cambridge 1915

[4] 'On Dispensing with Q' in *Studies in the Gospels*, ed. D. E. Nineham

[5] B. C. Butler, *The Originality of St Matthew*, Cambridge University Press, 1951

[6] Goulder *Midrash and Lection in Matthew*, London 1974

[7] John Drury, *Luke*, Collins Fontana, London 1973

[8] In Eusebius *Church History III.*39

[9] Excursus IV to C. F. D. Moule, *The Birth of the New Testament*, A. & C. Black, London 1966.

[10] Goulder, pp. 234f.

[11] At least, not to his modern interpreters. In his own world, where descent from gods was common enough, it was a telling embellishment.

[12] Goulder p. 241

[13] Goulder, pp. 233f

[14] Luke will deal with magicians at Acts 8:9ff., 13:6–8 and 19:19—and with evident disapproval. He may have failed to notice that Matthew's magi are not of this sort of 'evil professional consultants' but diviners and astrologers in the mould of Balaam, and so taken against them somewhat unjustifiably. See John Hull, *Hellenistic Magic and the Synoptic Tradition*, S.C.M. 1974, p. 126

[15] *The Four Gospels*. London 1930, p. 183

[16] Goulder, p. 460

[17] *The Four Gospels*, p. 183

[18] For another trio of woes see Ecclesiasticus (a favourite book of Luke's) 2:12–14

[19] C. F. Evans, 'The Central Section of St Luke's Gospel' in *Studies in the Gospels*, ed. D. E. Nineham, Blackwell, 1967, p. 41, quoting Streeter.

[20] pp. 42–50 of his essay 'The Central Section of St Luke's Gospel'

[21] See E. W. Heaton *The Hebrew Kingdoms*, Oxford 1968, pp. 209f.

[22] 'The Order of Q' , *Journal of Theological Studies*, 1953, p. 31

[23] Two lesser, or auxiliary, pillars are also noticeable. Immediately before the Christian Deuteronomy comes Jesus's over-ruling of the disciples exclusion of the unofficial exorcist, immediately after it his over-ruling of their exclusion of children (Lk 9:49–50 and 18:15–17.

[24] Five is another number which Luke likes. At 12:6 Matthew's two sparrows for a farthing (Mt 16:29) become five for two farthings. At 16:28 the rich man has five brothers.

[25] See also Deuteronomy 10:22: 'Your fathers went down to Egypt seventy persons; and now the Lord your God has made you as the stars of heaven for multitude'—an apt verse for Luke's theme of historical development. Add the tradition of the seventy translators of the Septuagint and the number is biblically inevitable.

[26] For fuller treatment of the Good Samaritan see p. 77f.

[27] Luke 11:22 is an addition to Matthew 12:29 of septuagintal references: the 'stronger' echoing Deuteronomy 9:1 and the stripping of armour recalling 1 Samuel 1:39, where the Philistines strip the vanquished Saul of his armour and 2 Kings 20:13 (=Isaiah 39:2) where the unwary Hezekiah shows a Babylonian envoy his storehouse and arsenal and is warned by Isaiah that it will be taken from him. Luke uses πάνοπλία instead of σχεύοι thus following the language of the Maccabean historian.

[28] Ecclesiasticus 32:1–13 also advises a modest diffidence and consideration at table.

[29] See p. 145 for details

[30] *Law in the New Testament*, London 1970, pp. 48–77

[31] See Creed, pp. 209f

[32] See Appendix D, 'Some Notes of Time in Matthew which are not in Mark'

[33] See Goulder, pp. 445ff. for details of these, as of all the passages discussed here

[34] Goulder, p. 415f.

[35] Using material from Mark 13:9–13

[36] Goulder (p. 416) invokes Revelation 19:8 where the bride's (Church's) fine linen 'is the righteous deeds of the saints'.

7

Historical Relativity and Christian Faith

ANY NEW TESTAMENT investigation by a believer is stimulated and embarrassed by belonging in the two worlds of historical investigation and contemporary faith. They are not separate but interact painfully and productively. At the present time the pain seems to predominate and is located where the relativity, which is integral to scientific history, grates against religion's longing for absolute authority. It often expresses itself in mutual hostility between the two camps. The theologian's task is to allay the pain—not simply by anaesthetics but by restoring the two parts into a productive relation with one another.

The study began by seeing Luke in relation to a particular time in the development of Christianity. He was part of a web in which a number of threads converged and were inter-woven, and was himself a weaver.

The findings of this investigation make it possible to draw a clear picture of him with a minimum of conjecture. He moved in three scenes which connected and interacted to form the context of his work. First are the weekly meetings of his Christian congregation over which he very probably presided as preacher. Readings of scripture were their main feature. In a world of much less communication and entertainment than our own, they were conducted in an atmosphere of expectant and imaginative concentration which we experience in the theatre or the concert hall, but hardly when the clergyman goes to the lectern. It is reflected in Luke's own scene of Jesus in the synagogue at Nazareth and survives today in that ceremonial bringing out of the scrolls in the synagogue which reminds a Christian of the exposition of the host at Benediction. The

Old Testament was the staple fare, to which was probably added the reading of one or other of the Christian books available: Mark, Matthew and possibly Paul's letters to Corinth. There followed a sermon—almost certainly by Luke himself—in which the readings were related to one another and to the life of the congregation by *midrash*. There would also have been prayer and eucharistic table fellowship. All these, and particularly the midrashic combination and interpretation of the writings, have left substantial traces in Luke's work. They also show the similarity of Christian and Jewish synagogue worship. Unmistakable traces of a symbolic or sacramental meal are found in *Joseph and Asenath*.[1]

The second scene is less precise. Luke moved in society. He picked up tags from non-Christian, gentile literature.[2] He was familiar with the intellectual dinner parties beloved of the writers of the *Letter to Aristeas* and Ecclesiasticus (32—they included music like the reunion party for the prodigal son and depended upon ceremonious etiquette: cf. Lk 14:7–14), the 'solemn little banquets' which 'were a normal feature of ancient life.'[3] It may have been here that he picked up the old Egyptian tale of the rich man and the poor man or the story of the crafty steward. He knew 'how the world wags', whether the running of a prosperous household or the business of officialdom, and an hospitably positive attitude to it runs through his work.

Third, and most immediately to our purposes, we can see Luke at his desk. Unlike his modern readers and critics, he is not surrounded by hundreds of books. He has his Old Testament scrolls, a rich and beloved collection, and two or three Christian writings: all the more important to him, and better known by him, for being so few. Possibly the notes of his sermons are also to hand.[4] He would need them for his Christian Deuteronomy unless (as is quite possible) his memory was very good. Last, but not least, there is the moral picture-book of life itself as he observed it, seeing God's traces not only in the epic sweep of history but also in the roadside inn, the steward's office, at the evening dinner-table and in the courts.

Fiercer spirits scorned such expansive hospitality, the writers of 2 Peter and Revelation seeing history's imminent doom and reviving the old apocalyptic *contra mundum*. John would construct a mystical theology which drew on history but transcended its limitations in an eternal communion. Luke, also standing at the latter end of the development of the New Testament gospel tradition, contented himself with a different and more mundane midrashic exercise: an ordered edition of that tradition which stuck relatively closely to its texts and showed the gospel working through history's distinct but connected phases under the direction of the one God. He preferred the horizontal, where sacred and secular mingle into a web of destiny, to the vertical, which puts sublunary affairs under an imperious question mark.

The second part of this study untangled the skeins of Luke's own tapestry by following his use of the Old Testament, Mark and Matthew, and investigating their relation to one another. His sense of history, and particularly his use of the old Jewish historiographical disciplines which operated by prophecy and fulfilment spaciously deployed within the secular, was found to be the governing pattern which he brought to bear on his Christian texts. Even for an ancient writer, the more the concentration on historical succession, the greater the relativity within his scheme of its particular events. Luke's lower christology is a consequence of this. He relates the time of the life of Jesus more firmly and delicately to the past and the future than his predecessors had done. It is a critical and definitive space in the historical scheme—the middle of time—but it was 'then' and not 'now'. There comes a point when the Spirit takes Jesus's place on the historical scene. He leaves it and continues to influence it, not by mystical indwelling, but by the strictly historical means of the telling of his life-story. He is not John's Word, present from all creation, to Abraham and to the true believer as to his disciples in the days of his flesh. Such mystical faith jumps out of time, but a more historical faith, by definition, cannot. Nor does Luke share the kind of belief expressed at 1 Corinthians 10:4 that Christ was the rock in the wilderness during Israel's exodus wanderings. He believes that before his time Christ was looked forward to in prophecy and that after it he was in heaven with God until the last judgement. There Stephen saw him and thence shone the light which converted Saul. The weight of Luke's argument falls decidedly on Jesus as a figure of the recent past who forms the critical link in God's historical chain. Having made the distinction, he exploits the connections which also impose a certain relativity as the (gladly paid) price of historical intelligibility. His Christ is a prophet like Elijah, applying himself to the momentous issues of his particular time and place. He was born like the heroes of old and lived like Moses, travelling with his people to the threshold of a new life. Like Moses (in extra-biblical tradition) and Elijah, he was received up into heaven. Pointing the other way, Luke's Jesus is the founder of Christianity. During his life-time he sets the Church on its way with a deliberate emphasis which would be otiose to Christ-mysticism. Just as patterns in the life of God's agents of old were repeated in his own, so patterns from his life recur in the story of his followers.

All this bears on the delicate task of combining history and uniqueness in thinking about Christ. They are not easy bedfellows. Luke shows that historical intelligibility encroaches on a thorough-going isolationist christology. In different ways the same problem of uniqueness and relevance confronted every major New Testament writer—even those who moved in a more mythological or philosophical atmosphere. The weight of Paul's doctrine falls on the single transforming event of Christ's death and resurrection but is by no means exclusively confined to it. If it were, it would be very difficult to see how it could connect with the faith and life of the believer. Abraham was justified by faith long before the 'Christ-event'. After it the Christian individual fills up the measure of Christ's sufferings, while the Christian Church is the body by which he is still present in the world. John believed that in Jesus of Nazareth God walked the earth for a generation. But at the point where that threatens to become absurdly irrelevant, suggesting that God had been thoroughly active only for a short time and among a privileged few, he makes the same excursions backwards and forwards in time. The Word incarnate in Jesus was with God from the beginning, is the light which lightens every man, and blesses those who have not, by accident of history, seen him yet believe. To the mystical temperament the God revealed in Christ is equidistant from every point in time, the 'scandal of particularity' relieved by doctrines of pre-existence and continuing presence in the faithful community.

Luke's closer attention to historical narrative allows a plurality-in-continuity which, in its own way, does justice to the significance of Jesus and to God's work in the world outside the short space of his ministry. An historian must see the most monumental historical figures growing out of the past which they inherited and into the future which they influenced. This does not abolish uniqueness but, by making it historically coherent, imposes a relitivity which makes 'distinctness' a more appropriate term. Mozart, for example, inherited the achievements of musical centuries. Haydn, acknowledging that a greater composer than himself had come on to the scene in his own lifetime, was his John the Baptist. Then Mozart opened the ways for Schubert and Beethoven, so that the uninformed listener can mistake passages in their earlier work for his. Similarly, Luke's historical typology can give his readers the impression that parts of his gospel are the Old Testament displaced, parts of Acts, repetitions of events in the gospel. Within the plurality of this temporal architecture of salvation history, there is a rich plurality of salvation histories in incidents and parables. Men and women are saved through their lively grasp of present issues, often without the aid of any christology at all. The good Samaritan, the prodigal son and the unjust steward simply respond resourcefully to the crises in front of their noses. The sinful woman of Luke 7:36–49 makes no christological confession, nor does Zacchaeus beyond the use of 'Lord' in talking to Jesus. In John, by contrast, encounters of this sort are overtly turned to perception of the divinity of Jesus. The reader of Luke is not so much confronted with one solitary 'scandal of particularity' as with dozens. As in the Old Testament, God is found in the narrative particulars, often scandalous enough, of what various human beings say and do in response to the situations in which they find themselves. Christ is historically central to all this, and so belongs with it rather than being isolated from it—the cornerstone of a *communio sanctorum* which extends deep into the secular. The signs and stories of the kingdom are not constricted by a positivism of unique revelation.

If we confine our attention to Luke we are moving in a generously catholic landscape with many witnesses to God's salvation, and Jesus its greatest paradigm. But within the New Testament he is not the only witness, so the plurality increases—biblically-based Christianity being a religion not of one book but of many. The Jesus of Luke is not precisely the same as the Jesus of the other evangelists, let alone the writers of the epistles. In each gospel he teaches in a distinct manner, Luke's stories contrasting in their shape with Matthew's, in their clarity with Mark's allegories, in their secular modesty with John's discourses of divine self-revelation. An overall, composite picture may form itself in the reader's mind, but it would be a logical jump to suppose this to be closer to the historical Jesus than the testimony of any of the New Testament witnesses. No more would a general picture of a Tudor monarch, drawn from reading about Henry VII, Henry VIII, Mary and Elizabeth I be closer to history than the sources which tell of any of them. The situation is profoundly irritating for a faith which longs to justify itself by appeal to the 'real' Jesus, recovered from the confusion of the testimony, as the clear and ultimate authority. We are no better off in Christology than in theology at large—believing, but unable to isolate a pure essence of divinity from the web of historical accidents by which it is accessibly incarnate to us. But seen in another light the situation is liberating, lively and the most telling tribute possible to Jesus's impact. The incarnation of God in history, it might be said, has worked all too thoroughly and inexorably for our convenience. Jesus has lost himself into the hearts and minds of his disciples like the grain of wheat which falls into the earth and 'dies' to produce new plants and new grain in an expanding vitality. The original seed is not recoverable precisely because it has germinated. This does not mean that Jesus is inaccessible to us. It means that, as with God, at no given point in time or space can we be absolutely certain that it is absolutely him, and no other, whom we encounter.

Nothing more is being said here than that Christianity works by tradition, the process of passing from mind to mind and heart to heart by which 'the words of a dead man are modified in the guts of the living'[5] in the constantly renewed task of imaginative appropriation which runs through all history. The reader of this book is being presented with one man's view, formed by the influence of many other people's views, of the work of another man similarly influenced. He will check it against the facts of the texts, take from it the things which his own previous history has disposed him to favour, quarrel with things which it has disposed him to dislike and have no recollection of things which it has not disposed him to notice or value at all. Tradition continues and is a long-winded, selective and creative process in which intuition and actualities interact, not a pantechnicon which transports the entire furniture of a past era by direct motorway into the present. Even if such a service were available—and it is one of the most obstinate fantasies of some New Testament scholarship to keep hoping that it might be —it would be less useful than was supposed, for

> We cannot revive old factions,
> We cannot restore old policies
> Or follow an antique drum.

—lines which were written by a poet[6] of a markedly conservative disposition which he submitted to a patient and searching meditation upon irrevocable historical process.

Eliot's lines are the cue for a task which admiration of Luke's skill and sympathetic powers has postponed: the indication of aspects of his work which belong among 'old policies' and need circumspectly delicate handling at the present time.

He had the massive confidence in history as the vehicle of God's will which was natural to him as an historian in the Old Testament mould and spirit celebrating Christianity's emergence into the light of morning. Now, when the Christian west has suffered two great wars and is in the middle of a pervasive economic and political crisis with intellectual and spiritual roots, it is harder for anybody who takes God and history as seriously as he did, to share it. Even if the field is limited to Church history, it is difficult to see it as the inexorable progress which runs in a great crescendo through the gospel and Acts. With an explosive increase in communications the idea of heathen lands as mission fields has waned, so that even Paul's liberal approach at Lystra and Athens seems high-handed to Christians who have learned a more open-minded appreciation of other religions. Nowadays it is as baffling to a believer within Luke's Judaeo-Christian tradition to see God working his cosmic purpose out through the fortunes of the Church with magisterial clarity, as it is for him to dissociate himself entirely from the hope that God guides historical destiny in some way. He may take Luke's story of the rich man and Lazarus as his programme, rather than the missionary sermons of Acts, and hand out material resources instead of dogmas. He may reflect that Luke's historical confidence is won at the expense of some distortion of the facts: the glamorising of the apostles and the denigration of the Jews both become more extreme as the two-volume work goes on. But the difficulty of a simple or unqualified assent to Luke's foremost theological assertion remains. His tactics may still be valuable. His strategic vantage point can now be taken up unreservedly only by the triumphalists— and even then seems to win only the most temporary victories. The only way to use it may be by a painful reversal (a Lukan enough strategy in itself) which would give the Church the Jewish role of an ancient and institutionalised religion, then call upon it to remember what happened to the dinosaur and repent by a radical change of mind and heart. This would make for a more demanding reading of Luke's work than usual, forced in obvious ways, but also able to appeal for its legitimacy to the use of some of Luke's leading convictions in conditions that he could not have foreseen. Church history has progressed from the dawn in which he rejoiced to a time which feels more like four in the morning.

The realism of a secular gospel is Luke's grand achievement, but here, too, time has told. Whoever marries the spirit of the age soon becomes a widow, and in some places where he has done so Luke has not entirely escaped that fate. The concrete and materialistic way in which he treats supernatural symbols can be embarrassing. At Jesus's baptism, Mark spoke of the spirit 'like a dove descending upon him'. The reader is surprised by the dynamic image of a bird's sudden, fluttering descent. Luke says 'there descended upon him the Holy Spirit in bodily form like a dove'. A clumsy and pedantic physicality has destroyed the effect. Likewise the resurrected Jesus is given a solid body which subsequently goes up into the sky and gives rise to the doctrine of the fourth of the Thirty-Nine Articles that 'Christ did truly rise from death and took again his body, with flesh and bones and all things appertaining to the perfection of man's nature, wherewith he ascended into heaven and there sitteth'. The mysterious appearances in Matthew and 1 Corinthians 15, the kind of powerfully mythic exaltation found in Philippians 2:9–11, have been transformed by a bluntness which shades into bathos, and confronts the modern reader (though he was not Luke's business) with gratuitous obstacles unless he translates them back into their more primitive poetry. Luke's marriage to the spirit of his age is most doomed to bereavement in the field of therapy. To the Mediterranean world of his day, this meant magic and the exorcism of demons. Mark gave him plenty to work on but he enhanced it. 'More than any other evangelist, Luke sees ordinary life as penetrated by diabolical agencies.'[7] Luke 8:43ff., for example, contains the addition, to Mark's account of the healing of the woman with the haemorrhage, of Jesus's saying 'someone did touch me for I perceived that power had gone out from me.' Following Preisigke,[8] Hull finds here 'the ancient idea of magical *mana*' which is basic to Hellenistic magic in a particularly outright expression, and argues convincingly that 'power' and 'authority' in Luke are not the spiritual generalities which a modern reader supposes, but the particular terms of magical art. This has been enthusiastically taken up by those who seek to answer the revival of black magic with the revival of white, repeating his marriage to the spirit of the age at a point which is far more questionable now than it was then. Similarly his account of Pentecost has given an authority to concrete demonstrations of spiritual possession to which Paul (1 Co 14) refused *carte blanche*. The irony is that aspects of Luke which were with him an advance into the world have become retreats into ecclesiastical enthusiasm. The historicism is skin deep.

We cannot transplant Luke into the twentieth century beyond saying that, if this impossibility were made possible, his secular sympathies and faith in historical development might lead him to prefer more scientific methods of therapy to exorcisms and be embarrassed (as writers often are) by those who follow him *au pied de la lettre*. His concrete attitude to the supernatural was, after all, in its time an appropriate product of his world-affirming realism and not an anxious revival of ancient rituals. In his approval of magic, he seized on Mark and a widespread phenomenon of practical popular religion and medicine which took him beyond his own biblical tradition.

For modern Christianity, however, the gains of Luke's realism far outweigh its embarrassments. Under the heading of contributions already received we can list the Christian year, popular Christian ethics got from his most popular parables, the popular picture of Jesus as 'a man who went about doing good', and, appropriately enough, the stock in trade of most Christian visual art. Luke is virtually the author, with a little help from Matthew and the apocryphal gospels, of the homely nativity plays which are done in schools and churches at Christmas—a time when Christianity is more popular than usual and cards and carols testify to continuing *midrash* on his work.[9] Without his psychological realism, Christianity would be a harsher, more exclusive and cruder religion. He is the explorer, in Old Testament vein, of the shortcomings of the virtuous, the redeeming commonsense and affections of sinners, the involuntary response to need and the perils of affluence. His appreciation of the mixed motives behind human action redeems Matthew's black and white—and Mark's black. His realism and plausibility have also cast their spell on the New Testament critics in their studies. Although investigation forces a distinction, not always applied, between these and authentic historical information, most scholarly reconstructions of Jesus and his work have drawn more heavily on him than on his colleagues. Jeremias and Dodd have taken his moral stories as normative parables of Jesus in need of little or no form-critical restoration— and this simply because they are realistic and narratively integrated. 'The Founder of Christianity' is a decidedly Lukan title for a book about Jesus. Kümmel's 'inaugurated eschatology', as a statesmanlike solution to the disturbance caused by Schweitzer's thorough-going eschatology, fits him better than any of the other gospel writers.

If the grand strategy of Luke's historical theology, his belief in the inexorable geographical progress of Christianity, has been battered by more recent historical experience, his tactics and the lesser tales within his tale (and following its threefold pattern) are still directly relevant. There is little for the preacher to add to the good Samaritan, the prodigal son or the walk to Emmaus. These are tales which say all that they have to say in the telling and need no morals attached. Underneath the assurance of his great scheme, Luke works through creative responses to God's historical surprises. Peter's three changes of mind mark the beginnings of three eras of Church history: the work with Jesus, the Easter axis and the admission of the Gentiles. The man or institution which fails to adapt imaginatively to the interruption of a new set of circumstances loses the future, which passes to those who have the inspired commonsense to get out of tight corners at the expense of dignity. Repentance, as Luke presents it in his stories, is that attention to the times and application of shrewd imagination to hard facts whereby a man comes back to himself, his fellows and his God. Its practical and theological implications still have force for historical understanding and historical action. The points at which Luke's larger scheme gears into minute particulars tease his readers into new departures, and new things may always be derived from him.

One of them could be a revival of the art of story-telling as a theological form. The anxiety for facts about Jesus has pulled the other way, as has the modern teaching of theology as a conceptual and critical rather than creative exercise, and led to an unnecessary alarm in the face of fiction and legend together with a certain incredulity at the notion that a narrative can be as good theology as a symbolic philosophical scheme. Under this view, Paul is a theologian but not Luke—a presupposition which has had much effect on the different ways in which they have been approached. Apologetically at least this is a misfortune. People live on stories. The average man hears dozens every day and uses them to persuade, explore and establish his whereabouts in the world. The theologian who stands aside from this loses custom as well as consenting to a regrettable break with centuries of tradition. The way forward is not by means of yet another life of Jesus—combining existing accounts as Luke did, but almost certainly without his freshness. It is for a renewal of his confidence that the signs of God's kingdom are present in the unregarded occurrences of secular existence, the contemplative patience to discern them and the skill to articulate them. This is something that can be learned, as Luke learned it from his scriptures. Such a disciplined cultivation of the imagination in the present hands the discoveries and revelations of the past on to the future in the most useful, truthful and promising way possible. Story-telling is one of the ways in which it expresses itself: not the only one, but the one which Luke chose and in which too few theologians of his ability have followed him in recent times. Its happy acceptance of historical relativities at least makes clear, as symbolic theology sometimes fails to do, that the absolute and ultimate is God alone. The earth, with its relativities, he has given to the children of men and made into the sacrament through which he reveals himself to human imaginations without violence to its freedom or its variety. This is where men like Luke belong and do theology in creaturely obedience to the providential dictates of time and place.

[1] See Philonenko's edition, pp. 89ff. and G. D. Kilpatrick 'The Last Supper' *Expository Times*, 64, 1952.

[2] Creed's commentary notes them *ad. loc.*

[3] Peter Brown *The World of Late Antiquity*, London 1971, p. 62

[4] See the plea of the contemporary pseudo-Pauline pastor for the return of 'the books, especially the parchments' (2 Tm 4:13). 'The parchments' could have been loose leaves—notes rather than a finished work. See C. F. D. Moule *The Birth of the New Testament*, London 1966, pp. 182f.

[5] W. H. Auden 'In Memory of W. B. Yeats' *Collected Shorter Poems*, Faber and Faber, London 1966, p. 141

[6] T. S. Eliot 'Little Gidding' in *Collected Poems*, Faber and Faber, London 1963. See also the haunting last pages (399–401) of A. Schweitzer's *The Quest of the Historical Jesus*, A. and C. Black, London 1911 etc.

[7] John M. Hull *Hellenistic Magic and the Synoptic Tradition*, Studies in Biblical Theology, S.C.M., London 1974, p. 100

[8] *Die Gotteskraft der Frühchristlichen Zeit*, Berlin 1922

[9] See Clare Drury 'Who's in, Who's out' in *What About the New Testament?—Essays in Honour of Christopher Evans*, ed. Morna Hooker and Colin Hickling, S.C.M., London 1975

Appendix A
Some Septuagintal Phrases in Luke 1 and 2

1:9   Κατὰ τὸ ἔθος (according to the custom) refers to Exodus 30:7 and uses phraseology similar to Daniel/Bel 15 (κατὰ τὸ ἔθος αὐτῶν) 1 Maccabees 10:89 and 2 Maccabees 13:4 (ὡς ἔθος ἐστὶν). 'The temple of the Lord' (though usually without the definite article) is widespread in the Septuagint.

1:13   Μὴ φοβοῦ (do not fear) is a stock answer to the stock reaction of fear at the presence of God. The parallel is most precise when the words are spoken by an angel as at Genesis 21:17 and Tobit 6:18 and 12:17 (plural).

1:15   ἐνώπιον (before/in the presence of) is a preposition used 22 times by Luke, once by John, not at all by the other evangelists. It is frequent in the Septuagint.

1:15   ἔτι ἐκ κοιλίας μητρὸς (even from his mother's womb) is closely similar to phrases in the LXX describing predestination: Psalm 21:10 'Thou art my God from my mother's womb' (ἐκ κοιλίας μητρὸς). Isaiah 49:5 'The Lord who formed me in the womb' (ἐκ κοιλίας).

1:28   ὁ Κύριος μετὰ σοῦ (the Lord is with you) is frequent. Judges 6:12 is the closest parallel 'The angel of the Lord appeared to him (Gideon) and said to him Κύριος μετὰ σοῦ.'

1:30   εὗρες γὰρ χάριν (for you have found grace) is a common phrase in the narrative and wisdom books of the Septuagint, e.g. Genesis 6:8. Νῶε δὲ εὗρεν χάριν ἐναντιον κυρίου τοῦ θεοῦ. (Noah found grace before the Lord God.)

1:35   ἐπισκιάσει σοι (will overshadow you) is used of God's protective presence at Exodus 40:35, Psalm 90 (91) 4 and Psalm 139:8. It is used by all three synoptics of the cloud at the transfiguration.

1:48   ταπείνωσιν (lowliness) describes the condition of Hagar

(Gn 16:11), Lea (Gn 29:32), Hannah (I Regn. 1:11), David (II Regn. 16:12) and Israel in general (I Regn. 9:16 and IV Regn. 14:26). Creed observes *ad loc* that it 'regularly suggests positive humiliation and distress'.

1:57 ἐπλήσθη ὁ χρόνος τοῦ τεκεῖν αὐτήν (the time was fulfilled for her to be delivered) follows closely Genesis 25:24: ἐπληρώθησαν αἱ ἡμέραι τοῦ τεκεῖν αὐτὴν (Rebecca). See also Lk 2:6.

1:66 ἔθεντο . . . ἐν τῇ καρδίᾳ αὐτῶν (laid them up in their hearts) is closely parallel to 1 Regn 21:13: ἔθετο Δαυιδ τα ῥήματα ἐν τῃ καρδίᾳ αὐτοῦ. Χεὶρ κυρίου (the hand of the Lord) is an extremely common phrase in the Septuagint, whether of the Lord or some human agent.

1:68 and 78 ἐπεσκέψατο (visited). The use of this verb *of God* is peculiar to Luke among the gospels and occurs elsewhere in the New Testament only in Hebrews (2:6). Matthew and James use it of human philanthropic visitation. It is very commonly used in the LXX of God visiting his people. So, too, but rarely, in the rest of Luke–Acts (Lk 7:16; Ac 15:14).

1:80 Τὸ δὲ παιδίον ηὔξανε, καὶ ἐκρατιοῦτο πνεύματι (the child grew and strengthened in spirit) is like Judges 13:24 ηὐξήθη τὸ παιδάριον (Samson) and I Regn. 2:26 καὶ τὸ παιδάριον Σαμουὴλ ἐπορεύετο καὶ ἐμεγαλύνετο καὶ ἀγαθόν καὶ μετὰ κυρίου καὶ μετὰ ἀνθρώπων.

2:40 and 52 (of Jesus) should be included in comparison. The note of growth is as characteristic of Old Testament narrative as of Luke's.

2:25 Προσδεχόμενος παράκλησιν τοῦ Ἰσράηλ (waiting for the comforting of Israel) echoes Isaiah 40:1: παρακαλειτε, παρακαλεῖτε τὸν λαόν μου λέγει ὁ θεός. (Comfort, comfort my people, saith God.)

2:26 Καὶ Πνεῦμα ἦν Ἅγιον ἐπ' αὐτόν (the Holy Spirit was upon him) resembles Judges 11:29: ἐγενήθη ἐπὶ Ἰεφθάε πνεῦμα κυρίου and Judges 15:14: κατηύθυνεν ἐπ' αὐτὸν πνεῦμα κυρίου (Samson), etc.

2:29 ἀπολύω (release) is also used for death at Genesis 15:15 (Abraham) Numbers 20:29 (Aaron) Tobit 3:6 (Tobit) and 2 Maccabees 7:9 (a martyr). Ἐν εἰρήνῃ (in peace) echoes Genesis 15:15: Σὺ δὲ (Abraham) ἀπελεύσῃ πρὸς τος πατέρας σου μετ' εἰρήνης—a text which seems to lie behind this verse.

2:49 ἐν τοῖς τοῦ πατρός μου (in the things of my father) resembles the phrase used by Joseph in naming his son Manasseh at Genesis 41:51, καὶ πάντων τῶν τοῦ πατρός μόυ.

Appendix B
Psalmody in Luke 1 and 2 (RSV)

Do not be afraid Zechariah,
    for your prayer is heard,
And your wife Elizabeth will bear a son,
    and you shall call his name John. (1:13)

I am Gabriel,
    who stand in the presence of God;
And I was sent to speak to you,
    and to bring you this good news.
And behold, you will be silent and unable to speak
    until the day that these things come to pass,
Because you did not believe my words,
    which will be fulfilled in their time. (1:19–20)

How shall I know this?
    for I am an old man
    and my wife is advanced in years. (1:18)

Thus the Lord has done to me in the days when he looked upon me,
    to take away my reproach among men. (1:25)

Hail, O favoured one;
    the Lord is with you. (1:28)

Do not be afraid, Mary,
    for you have found favour with God.
And behold, you will conceive in your womb and bear a son,
    and you shall call his name Jesus. (1:30, 31)

How can this be
    since I have no husband? (1:34)

And behold your kinswoman Elizabeth,
>   has also conceived a son, in her old age;
And this is the sixth month
>   with her who was called barren.
For with God nothing will be impossible.   (1:36, 37)

Behold I am the handmaid of the Lord;
>   let it be to me according to your word.   (1:38)

Blessed are you among women,
>   and blessed is the fruit of your womb!
And why is this granted me,
>   that the mother of my Lord should come to me?
For behold, when the voice of your greeting came to my ears,
>   the babe in my womb leaped for joy.
And blessed is she who believed,
>   for there will be a fulfilment of what was spoken to her from
>   the Lord. (1:42–45)

Be not afraid, for behold I bring you good news of great joy,
>   which will come to all the people;
For to you is born this day a saviour,
>   who is Christ the Lord, in the city of David.
And this will be a sign for you:
>   you will find a babe wrapped in swaddling clothes
>   and lying in a manger.   (2:10–12)

Let us go over to Bethlehem and see this thing that has happened,
>   which the Lord has made known to us.   (2:15)

Son, why have you treated us so?
>   behold, your father and I have been looking for you anxiously.
How is it that you sought me?
>   did you not know that I must be in my Father's house?
>   (2:48, 49)

Appendix C
The Census

Luke seems to have jumbled various historical incidents:

1) The census (ἀπογραφή) of the Judean lands of the ethnarch Archelaus made by Quirinius when he became Governor of Syria in A.D. 6 and this territory was annexed to his province. Luke refers to this census again at Acts 5:37 together with the revolt under Judas which it provoked and which made it memorable.
2) Herod the Great imposed taxes (Josephus *Ant.* 17:204–5; 308) and gave a summary of the resources of his kingdom in his will—but that is by no means a census.
3) C. Vibius Maximus, the Roman Prefect of Egypt in Alexandria, troubled by over-population brought about by the migration of peasants into the city, tried to deal with the problem by sending them all back to their own places for a census in A.D. 104. The text is given by Creed, p. 33.

The first of these is obviously the most important to Luke: the 'first' (2:2) census whose novelty caused such a stir. But it was not made, as he certainly infers, 'in the days of Herod, King of Judea' (1:5) who died in 4 B.C., nor is there a shred of evidence that it involved 'everyone' going to 'his own city' (2:3)—it would scarcely have been in the interests of *Pax Romana* to have the population of 'all the world' (2:1) involved in a vast game of 'general post'. Inhabitants of Galilee would have come under Luke's imaginary census of the entire empire, but not under the real one under Quirinius. The hypothesis that Joseph had some land within Quirinius's province seeks to abolish the difficulty, but in Luke's text the reason for Joseph's journey is quite different—and the other contradictions remain. If there was an earlier census Quirinius could have had nothing to do with it officially, and if it was made by Herod then it was not by 'a decree from Caesar Augustus'. There is a gap in our knowledge of the governors of Syria between 4 B.C. and A.D. 6 and attempts have been made to get Quirinius into it, but they ignore Luke's statement that all this took place in the time of King Herod, and so fail.

It is best to acknowledge that Luke, unable to check his facts with the thoroughness of his critics, has made one of his muddles (compare his confusion of infancy rituals in the prologue) while going about the more exalted task of giving his story a world-wide frame of reference for theological reasons.

Appendix D

Some notes of Time in Matthew which are not in Mark

3:1	'And in those days cometh John the Baptist.'
4:11	'Then the devil leaveth him; (and behold, angels came and ministered unto him).'
4:17	'From that time began Jesus to preach . . .'
8:1	'And when he was come down from the mountain . . .'
8:29	'Before the time . . .'
9:33	'It was never so seen in Israel . . .'
11:1	'When Jesus had made an end of commanding his twelve disciples . . .'
12:28	'But if I by the spirit of God cast out devils, then is the kingdom of God come upon you.'
12:36	'Every idle word that men shall speak, they shall give account thereof in the day of judgement . . .'
13:14f.	The fulfilment of prophecy gives an historical cause for hardness of heart.
21:4f.	Again fulfilment of prophecy gives the historical reason for Jesus riding 'upon an ass and upon a colt, the foal of an ass'.
21:32	'For John came unto you in the way of righteousness and ye believed him not: but the publicans and the harlots believed him: and ye, when ye saw it, did not even repent yourselves afterward, that ye might believe him.'
21:39	The son is first thrown out of the vineyard and then killed to fit the order of events in Jesus's passion.
22:34	'But the Pharisees, when they heard that he had put the Sadducees to silence, gathered themselves together . . .'
22:46	'Neither durst any man from that day forth ask him any more questions.'

24:3	'. . . And of the end of the world.'
24:9	'*Then* shall they deliver you up . . .'
24:10–14	Matthew adds a series of events in history which will precede the end.
24:15	The fulfilment in history of Daniel's prophecy makes 'the abomination of desolation' more intelligible.
24:37–41	The suddenness of the end deduced from the suddenness of Noah's flood, this section being followed by extra injunctions to vigilance. (24:43—25:46).
26:68	'Who is he that struck thee?' gives a reference to the vague 'prophesy!'
27:19	Pilate's wife's dream, though not given in detail, is clearly prophetic.
27:52	The resurrection of the saints at Christ's death marks it as a culmination of sacred history. Matthew's attention to time results curiously in the risen saints waiting in their tombs until Jesus's resurrection before they enter the holy city and appear to many.

Select Bibliography

This is a list of books and articles which have been found particularly useful in the composition of this book.

ALAND, K. (ed.) *Synopsis Quattuor Evangeliorum*, Württembergische Bibelanstalt, Stuttgart 1967.

BARNABAS *Epistle* in *Early Christian Writings*, tr. and ed. M. Staniforth, Penguin, 1968.

BARRETT, C. K. *Luke the Historian in Recent Study*, Epworth, 1961.

BAUER, W. *A Greek–English Lexicon of the New Testament*, tr. and ed. W. F. Arndt and F. W. Gingrich, University of Chicago Press and Cambridge University Press, 1952.

BLOCH, R. 'Midrash' *Dictionnaire de la Bible*. Supplement V. cols. 1263–81.

BULTMANN, R. *The History of the Synoptic Tradition* (tr. from the second German edition of 1931 by John Marsh), Blackwell, 1968.

BUTLER, B. C. *The Originality of St Matthew*, Cambridge University Press, 1951.

CADBURY, H. J. *The Making of Luke–Acts*, S.P.C.K., 1968.

CAMPENHAUSEN, H. von *The Formation of the Christian Bible* (E.T. by J. A. Baker of *Die Entstehung der Christlichen Bibel*) Black, 1972.

CHADWICK, H. 'Ephesians' *Peake's Commentary on the Bible* (ed. M. Black and H. H. Rowley) Nelson, 1962.

——'Justin Martyr' in *Bulletin of the John Rylands Library*, 1965.

CHARLES, R. H. (ed.) *Apocrypha and Pseudepigrapha of the Old Testament*, Oxford University Press, 1913.

CLEMENT *Epistles* in *Early Christian Writings* tr. and ed. M. Staniforth, Penguin, 1968.

CONZELMANN, H. *The Theology of St Luke* (E.T. of *Die Mitte der Zeit*), Faber, 1960.

CREED, J. M. *The Gospel according to St Luke*, Macmillan, 1930.

DERRETT, J. D. M. *Law in the New Testament*, Darton, Longman and Todd, 1970.

DIBELIUS, M. *From Tradition to Gospel* (E.T. by B. L. Woolf) of *Die Formgeschichte des Evangeliums*, James Clarke, 1971.

DRURY, J. *Luke*, Fontana, 1973.
'The Sower, the Vineyard and the Place of Allegory in the Interpretation of Mark's Parables' *Journal of Theological Studies*, October 1973.

EISSFELDT, O. *The Old Testament, an Introduction* tr. by P. R. Ackroyd, Blackwell, 1966.

EUSEBIUS *Ecclesiastical History*, ed. with translation by K. Lake, 2 vols., Loeb/Heinemann, 1926–32.

EVANS, C. F. 'The Central Section of St Luke's Gospel', *Studies in the Gospels* ed. D. E. Nineham, Blackwell, 1955.

FARMER, W. R. *The Synoptic Problem, A Critical Analysis*, Macmillan, New York, 1964.

FARRER, A. *A Study in Mark*, Dacre Press, 1951.
'On dispensing with Q' *Studies in the Gospels*, ed. D. E. Nineham, Blackwell, 1955.

FLENDER, H. *St Luke, Theologian of Redemptive History* tr. R. H. and I. Fuller, S.P.C.K., 1967.

FRASER, P. M. *Ptolemaic Alexandria*, Oxford University Press, 1972.

GOULDER, M. D. *Midrash and Lection in Matthew*, S.P.C.K., 1974.

HAENCHEN, E. *The Acts of the Apostles* (E.T. of 14th German edition), Blackwell, 1971.

HARNACK, A. *Luke the Physician* tr. J. R. Wilkinson, London, 1907.

HATCH, E. and REDPATH, H. A. *A Concordance of the Septuagint* originally Oxford University Press, 1897, reprinted Akademische Druck U. Verlagsanstalt, Graz, 1954.

HEATON, E. W. *The Hebrew Kingdoms*, Oxford University Press, 1966.

HENNECKE, E. (ed.) *New Testament Apocrypha* ed R. McL. Wilson, Lutterworth, 1963.

HOULDEN, J. L. *Paul's Letters from Prison*, Penguin, 1970.

HULL, John M. *Hellenistic Magic in the Synoptic Tradition*, S.C.M., Studies in Biblical Theology, Series 2, No. 28, 1974.

IGNATIUS *Epistles*, in *Early Christian Writings*, tr. and ed. M. Staniforth, Penguin, 1968.

JAMESON, H. G. *The Origin of the Synoptic Gospels: A Revision of the Synoptic Problem*, Blackwell, Oxford, 1922.

JEREMIAS, J. *The Parables of Jesus* (E.T. of *Die Gleichnisse Jesu*) S.C.M., 1954.

JONES, C. P. M. 'The Epistle to the Hebrews and the Lucan Writings' *Studies in the Gospels*, ed. D. E. Nineham, Blackwell, 1955.

JOSEPHUS *Jewish Antiquities*, ed. H. St J. Thackeray, Loeb/ Heinemann, 1930.

JUSTIN, St *Works*, tr. T. B. Falls, Fathers of the Church, Washington 1965.

KECK, L. E. and MARTYN, J. L. (eds.) *Studies in Luke–Acts*, S.P.C.K., 1968.

LAURENTIN, R. *Structure et Théologie de Luc I–II*, Gabalda, Paris 1964.

LIGHTFOOT, R. H. *The Gospel Message of St Mark*, Oxford University Press, 1950.

LUMMIS, E. W. *How Luke was Written*, Cambridge University Press 1915.

MOMIGLIANO, A. 'Time in Ancient Historiography' *History and Theory*, Wesleyan University Press, Middletown 1966.

MOULE, C. F. D. *The Birth of the New Testament*, Black 1966.
'The Problem of the Pastoral Epistles', *Bulletin of the John Rylands Library*, 1965.

MOULTON, W. F. and GEDEN, A. S. *A Concordance to the Greek Testament*, T. & T. Clark 1963.

NEIRYNCK, F. (ed.) *L'Evangile de Luc—Problèmes Littéraires et Théologiques* (Mémorial Lucien Cerfaux), J. Duculot, Gembloux (Belgium) 1973.

NINEHAM, D. E. *St Mark*, Pelican, London 1963.
—— (ed.) *Studies in the Gospels*, Blackwell, 1955.

NOCK, A. D. *Conversion*, Oxford University Press, 1933.

O'NEILL, J. C. *The Theology of Acts in its Historical Setting* (second edition), S.P.C.K., 1970.

ORIGEN, *Contra Celsum*, tr. and ed. H. Chadwick, Cambridge University Press 1953.

PERROT, 'Les Récits d'Enfance' *Recherche des Sciences Religieuses*, 1967.

PERRY, B. E. *The Ancient Romances*, University of California Press, 1967. *Aesopica*, Urbana 1952. *Phaedrus and Babrius* (ed.) Heinemann/Loeb 1965.

PHILONENKO, M. (ed.) *Joseph et Aséneth*, Brill, Leiden 1968.

PHILOSTRATUS *Life of Apollonius*, tr. C. P. Jones, ed. G. W. Bowersock, Penguin 1970.

PLUMB, J. H. *The Death of the Past*, Pelican 1973.

PLUTARCH *The Fall of the Roman Republic* (some of his *Lives*), tr. and ed. R. Warner, Penguin 1958.

QUESNELL, Q. *The Mind of Mark*, Pontifical Biblical Institute, 1969.

RAHLFS, A. (ed.) *Septuaginta*, Wurttembergische Bibelanstat, Stuttgart 1965.

ROHDE, J. *Rediscovering the Teaching of the Evangelists*, tr. by D. M. Barton, S.C.M. 1968.

ROPES, J. H. *The Synoptic Gospels*, Harvard 1934 and Oxford University Press 1960.

SIMON, M. *Hercule et le Christianisme*, University of Strasburg, Paris 1955.

SMITH, Morton 'Aretalogies, Divine Men, The Gospels and Jesus' *The Journal of Biblical Literature* 1971.

SPARKS, H. F. D. 'The Semitisms of Luke's Gospel' *Journal of Theological Studies*, 44 1943.

—— (ed.) *A Synopsis of the Gospels*, A. & C. Black 1964.

STREETER, B. H. *The Four Gospels—A Study of Origins*, Macmillan, 1924.

STROBEL, A. 'Schreiben des Lukas' u.s.w. *New Testament Studies* 1968.

TAYLOR, V. *The Passion Narrative of St Luke*, Society of New Testament Studies Monograph, Cambridge University Press 1973.

'The Order of Q' *Journal of Theological Studies*, 1953, pp. 27–31.

VERMES, G. *Scripture and Tradition in Judaism*, Brill, Leiden 1973.

—— *Jesus the Jew*, Collins 1973.

—— Chapter 8 of *The Cambridge History of the Bible*, Vol. I, Cambridge University Press.

WEINFELD, M. *Deuteronomy and the Deuteronomic School*, Oxford University Press 1972.

WREDE, W. *The Messianic Secret* (E. T. of *Das Messiasgeheimnis in den Evangelien* by J. C. G. Greig), James Clarke, 1971.

Index of Scriptural References

Old Testament

GENESIS	PAGE	NUMBERS	PAGE
6:8	59	11:16	68
7:1	56	23:25	50
10	102		
11:30	56	DEUTERONOMY	
15:8	59	1:21–35	68
18:7	76	3:23	149
18:8–11	56	3:26	111
18:14	59	4:36	149
21:1–21	51	6:15	77
25:22	60	8	149–50
25:29	77	8:15	145
30:23	57	9:10f	150
41:42	76	10:2–11	152
41:45	5	11:18	152
		12	152
		12:1–16	140
EXODUS		12:17	140
3:1	55	13:3	154
8:19	150	13:6–11	140, 154
13:1	62	15:1–18	140, 155
15	50	16:16	156
15:13	62	17:2–7	156
19:10	70	18:1–5	157
19:15	51	18:18	147
23:20	147	20:5–8	140
24:4	102	20:10	157
31:18	150	20:29	157
40:35	59	21:15–22:4	75, 140, 158
		23:15f	159
		23:19f	159
LEVITICUS		23:15–25	160
12:6	62	24:1–4	160
13:49	162	24:5–9	160
19:18	77		

Deuteronomy–*cont.*	PAGE		PAGE
24:6	161	17	66, 86
24:6–25:3	140	17:8–24	70
24:15	162	19:19	68, 74
24:17–22	161, 162	21:25	51
25:4	6		
26:12–16	164	II KINGS	
33	50	1:10	67, 148
		2:4	73
JOSHUA		2:9	130
2	73	4:1–7	66
2:2	51, 73	4:38–44	66
2:21	60	5	163
6	73	7	78
		9:57–62	74
JUDGES		10:6	60
3:10	59	12:17	67
4	50, 51	14:25	60
5	50, 51		
6:12	59	II CHRONICLES	
6:34	59	24:22	169
11:10	60	28:15	77
13:2	56		
13:7	57	NEHEMIAH	
13:24	60	4:18	110
16	51		
		ESTHER	
RUTH	51	8:2	76
I SAMUEL		PSALMS	
1	51	14:1	153
1:20	7	23:5	68
1:24	62	31:6	69, 114
2:1–10	58	78:2	165
2:26	60	132:11	59
10:6	59	145:14	155
16:13	61	146:8	155
21:12	60, 62		
25:1	58	PROVERBS	
28:24	76	1:8	52
		6:20	52
II SAMUEL		15:20	52
2:1	60	25:6	157
7:6	61	29:3	79
12:1–6	79	30:27	52
15:20	68	31:10–31	52
22	50		
23	50	ECCLESIASTES	
		2:24	76
I KINGS		3:1	98
8	51		
8:47	76	ISAIAH	
10:1–3	51	1:3	60
11	51	7:14	59

	PAGE		PAGE
8:14f	168	10:8	69, 113
9:2	165		
9:7	59	AMOS	
16:5	59	3:2	154
28:16	63		
40:1	62	OBADIAH	
42:1–4	165	21	55
50:7	67, 110		
53:4	165	JONAH	50
53:12	69		
61:1	63		
		MICAH	
JEREMIAH		5:2	124, 61
14:8	61		
21:10	10	HABAKKUK	
		2:9–11	105
EZEKIEL			
16:10	76	ZECHARIAH	
20:47	113	1:17	52
21:2	67	3:3–5	76
		12:6	59
DANIEL		12:10	69
9:21	56		
10:15	57		
		MALACHI	
HOSEA		3:1	55, 129, 166
2:7	76	4:5–6	37, 71

Apocrypha

TOBIT		16:22	61, 63, 64
1:6	65		
2:2	65	SONG OF THREE	
2:6	65	whole book	51
12:17	65		
13	64		
		ECCLESIASTICUS	
JUDITH		32	77, 175
whole book	51	33:19–23	76
13:18	65	48:1–14	148

New Testament

MATTHEW		2:13–15	127
1:1–17	51, 125	2:22	165
1:20	123	3:7–4:11	128, 131
2:1	124, 165	3:7–10	166
2:1–12	125	3:8	155
2:5	62	3:10	168
2:6	124	3:14f	166

199

Matthew—*cont.*

	PAGE		PAGE
4:14–16	165	13:31–35	155
5:1–7:27	131–8, 142–5	13:34	165
5:15	152	13:36–43	171
5:18	160	13:47–50	87
5:25	44	15:14	136
5:26	154	16:1–4	100
5:27	160	16:2	154
5:32	160	16:5f	152
6:6	164	16:11	83
6:19	19	16:17–19	170
6:22f	152	17:10–13	166–7
6:24	160	17:20	162
6:25–34	153	18	161, 162
6:27	72	18:2	163
7:15	170	18:12f	158
7:21	150	18:14	150
8:1–4	162	18:23–35	92
8:5–13	170	19:28	110
8:11	168	20:30	163
8:17	165	21:21	162
9:22	163	21:23–32	74, 75, 167
9:32–4	150	21:28–32	146, 158
9:37f	148	21:43	168
10	142–5	22:1–4	79, 157, 168, 171
10:5–42	170	22:34–40	78, 149
10:9–14	148	23	142–55
10:10	19	23:6	146, 156
10:16	148	23:23	152
10:17	153	23:25f	152
10:26f	152	23:29–36	169
10:31f	153	23:37–9	156, 169
10:34–6	154	24	142–5
10:36f	153	24:42–4	153
10:37	157	24:45–51	154, 159
10:40	148	25:14–30	104
11:2–19	166	25:31–46	161
11:12	160	26:53	117
11:19	92	27:3–10	165–6
11:20–4	148, 168, 169	27:24	169
12:9–13	155	27:52	169
12:17	165	27:62–6	165
12:24–30	150	28:11–15	165
12:30–42	152		
12:31f	153		
12:33–5	137	MARK	
12:35f	153	1:1–15	46, 126
12:38–45	168	1:5	168
12:40	151	1:6	58
12:43–7	151	1:9	124
12:46–50	151	1:10	130
12:50	150	1:14–45	85, 87
13:23–30	79	1:15	6
13:26–29	171	1:16–20	86, 131

	PAGE	LUKE	PAGE
1:40–3:19	89	1:1–4	36, 46, 82
1:40–5	162	1:1–25	46, 47, 51
2:4	72	1:3	4
2:16	92	1:10	150
2:23–3:6	99	1:14–17	49
3:7	131	1:26	52, 123, 125
3:13	90, 91	1:26–38	58, 59
3:20–4:34	93	1:31	123, 124
3:31	72	1:32	54, 55
3:31–5	63	1:34	123, 125
4:1	87	1:35	123
4:1–20	79	1:39	52
4:12	93	1:42	151
4:33	94	1:46–55	49
4:35–6:44	94–5	1:55	53
4:35–41	99	1:68–79	49
5:34	163	1:69	55
5:41	71	1:70	23
6:1–6	86, 91	1:71	55
6:7–11	166	1:73	53
6:45–8:22	97	1:76	55
7:24–8:26	98	1:79	80
7:28	161	2:1–3	124
8:14–21	83	2:4	124
9:1	89	2:7	72
9:9–13	167	2:10–12	125
10:13–13:37	103	2:11	55, 70
10:21	19	2:12	62
10:35–45	110	2:16	72
10:38	35	2:17	62
10:45	19	2:22	52, 55
10:46	73	2:26	55
10:46–52	100	2:29–32	49
10:47	124	2:35	62
10:52	163	2:41	52
11:27–12:34	107	2:41–52	63
12:1–12	75, 79, 168	2:51	124
12:3–5	145	2:52	72
12:40	151	3:1:2	124
13	34, 106	3:7–4:13	128–30
13:8	107	3:10–14	167, 168
13:14–19	168	3:15	58
14:1–31	109, 110	3:21	150
14:3–9	74, 91	3:22	70
14:21	165	3:23	123
14:23	35	4:1–5:16	85–9
14:30	70	4:16–30	11, 66
14:32–15:1	111	4:21	70
14:36	35	4:22	123
15:22–41	114	4:23	79
15:30	114	4:25	147
15:37–9	116	4:26	71
16:7	165	5:1–11	10, 17, 66, 74

Luke–*cont.*	PAGE		PAGE
5:12–16	6, 19, 162, 163	11:5–13	163
5:16	150	11:12	145
5:26	70	11:14	150
5:36	79	11:14–26	139, 145
6:11–17	71, 95	11:20	150
6:12	150	11:26–32	152
6:20–49	131–42	11:27	69, 151
6:30	16	11:36	152
7:1–10	98	11:37–44	140
7:9	162	11:39–52	141, 145
7:11–17	71, 95	11:41	152, 163
7:16	147	12:1	83, 100
7:18–35	167	12:1–3	152
7:29–30	92	12:1–59	142
7:30	16	12:4–7	153
7:36–39	178	12:10–12	153
7:36–50	74, 109	12:13–15	140
7:50	163	12:19	76
8:1–3	82, 92	12:1–12	160
8:2, 3	52	12:22–34	153
8:9–9:17	92–6	12:25	72
8:16	152	12:35, 36	153
8:19	72	12:35–13:9	154, 155
8:21	150	12:39, 40	153
8:24	96	12:41-8	154
8:25	96	12:47	20
8:29	96	12:49–53	154
8:43:44	181	12:51–53	140
8:45	96	12:58	44, 145
8:46–50	100–2	13:6–9	106
8:47	96	13:10–21	140
8:48	163	13:16	155
8:54	71	13:18	94, 141
9:1, 2	96	13:22	138
9:7–9	84	13:24–9	142
9:9	72, 95	13:26	137, 142
9:18	150	13:31–3	70, 95
9:24	96	13:34, 35	144, 156
9:28	152	14:1–25	146, 156, 157
9:43–50	141	14:7–14	175
9:51	10, 56, 67, 84,	14:15–31	140
	94, 127, 138, 147, 148	14:25–33	157
9:51–18:14	138–64	15:1–10	146, 150, 158
9:57–62	19	15:10	54
10:1	148	15:11–32	75, 76, 140, 144,
10:1–12	101, 102		146, 150, 158
10:2–16	141, 142	16:1–9	78, 142, 158
10:7	19	16:10–18	160
10:12–15	168	16:19–31	140, 144, 146, 161
10:29–57	77, 144, 149	17:1–4	142, 161
10:38–42	149	17:5, 6	63, 162
11:1	150	17:6	73
11:1–13	139, 145	17:7–10	146, 162

	PAGE
17:11	138
17:11–19	78, 162
17:19	163
17:21	152
17:22–37	141, 142, 144, 163, 164
18:1–8	78, 164
18:9–14	144, 164
18:13	114
18:15–21:38	103–9
18:42	163
19:1	73
19:1–10	72, 104
19:5	70
19:7	72, 73
19:9	70
19:11–27	104
19:37	105
19:40	105
19:41–4	105
19:42	17, 112
19:45–7	106
20:1–8	106
20:9–18	106
20:19–36	107–12
20:29–38	107
21:1–4	107
21:1–38	107, 109
21:20–4	53, 105
21:24	98
22:1–23:48	109–17
22:3	110
22:16–19	109
22:21–33	68
22:27	110
22:32	11, 88, 162
22:35–8	69, 110, 111
22:43	54
22:51	111
22:53	69, 111
22:61	70, 106
22:62	112
23:2	112
23:8–12	16, 17, 95
23:18, 19	112
23:24	113
23:27–31	66, 69
23:28	71
23:32	10, 66
23:36	115
23:39	115
23:43	70, 160
23:46	114

	PAGE
23:54:55	117
24:6	69
24:11	127
24:21	70
24:23	55
24:25	69
24:27	73
24:38	128
24:45	69
24:47	128

JOHN

1:11	170
1:19–23	130
1:29	113
12:14	113
12:31	170
13:1–11	153

ACTS

1:10	117
1:14	127
2:23	113
3:17	20, 114
3:21	9
3:24	82
5:19	54
5:34	117
7:52	10, 113
7:56	128
8:26	54
10	18
10:30–48	88, 126
10:45	12
11:4	82
11:18	11
11:31	55
12:23	55
14:15–17	8
15	12
15:5	99
16:3	99
17:22–31	8, 12
17:30	20
18:23	82
19:23	157
22:4	157
23:6	161
24:21	161
26:8	161
26:26	86, 134
27:23	55
27:33–8	89

Acts–*cont.*

	PAGE
27:34	108
28:25–8	16

ROMANS

1:3	33
5:8	33
6:3f	34
9:33	62
13:1–7	18

I CORINTHIANS

2:6	33
4:2	160
9:9	6
10:4	176
11:24	109
15:3	6

GALATIANS

3	12
4:4	33
4:25–31	75
4:29	6

EPHESIANS

1:10	16
2:13–16	16
2:17	17

	PAGE
2:20	17
3:8–11	16
4:11	17
4:32	17

PHILIPPIANS

2:1–11	50
2:5–11	33

I TIMOTHY

1:15	20
2:1–4	18
2:5	19
3:1–3	18
3:16	19
4:1–5	18
4:8	19
5:3–8	18
5:5	63

HEBREWS

2:3	21
11:31	73
13:1–17	21

JAMES

2:25	73

General Index

not including the Appendices

AARON, 56
Abel, 75
Abraham, 2, 7, 31, 32, 50, 56, 58, 59, 85, 125, 155, 161, 176, 177
Adam, 2, 3, 31, 85, 125
Aesop, 28, 29
Akiba, 35
Alexandria, 5, 25, 31, 48, 190
Alfred, King, 2
allegory, 72, 79
angels, 8, 54, 55, 56, 59, 65, 67, 117, 123, 161
Antiochus Epiphanes, 107
Apollonius of Tyana, 29
Archelaus, 104, 190
aretalogy, 27
Aristeas, Epistle of, 37f, 68n, 90, 146, 175
Aristophanes, 79
Asclepius, 28

BABRIUS, 29
baptism, 34f
Barnabas, Epistle of, 24
Barr, J., 5n
Barrett, C. K., 8
Barth, K., 12
Beare, F. W., 33
Beethoven, L. von, 178
Benjamin, 75
Bethsaida, 97f, 100
biography, 27–30, 32, 47
blind guide parable, 136
brothers, 75, 158
Brown, P. L., 175
Bultman, R., 41

Bunyan, John, 57

CAIN, 75
Campenhausen, H. von, 15
Celsus, 27
census, 60
Chadwick, H., 16, 23, 24
Charles, R. H., 48
Christ, 55
christology, 9, 12, 21, 23, 55f, 123, 176, 178
Chronicler, 44
Church, 9, 10, 16, 21, 85, 88, 101, 110, 117, 144, 170, 177
church order, 17, 20, 24, 110, 170
Clement of Rome, 24
compassion, 71, 77
conversion, 11
Conzelmann, H., 73
Cornelius, 55
Creed, J.M., 97, 98, 99, 100, 111, 163
cuckoo, 27

DAHL, N. A., 72n
dates, 49, 56, 64, 124, 129, 165
David, 9, 54, 55, 56, 58, 60, 61, 62, 68, 75, 78, 79, 124
Dead Sea Sect, 5, 31, 50
death, 33–5
debtors, two – parable, 92
Delphi, 29
Derrett, J. D., 159
Deuteronomist/Deuteronomic historian, 4, 51, 70, 75–7, 82, 84, 87, 103, 135, 139ff, 140
Dibelius, M., 36

205

dinner table, 77, 89f, 90f, 97, 109, 110, 146, 156f, 161
Dionysus, 28
Dodd, C. H., 12, 39, 40, 182
doublets, 99f
drag-net – parable, 87
dropsical Man, 146
Drury, C., 182n
Drury, J., 79n, 93n, 120

ECCLESIASTICUS, 37
Elijah, 9, 10, 29, 31, 57, 66, 67f, 69, 71, 73, 76, 86, 112, 129, 145, 147f, 167, 176
Eliot, T. S., 179
Elisha, 9, 66, 67f, 71, 73, 86, 130, 145
energy and fatigue, 91, 96, 134, 137, 142, 162
Enoch, 67
Esau, 75, 77
eschatology, 9, 21, 42, 72, 87, 93, 106, 107f, 144, 153, 154, 161, 163f, 170, 182,
Esther, 31, 51, 54, 60, 64, 65, 90, 146
Eusebius, 23, 121n
Evans, C. F., 25, 67, 138n, 140, 145
Ezra, 4

FAITH, 162
family, 17, 18, 63, 93, 94, 151
Farrer, A., 43, 83, 84n, 139
feeding of 5000, 96
forgiveness (see also repentance), 91f
friend, the reluctant, parable, 78, 150

GENESIS Apocryphon, 48
gentiles, 10, 13, 16, 88, 97–100, 126, 175
Gideon, 59, 75
good samaritan parable, 71, 149
Gospel of Truth, 27
Gospels, singularity of, 25ff
Goulder, M. D., 99n, 120, 125, 130, 141, 169n

HAENCHEN, E., 8, 99n
Hannah, 7, 51, 58, 60
Harnack, A., 7, 12
Haydn, J., 177

Heaton, E. W., 140n
Hebrews, Epistle to, 20–2
Hellenistic Judaism, 5, 47f
Heracles, 28
Hermes, 28
Herod, King, 190
Herod Agrippa I, 95
Herod Antipas, 95, 130
Hillel, 35
historiography, Greek, 5, 8, 31
historiography, Jewish, 2–5, 8, 31, 49, 51, 53
Homer, 30
Hort, F. J. A., 24n
hospitality, 21, 73, 90
Houlden, J. L., 99n
Hull, J. M., 96 n, 126 n, 181n

IGNATIUS of Antioch, 25
infancy stories, 47f, 165
Isaac, 2, 31

JACOB, 2, 31, 54, 60, 75, 77, 78
James, Protevangelium of, 7, 27
Jameson, H. G., 40, 120
Jeremias, J., 12, 40, 75n, 182
Jericho, 73, 78, 104
Jerusalem, 10, 49, 51, 52 f, 54, 66, 67, 69, 104, 105, 108, 127, 130, 138, 144, 156
Jewish nation, 10, 11, 49, 53n, 61, 78, 105, 113, 127, 144, 151, 153, 154, 155, 168ff
Johannan ben Zakkai, 35
John Baptist, 6, 7, 29, 31, 56f, 60, 63, 64, 66, 84, 95, 147, 165f, 177
John Evangelist, 7, 9, 27, 39, 44, 51n, 127, 128, 163, 169f, 175, 176, 177, 178
Jonah, 50, 77, 151
Jones, C. P. M., 9, 36
Joseph, 75, 76, 77, 123
Joseph and Asenath, 5, 8, 9, 31, 48, 51, 54, 55
Josephus, 5, 8, 31, 47f, 104, 190
Joshua, 73
journeys, 77, 104, 124, 127, 138, 140
joy, 50, 72, 140
Jubilees, Book of, 31, 48, 50
Judas Iscariot, 165f
judge, the unjust – parable, 78
Judith, 7, 31, 50, 51n, 60, 62, 64, 65

Justin Martyr, 22–4, 28

KILPATRICK, G. D., 175n
Kümmel, W. G., 182

LAW, 16, 20, 21, 24, 62, 63, 76,
    77, 99, 117, 134, 160, 162
leaven parable, 155
lepers, ten, 103
light parable, 94, 152
Lightfoot, R. H., 34
lodging, 61, 73
Loisy, A., 12
lost coin parable, 146
lost sheep parable, 146
love, 77
Lud, King, 2
Lummis, E. W., 120

MACCABAEUS, Judas, 75
Maccabees, 31
magic, 100, 126n, 181
Malachi, 58
Mann, Thomas, 2
Manoah, 7, 48, 56
Mark, 6, 10, 25, 27, 29, 30, 32, 34,
    35, 40, 44, 65, 82–119 passim,
    120–2, 182
marriage, 17, 20, 160f
marriage feast parable (see also
    supper parable), 79, 168
Martha, 103
Matthew, 6, 10, 25, 27, 35f, 44,
    65, 88, 103, 120–12, 123–72
    passim, 182
midrash, 4, 5, 44f, 48, 50, 65, 66,
    84, 86, 94, 116, 126, 150, 162,
    164, 168, 175, 182
miracles, 66f, 87, 89, 90
Momigliano, A., 3
monotheism, 8, 9, 12, 19, 23, 54,
    71f
Morton Smith, 24n
Moses, 10, 24, 31, 47f, 54, 55, 62,
    67, 71, 102, 112, 130, 147f, 161,
    176
Most High, 8, 54, 55, 59
Moule, C. F. D., 19, 175n
Mozart, W. A., 177
mustard seed parable, 94, 155
myth, 33

NAAMAN, 88, 162
Nain, resurrection at, 71f

Nineham, D. E., 73n, 98, 99n
Noah, 48, 56
Nock, A. D., 11n
Novel, 27

OG, 148
O'Neill, J. C., 22

PAIRS, 71, 74
Papias, 121
parables (see also under individual
    titles, e.g., 'sower'), 11, 40,
    75–9, 90, 92, 136, 165
passover, 63, 105
Pastoral Epistles, 15f, 18–20, 51
Paul, 3, 4, 6, 12, 15, 33, 42, 65, 99,
    117, 183
Perrot, F., 47n
Perry, B. E., 27
Pesch, R., 67n
Peter, 10, 121
Phaedrus, 29
Philo, 31
Philonenko, M., 175n
Philostratus, 29, 32
Plato, 23, 30, 90
Plumb, J. H. 2, 3
Plutarch, 30
popular literature, 27
Pound, Ezra, 6
pounds parable, 104
prayer, 91, 150, 164
prodigal son, parable, 71, 146
prophecy and fulfilment, 4, 7, 17,
    21, 50, 52, 56, 63, 64, 66, 69, 72,
    82, 86, 87, 98, 102, 105, 109,
    110, 113, 114, 117, 129, 144,
    155, 156, 165, 168, 169
prophet(s), 9, 10, 11, 23, 24, 53n,
    55, 62, 70, 71, 86, 137, 147, 151,
    154, 161
Proto-Luke, 41, 66, 68, 115
Proverbs, 79, 86, 136
psalms and canticles, 7, 49f, 54, 58,
    64, 65, 69, 87
Pseudo-Matthew, 60

Q, 22, 40, 74, 120, 128f, 132, 137,
    138f, 143, 151

RAHAB, 51, 73f, 78
Repentance, 11, 69, 72, 76, 77, 88,
    89, 90, 91, 116, 155, 158, 183
ressurrection, 107, 161

207

reversal of fortunes, 50, 53f, 64, 77, 104, 135, 136
rich fool parable, 106, 153
Robinson, J. A. T., 12
Roman Empire, 24, 55, 95, 104, 108, 112, 155, 190
Ropes, J. H., 40, 120
Ruth, 51, 76

SAMARIA, 77f, 78, 138
Samaritan, the good – parable, 77f
Samaritans, 77f, 78, 163
Samson, 48, 56, 58, 60
Samuel, 7, 58, 60, 61
Saul, 75
saviour, 50, 55
Sawyer, J. F. A., 116n
Schneemelcher, W., 25
Schubert, F., 178
Schweitzer, A., 182
scorpions, 145
scripture, authority of, 20, 22, 23, 24, 25, 30f, 57, 64, 65, 66, 69
Septimius Severus, 30
septuagint, 44, 49, 59, 60, 65, 66, 67, 68, 69, 72, 74, 77, 86, 105, 109, 111, 113, 123, 129, 138, 161, 163
servants, hired, 76
Sethy the First, 2
Sihon, 148
Simeon (Son of Jacob), 62
Simon Magus, 28
Solomon, 3
Son of God, 9, 28, 32, 33, 34, 52, 55, 136 (plural)
sower parable, 79, 93
Sparks, H. F. D., 7
speeches and soliloquies, 4, 64, 65, 76, 77, 78, 84, 105, 106, 107, 141f, 146, 152
Stephen, 176

steward, the unjust – parable, 78f, 106, 159ff
Strauss, D. F., 43
Streeter, B. H., 40, 45, 120, 128, 131f, 138n
Styler, G. M., 122
supper parable (see also marriage feast), 145, 157
Syria, 30, 77, 78f, 190

TANNAITIC rabbis, 8, 36
Taylor, V., 40f, 142
Temple, 51, 55, 56, 63, 106
Thackeray, H. St. J., 48
Thomas, Gospel of, 27
Titus, 168
Tobit, 7, 50, 54, 64, 65
today, 70 f, 72
tradition, 179
typology, 57 f

VERMES, G., 37, 44
vineyard parable, 75, 79, 106, 168
virgin birth, 123

WARNER, R., 30n
wealth, 17, 19, 20, 65, 72, 76, 77, 78, 92, 104, 109, 153f, 161
Weil, S., 12
Weinfeld, M., 4, 51, 52n
wheat and tares parable, 79, 93, 171
widows, 18, 63, 65, 88
women, 51f, 55, 65, 73, 96, 124, 127, 151
Woollcombe, K., 71n
Wrede, W., 40, 43

YEATS, W. B., 179n

ZACCHAEUS, 72–5
Zechariah the prophet, 58f
Zeus, 28